Press Reviews

Best Business Book of 2016
strategy+business Magazine

'If you read only one thing …'
Politico

'A landmark new book.'
The Guardian

'Far-sighted … Age of Discovery succeeds in convincing that this is an uncommonly interesting time to be alive, with unusual levels of promise – and peril.'
Times Higher Education Supplement

'A highly stimulating, indeed challenging book.'
Forbes

'A bold mega-analysis of global education, health, prosperity and technology … Incisive and rich.'
Nature

'Enlightening.'
The Sunday Telegraph

'*Age of Discovery* will leave its readers drained by the scale of the problems we face … but its scope and authority reward the effort.'
Daily Telegraph

'Breathless.'
New Statesman

'[A] lively account of both Renaissance and modern history … Maybe someone should send Mr. Trump a copy of this book; it might yield some thought-provoking tweets.'
Financial Times

'Urgent reading everywhere.'
Shanghai Review of Books

'This book completely blows my mind.'
'Tell Me Everything with John Fugelsang' on Sirius/XM

'Wow.'
ABC Afternoons with James Valentine

'Audacious.'
Salon.com

'Charts the birth of a brave new world … Impressive.'
Morning Star

'A rallying cry for an aspirational future.'
CBC News

'A fantastic new book.'
Breitbart.com

'Urgent and compelling.'
Knowledge@Wharton on Siriux/XM

'Edifying and thoroughly entertaining.'
Inside Higher Ed

'A brilliant, "big-think" read of serious scholarship and keen observation of our present moment. It is a prescient warning, a call to action to the better angels of our nature, and a map for a new age of discovery.'
800-CEO-READ

'The best book I've read in the past five years.'
33Voices.com

'Important. Powerful.'
FutureSquared

'An immense contribution to rethinking our epoch.'
Cambridge Business Review

PRAISE FOR *AGE OF DISCOVERY*

In a time of big global challenges and unprecedented opportunities, *Age of Discovery* is an essential guide – and a superb ride – through our current stormy moment. In their timely and lively book, Ian Goldin and Chris Kutarna chart a course to a new golden age of human creativity, ingenuity, and potential.

—ARIANNA HUFFINGTON, *Founder, Huffington Post*

Age of Discovery is an important book in a time where the world is dividing and retreating. Ian and Chris take us on a powerful journey and remind us of our common humanity and the importance of collaboration, compassion and genius. We must not build walls, pull up the drawbridge and live in fear. This book will help the world courageously embrace the potential of collective intelligence and ensure we understand the lessons from the past and realise the opportunities ahead of us in this New Renaissance.

—RICHARD BRANSON, *Founder, Virgin Group*

There are many things to admire in this wonderful book. The Renaissance brought a crescendo of new ideas in the full range of human endeavor, and with them a century of transformational change. It also brought interdependence, risk, instability, confusion and fear. The present age feels similar. The authors convincingly argue there is no way to chart a precise course amidst this level of complexity. Navigational skills, humility, and embracing fundamental values, most importantly our capacities for creativity and empathy, will help us, individually and societally. Everyone should read it.

—PROFESSOR MICHAEL SPENCE,
Nobel Laureate in Economics

In this superb account of the parallels between our own time and the Renaissance the authors show what we can learn, both as guide and warning; if we hark to what they say, we can unleash the best of today's potentials and avoid its pitfalls. Their book is an education and a great read in one.

—PROFESSOR AC GRAYLING, MASTER,
New College of the Humanities

This fascinating book covers a remarkably broad canvas. The authors set today's global trends in a historical perspective while assessing current challenges and policy options. They argue that we live in an era where the stakes are higher than ever before – but they are neither techno-utopians nor doom-mongers. This balanced analysis should interest all who care about the future of humanity.

—LORD MARTIN REES, *former President of Royal Society and Astronomer Royal*

In an age of quick and often simplistic analysis, Ian and Chris paint a rich and instructive portrait of our current moment. Drawing on powerful Renaissance-era parallels to diagnose the opportunities and challenges that lie before us, *Age of Discovery* offers essential insights for all of us including every emerging Michaelangelo and Da Vinci.

—REID HOFFMAN, *Founder, LinkedIn*

Age of Discovery identifies the pivotal choices we all face, and issues a call to action that we all need to hear. I strongly recommend this timely and immensely important and readable book.

—KUMI NAIDOO, *International Executive Director, Greenpeace and former Secretary General, Civicus*

Age of Discovery is a much needed dose of perspective in our increasingly short-term focused world. The authors step back from the day-to-day to illustrate how our current period – with its relentless pace, new technologies, and heightened connectedness – is a New Renaissance. The reader learns the lessons of the original Renaissance, such as the need to look out for new systemic risks, and the necessity to 'embrace genius' – the innovative and frequently controversial ideas that originate from these unique points in time. With this perspective, leaders can learn to make prudent decisions for the long-term without being over-biased by near-term volatility.

—DOMINIC BARTON, *Managing Partner of McKinsey*

Age of Discovery is a fascinating book that seeks to make links from the remarkable period of crisis and creativity that was the Renaissance to the dramatic changes that we are all experiencing in the world today. Compelling parallels are drawn between the rapid developments in technology and culture that occurred or are occurring, and the challenges faced by the societies in absorbing them. The book offers outstanding insights for all those interested in the stresses of the modern world and how other ages have confronted them in their own time.

—PROFESSOR ANDREW HAMILTON,
President, New York University and former Vice-Chancellor, University of Oxford

Along with being fascinating reading, *Age of Discovery* provides the big picture view required to understand the challenges being created by the constant waves of innovation we face today. Our wonderful new technologies are agnostic, capable of being used for good and for evil, to save lives and to end lives. The book illustrates well that in life, as in chess, every advance creates both opportunities and dangers – and the winners will be those who best embrace the new while still learning from the old. I know better than most that 'genius' is an overused word, but the authors effectively rehabilitate it in *Age of Discovery* by showing how individual brilliance becomes collective success when individual freedom spreads opportunity throughout society.

—GARRY KASPAROV, *Chairman of the Human Rights Foundation, 13th World Chess Champion and Author of Winter Is Coming*

Ian Goldin and Chris Kutarna have dared to look up from the spreadsheets and put aside for the moment the safe, incremental studies to ask – and answer – essential big questions: where do we come from, what are we doing wrong – and right! – and where are we trying to go? We should thank them for their audacity and accept their challenge to take risks, push the boundaries of the possible, be sober about the challenges, and perhaps most importantly, to be optimistic for what the future may hold.

—CHRISTINE LAGARDE, *Managing Director,*
International Monetary Fund

Are we living through a new Renaissance? In this hugely stimulating book, Ian Goldin and Chris Kutarna look at today's hubs of innovation and sees new versions of Florence in the age of the Medici. Ours, he argues, is a new era of exploration. But, as in the da Vinci and da Gama, new technology and global integration bring with them new perils as well as new prosperity: pandemics, religious manias, war. Everyone should read the authors' call for a new humanism that is ready to defend our modern Renaissance against attacks that have already begun.

—PROFESSOR NIALL FERGUSON, *Laurence A. Tisch*
Professor of History, Harvard University

Age of Discovery offers a refreshing change from the shallow analyses and sterile nostrums of the right and the left. Its vision is that the current wave of advances – in communications and science among others – are fast presenting opportunities for a worldwide outpouring of creativity. Its wisdom is that these possibilities will be largely missed if citizens do not act and nations do not organize to take advantage of them. An impressive and important book.

—PROFESSOR EDMUND PHELPS,
Nobel Laureate in Economics

Age of Discovery provides a very important reminder to see and to grasp the opportunities in the many challenges we are facing today, as we have done successfully in past times. We have made enormous progress by coming up with new solutions time and again. There is no reason to be pessimistic.

—HANS-PAUL BUERKNER, *Chairman,*
The Boston Consulting Group

In a time of loose rhetoric and gloomy headlines, *Age of Discovery* shines the hope that, working together, we can promote learning societies that will help us navigate our tangled 21st century. Will we flounder or flourish? With a brilliant mix of fresh wit and sober thinking, Ian and Chris challenge and inspire us all. A must-read for present and future leaders everywhere.

—PROFESSOR ASHA KANWAR, *President,*
Commonwealth of Learning

In *Age of Discovery*, Ian Goldin and Chris Kutarna deliver a masterpiece with a very important message: how to weather today's crises and achieve greatness.

—VIJAY GOVINDARAJAN,
NYT Bestselling Author

This is the best book I have read in recent years – highly educational, enlightened and entertaining. The evolution of our society's achievements and challenges over generations, explained in wonderful clarity and simplicity, provides a valuable guide for present and future generations to navigate the growing risks and complexities facing humanity. A must-read!

—VICTOR L.L. CHU, *Chairman,*
First Eastern Investment Group

At the time of the rise of China, the reversal of globalization and the remaking of world order, *Age of Discovery* provides readers wisdom and enlightenment by foreseeing the future through reviewing the past.

—JUSTIN YIFU LIN, *former Chief Economist, World Bank*

'Bold, challenging and invigorating'.

—PETER FRANKOPAN, *Author, The Silk Roads*

With their magical pen, Ian and Chris take us through a thrilling and unforgettable 500 years of human history: from the Renaissance to today. As 500 years ago, today is indeed an age of discovery. In the face of rapid technological, cultural and ideological changes, faced with surging opportunities and risks, faced with great uncertainty, where can we find hope and determination? How can we become active players in innovation? How can we achieve a new "Renaissance"? The authors implant into our present perspective not only history, but also openness, humility, innovation and insight. What we're left with is faith for the future. Reading this book is a shocking and beautiful voyage of discovery.

—ZHU MIN, *former Deputy Managing Director,*
International Monetary Fund

Civilizations, epochs, eras, ages – whatever – cannot see their own effect on history. The 'roostertails' of the Age of Enlightenment or Renaissance Era are unknowable to those living then. What Ian Goldin and Chris Kutarna have done is nothing less than to capture a freeze frame of the rapidly moving innovations and discoveries of today, examine its risks and benefits, and extrapolate our own roostertail. That they have done this while the plane is flying, the computer code being written, the achievements being celebrated and their side-effects and knock effect not yet realized is a remarkable feat of both history and prophecy. They have given us a gift of self-reflection that is indeed rare. I can't believe the book is so light and small for accomplishing such a heavy lift.

—LARRY BRILLIANT, *President of Skoll Urgent Threats Fund and former Executive Director Google.org*

AGE OF DISCOVERY

Revised edition

AGE OF DISCOVERY

Navigating the Storms of our Second Renaissance

Revised edition

IAN GOLDIN AND CHRIS KUTARNA

Bloomsbury Business

An imprint of Bloomsbury Publishing Plc

B L O O M S B U R Y

LONDON · OXFORD · NEW YORK · NEW DELHI · SYDNEY

Bloomsbury Business

An imprint of Bloomsbury Publishing Plc

50 Bedford Square	1385 Broadway
London	New York
WC1B 3DP	NY 10018
UK	USA

www.bloomsbury.com

**BLOOMSBURY and the Diana logo are trademarks
of Bloomsbury Publishing Plc**

First published in 2016

This revised paperback edition published 2017

© Ian Goldin and Chris Kutarna, 2017

Ian Goldin and Chris Kutarna have asserted their rights under
the Copyright, Designs and Patents Act, 1988, to be identified as
Authors of this work.

British Library Cataloguing-in-Publication Data
A catalogue record for this book is available from the British Library.

ISBN:	HB:	978-1-4729-3637-0
	PB:	978-1-4729-4352-1
	ePDF:	978-1-4729-3639-4
	ePub:	978-1-4729-3638-7

Library of Congress Cataloging-in-Publication Data
A catalog record for this book is available from the Library of Congress.

Cover design by Alice Marwick

Typeset by Integra Software Services Pvt. Ltd.
Printed and bound in Great Britain

To find out more about our authors and books visit www.bloomsbury.com. Here you
will find extracts, author interviews, details of forthcoming events and the option to
sign up for our newsletters.

To Olivia and Alex
And their flourishing in the New Renaissance
Ian Goldin

To my father
The most Renaissance man I know
Chris Kutarna

CONTENTS

PREFACE TO THE PAPERBACK EDITION

'The present age is a *contest*. Hand in hand with its recognition comes the urgent responsibility to join it.' (*Age of Discovery*, p. 2).

We led the hardcover edition of this book with an urgent call to action, because our research showed that rapid social, demographic and technological change was likely to shock much of the 'status quo' that we all take for granted every day. On that basis we predicted both that Britain would vote to 'Brexit' from the European Union and that Donald Trump would be elected President of the United States.

Shock – a seemingly relentless theme nowadays – is personal proof that whatever lens we've been looking through to see the world no longer shows things as they really are. We need to shatter that lens – and with it, binary divisions that can warp our sight: globalization versus nationalism; open doors versus xenophobia; information abundance versus fake news; the lifted up versus the left behind.

We need to develop for ourselves a wider way of seeing the world. The sooner we do that, the less time we'll waste frozen in disbelief, and the more time we'll spend helping ourselves, our families, our organizations and communities to thrive through the upheavals to come.

This book is our lens for seeing the moment we're in. Every shocking day since the first edition's release has offered new proof of its urgency.

The title, *Age of Discovery*, plays on our misconceptions of both the past and the present. It evokes an optimistic vision of humanity blown by scientific, economic and social winds – zigging and zagging, surely, but always *progressing* toward a better, New World. In hindsight, that's how many of us viewed our present circumstances. We thought we were passengers on a ship at sea, with little control over the weather, yet lulled into complacency by our general heading and the apparent competence of our captains.

Now, recent reversals have made us wise to our true predicament. In an age of discovery, there is no inevitable path of progress, and there are no passengers. We all need to learn how to pilot the ship: between the good and bad consequences of global entanglement; between forces of inclusion and exclusion; between flourishing genius and flourishing risks. The present seems a constant struggle to navigate these awesome, paradoxical forces.

But we've been here before.

And the wisdom of history can be our compass, if we choose to receive it.

We hope that this book empowers readers to make sense of the extraordinary moment we are in, and to chart a course toward a thriving future.

Chris Kutarna and Ian Goldin
Oxford
July 2017.

ACKNOWLEDGEMENTS

This book covers an unusually broad set of subjects, historical references and disciplines. It would not have come together without the expert guidance, research assistance, friendship and support of many people. And we could not have wished for a richer and more stimulating community, or more generous and knowledgeable sources, than our colleagues in the Oxford Martin School and across the University of Oxford.

Drawing on the Renaissance helps make sense of the present and of the choices we all face. Seeing our time through a long-term lens helps put our often confusing world in perspective. But history needs to be interpreted with care, since many concepts that are core to the present day – say, 'science' – were understood very differently half a millennium ago. We are most grateful to Diarmaid MacCulloch and Howard Hotson, both professors of history at Oxford, who generously offered guidance. Their extraordinary knowledge of the fifteenth and sixteenth centuries helped us to find the balance between the wisdom of past centuries that is relevant to today by virtue of our shared humanity, and that which has been rendered irrelevant by social and technological change.

On the contemporary side of this story, we are grateful to Eugene Rogan for introducing us to Nadia Oweidat, whose insights have deepened our understanding of extremism. Angus Deaton generously shared wisdom and figures from his work in economics. Terry Dwyer and Kazem Rahimi helped us understand medical matters. Recent graduates from the history, theology, physics, chemistry, medicine, economics, politics and philosophy departments at the University of Oxford have provided research assistance to check and supplement our facts, sources and arguments, and for this we thank Ernesto Oyarbide, Jonathan Griffiths, Julian Ratcliffe, Paul Taylor and Gerhard Toews. We owe special thanks to Maximilia Lane, who expertly hunted down facts that others could not, and offered numerous improvements to the text. Needless to say, we alone are responsible for any errors that remain.

The Bodleian Library is an international treasure, and we are most grateful to Richard Ovenden, the Bodleian Librarian, for his enthusiastic support, to Nick Millea, Map Librarian, and to Michael Athanson Deputy Map Librarian, for the historical maps that are presented in this book. We are grateful to the publishers who have permitted us to reproduce their material, to Claire Jordan for securing our necessary permissions, and to Diarmaid MacCulloch once again, for sharing his maps of Europe in the 1500s.

Ian's work on this book hinged on help from Lindsay Walker, who managed his diary, and from Laura Lauer, administrator of the Oxford Martin School, whose smooth running of the school freed Ian to focus on the questions raised, and the answers given, in this volume.

Chris could not have devoted years to this book without the immense patience of his business partner, Dave Anderson, and of his doctoral supervisor, Vivienne Shue. Both sacrificed their own milestones for this one. He also owes a deep debt to Jim Gallagher, who taught him how to write, and to Rick Boven at the Boston Consulting Group, who taught him how to make words mean something.

Our agent Esmond Harmsworth has been part of this book since its inception, helping us to define the topic and then to secure publishers. We are most grateful to the chief executive of Bloomsbury, Nigel Newton, for taking an enthusiastic interest in our manuscript, and to Ian Hallsworth, who has proven to be an outstanding editor, working with his colleagues in what we regard as an exemplary partnership.

Finally, our deepest gratitude is due to our family and friends, who have stood by us through the many long hours that this book has absorbed.

Ian Goldin and Chris Kutarna
Oxford
July 2017.

1

To Flounder or Flourish?

The moment we're in

If Michelangelo were reborn right now, amidst all the turmoil that marks this shocking moment we're in, would he flounder, or flourish again?

Every year, millions of people file into the Sistine Chapel to stare up in wonder at Michelangelo Buonarroti's *Creation of Adam*. Millions more pay homage to Leonardo da Vinci's *Mona Lisa*. Through five centuries, we have carefully preserved such Renaissance masterpieces, and cherished them, as objects of beauty and inspiration.

But they also challenge us.

The artists who crafted these feats of genius 500 years ago did not inhabit some magical age of universal beauty, but rather a tumultuous moment – marked by historic milestones and discoveries, yes, but also wrenching upheaval. Their world was tangling together in a way it had never done before, thanks to Gutenberg's recent invention of the printing press (1450s), Columbus' discovery of the New World (1492) and Vasco da Gama's discovery of a sea route to Asia's riches (1497). And humanity's fortunes were changing, in some ways radically. The Black Death had tapered off, Europe's population was recovering and public health, wealth and education were all rising.

Genius flourished under these conditions, as evidenced by artistic achievements (especially from the 1490s to the 1520s), by Copernicus' revolutionary theories of a sun-centred cosmos (1510s) and by similar advances in a wide range of fields, from biology to engineering to navigation to medicine. Basic, common-sense 'truths' that had stood unquestioned for centuries, even millennia, were eroding away. The earth did not stand still. The sun did not revolve around it. The 'known' world wasn't even half of the whole. The human heart wasn't the soul; it was a pump. In mere decades, printing boosted the production of books from hundreds to millions per year, and these weird facts and new ideas travelled farther, faster than had ever been possible.

But risk flourished, too. Terrifying new diseases spread like wildfire on both sides of the now-connected Atlantic. The Ottoman Turks – backed by a 'new' weapon, gunpowder –

conquered the eastern Mediterranean for Islam in a stunning series of land and naval victories that cast a threatening gloom over all of Europe. Martin Luther (1483-1546) leveraged Gutenberg's press to broadcast a new narrative—that society's hallowed institutions served only to fatten their own hierarchies. It spread faster than complacent elites could fathom. Europe broke into Protestant and Catholic halves; war and refugee crises ignited continent-wide.

Meanwhile, the populist priest Girolamo Savonarola (1452-1498) ignited a real fire—the Bonfire of the Vanities—in Florence, the very heart of Renaissance Europe. With apocalyptic sermons, Savonarola stoked people's worst reactions to rapid change. He promised Florentines a return to past glories if only they would join him in his campaign to burn away weak elites and their corrupt agendas. Enough did so that he was able to lord over the republic as de facto king (until, four years later, his political enemies crucified him).

Such was the age in which, on 8 September 1504, in Florence, Italy, Michelangelo unveiled his statue of *David* in the city's main square. Standing over 5 metres tall, weighing in at over 6 tons of fine Carrara marble, *David* was an instant monument to the city's wealth and to the sculptor's skill. See Figure 1.1.

David and Goliath was a familiar Old Testament story, about a brave young warrior who, in true underdog fashion, improbably defeated a giant foe in single combat. But with hammer and chisel,

FIGURE 1.1 *A moment etched in marble.*
Michelangelo Buonarroti (1501–1504). David – detail. Florence. Photo credit: Art Resource.

Michelangelo fixed into stone a moment that no one had seen before. It must have caused some confusion for those present at the unveiling. David's face and neck were tensed. His brow was furrowed and his eyes focused determinedly upon some distant point. He stood, not triumphant atop the corpse of his enemy (the standard portrayal), but ready, with the implacable resolve of one who knows his next step but not its outcome. And then they saw the artist's meaning clearly: Michelangelo carved David in that fateful moment between decision and action, between realizing what he must do and summoning the courage to do it.

They knew that moment. They were in it.

The past is prologue

We are in it, too.

The present age is a contest: between the good and bad consequences of global entanglement and human development; between forces of inclusion and exclusion; between flourishing genius and flourishing risks. Whether we each flourish or flounder, and whether the twenty-first century goes down in the history books as one of humanity's best or worst, depends on what we all do to promote the possibilities and dampen the dangers that this contest brings.

The stakes could not be higher. We each have the perilous fortune to have been born into a historic moment – a decisive moment – when events and choices in our own lifetime will dictate the circumstances of many, many lifetimes to come.

Yes, it is the conceit of each generation to think so, but this time it's true. The long-term facts speak more loudly than our egos ever could. Humanity's shift into cities, begun some 10,000 years ago by our Neolithic ancestors, crossed the half-way mark in our own lifetimes.[1] We are the first generations of the urban epoch. Carbon pollution has pushed atmospheric greenhouse gases today to concentrations not seen since those Neolithic days; fourteen of the fifteen hottest years in our climate record have all come in the twenty-first century.[2] For the first time ever, the number of poor people in the world has plummeted (by over one billion people since 1990) *and* the overall population has swelled (by some two billion) at the same time. Scientists alive today outnumber all scientists who ever lived up to 1980, and – in part thanks to them – average life expectancy has risen more in the past fifty years than in the previous 1,000.

In the short term, too, history is being made. The Internet, effectively non-existent twenty years ago, linked one billion people by 2005, two billion people by 2010 and three billion people by 2015. Now, over half of humanity is online.[3] China has erupted from autarky to become the world's biggest exporter and economy. India is close behind. The Berlin Wall is gone, and the clash of economic ideologies that defined the second half of the twentieth century is gone with it. All this feels like old news when set against the headlines since the turn of the new millennium: 9/11; devastating tsunamis and hurricanes; a global financial crisis that struck dumb the world's highest-paid brains; a nuclear meltdown in hyper-safe Japan; acts of terrorism from Montreal to Manchester; Britain's vote to 'Brexit' the EU; America's vote to elect Donald Trump celebrity-in-chief – and other events that surprise us in a different way, like the explosion of mobile and social media, cracking the human genome, the advent of 3D printing, the breaking of long-standing taboos on gay marriage, the detection of gravitational waves and the discovery of earth-like planets orbiting nearby stars.

It seems that every day we wake up to a new shock. And *shock* itself is the most compelling evidence that this age is very different, because it's data that comes from within. Shock is our own personal proof of historic change – a psychic collision of reality and expectations – and it has been the relentless theme of all our lives. It agitates and animates us. It will continue to do so. Right now we don't talk much about geoengineering, organic energy, super-intelligent machines, bioengineered plagues, nanofactories or designer babies, but someday soon – surprise! – it may seem that we talk about little else.

We lack – and need – perspective

We don't know where we're headed, and so we let ourselves get pushed around – bullied even – by immediate crises and the anxieties they evoke. We retreat rather than reach out. In an age when we *must* defy fear with courage, we hesitate instead. Globally, that's the present mood. The US and UK governments, once the world's chief promoters of free trade, now rally their citizens against it.[4] Industry around the world is accumulating or distributing record levels of cash, rather than investing it. By late 2015, it was estimated that global corporations held over \$15 trillion in cash and cash equivalents – four times as much as a decade earlier.[5] The S&P 500 companies as a group gave almost all their 2014 profits back to shareholders (via dividends and share buybacks), rather than bet on new projects and ideas.[6] Both the political far right (which seeks to reverse society's opening up to gays, immigrants and global responsibilities) and the far left (which seeks to reverse society's opening up to trade and private enterprise) enjoy electoral success across much of the developed world. In the 1990s, the word 'globalization' was ubiquitous. For many, it implied a global coming together, and it captured grand hopes of a better world for everyone. Today, the term is anathema (except among politicians, who blame it for the problems they can't solve). See Figure 1.2.

What we lack, and so urgently need, is *perspective*. With it, we can see the contest that defines our lifetime and better assert our own will upon the wider forces rocking the world. When the next shocks hit, we can step back from their immediacy and place them in a broader context, in which we have more leverage over their meaning (and our response). Civic and political

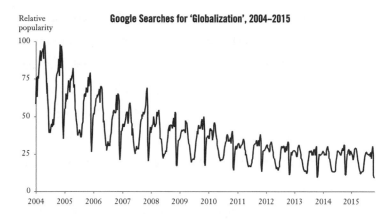

FIGURE 1.2 *Google searches for 'globalization' have been declining for a decade.*

Source: Google Trends (2015). 'Interest over Time: Globalization'. Retrieved from www.google.com/trends.

leaders need perspective to craft a positive vision that connects the big drivers of change with our daily lives. Businesspeople need perspective to cut through the chaos of 24/7 news and information to make capable decisions. Youth need perspective to find answers to their big, burning questions and a pathway for their own passions. Perspective is what enables each of us to transform the sum of our days into an epic journey. And it's what improves our chances of together making the twenty-first century humanity's best.

'Perspective is the guide and the gateway, and without it nothing can be done well.'[7] When he wrote these words, Leonardo da Vinci (1452–1519) was counselling artists, but he could easily have been counselling his whole generation. A contemporary of Michelangelo (1475–1564), Leonardo lived in the same moment of fateful contest that his peer had captured in marble. To gain perspective on the present age, we need only step back, look to the past, and realize: *We've been here before.* The forces that converged in Europe 500 years ago to spark genius and upend social order are present again in our lifetime. Only now they are stronger, and global.

That is the main message of this book. It should fill us with a mix of hope and determination. *Hope*, because amidst chaos the Renaissance left a legacy that we still celebrate, 500 years on, as one of history's brightest. We, too, can seize this moment. We can realize a new flourishing that in magnitude, geographic scope and positive consequences for human welfare will far surpass the first Renaissance – or, indeed, any other flourishing in history. *Determination*, because this new golden age will never simply arrive. We have to achieve it, in open defiance of the forces tearing it apart.

In 1517, Niccolò Machiavelli (1469–1527), one of the chief philosophers of his age and a founding father of modern political science, wrote:

Whoever wishes to foresee the future must consult the past; for human events ever resemble those of preceding times. This arises from the fact that they are produced by men who have been, and ever will be, animated by the same passions. The result is that the same problems always exist in every era.[8]

We've been warned. The first Renaissance was a time of tremendous upheaval that strained society to, and often past, the breaking point. Now, we risk fumbling badly again, as individuals, as society and as a species – and we've had some big stumbles already. It's made many of us cynical and fearful for the future. If we want to attain the greatness for which humanity is once again eligible, we must keep faith in its possibility. We must broaden and share more widely the benefits of progress. We must combat ignorance with evidence, and fear with courage. And we must help one another to cope with the shocks that none of us will see coming.

The way forward

We reframe this present age as a second Renaissance in four parts.

Part I lays out the big, hard facts of the age, and rebuts the loose and often irresponsible rhetoric that pervades today's public discourse. We step back and make clear the connective and developmental forces that defined the Renaissance 500 years ago and which, over the past quarter-century, have completely remade the world we live in now. Columbus' voyages of discovery, the fall of the Berlin Wall – both events highlighted the breakdown of long-standing barriers of ignorance and myth, and the opening of fresh, planet-wide systems of political and economic exchange. The Gutenberg press, the internet – both shifted the whole of human communication to a new normal: information abundance, cheap distribution, radical variety and wide participation.

Developmental forces – gains in health, wealth and education – also underlay human progress then, and lift us now. War and disease, throughout history the two heaviest drags on human progress, subsided in the decades leading up to the Renaissance. Today, overall battlefield deaths are in steep retreat – even taking into account the violence surrounding the Syrian civil war – and successful campaigns against disease and aging have added nearly two full decades to global life expectancy.[9] Then, literacy and numeracy skills were transformed from elite luxuries to precious commodities. Now, the incoming generation of adults is the first in history to be near-universally literate.

These revolutions in technology, demography, health and economics add momentum and vitality to the sum of human activity. With each turn, we accumulate and reinvest more human capital, and exchange and act with ever-rising intensity, until, as we show in Part II, a flourishing of genius accelerates us even more.

The positive legacy of the Renaissance was an eruption of genius – exceptional achievements in European art, science and philosophy unrivalled in the preceding millennium, which set Europe on course towards the Scientific Revolution and Enlightenment in the centuries that followed. We are in the midst of another such eruption, in scale and scope far surpassing theirs. We know this, first because the conditions match and second, from the roll call of fundamental breakthroughs we've already begun to ring up. We show how the forces identified in Part I are helping genius to blossom now, and we foreshadow the deep changes this flourishing will work upon humanity. We also probe humanity's expanding powers of *collective* achievement: our new, disruptive capacity for sharing and collaboration that inflates the boundaries of the possible. During the Renaissance, collective efforts raised the world's largest cathedrals; today, mass collaborations are finding new cures for diseases, making humanity's knowledge base multilingual and mapping the visible universe.

Part III, Flourishing Risk, balances hope with caution. The same connective and developmental forces that fuel human imagination also breed complexity and concentrate our activities in dangerous ways. These twin consequences heighten our exposure to an especially perilous species of risk – 'systemic' risk. Five hundred years ago, systemic shocks caused some of the moments of greatest grief – strange new diseases that struck and spread with terrifying speed; ruinous financial collapses in new credit markets; the obsolescence of whole communities built along the Silk Roads as the new sea route to Asia diverted trade away. The 2008 financial crisis has already taught us to respect this class of threat, but we do not yet appreciate how widespread it has become.

We are, however, becoming familiar with the systemic risks brewing within our national- and geo-politics. A Renaissance age creates big winners and big losers. Our social bargain is weakening, just when the technologies to summon solidarity, or rally rebellion, are made common and powerful. Five hundred years ago, the Bonfire of the Vanities, religious wars, the Inquisition and ever more frequent popular revolts tore at the peace in which genius laboured and smothered some of the brightest lights of the age. Now, voices of extremism, protectionism and xenophobia likewise tear apart the same connections that spark present-day genius, and popular anger has sapped our public institutions of the legitimacy needed to take bold actions.

The journey ends in Part IV, The Contest for Our Future. We lay out what we all need to do – government, business and civil society, all of us – to achieve the greatness and weather the crises that this age makes possible. Will we repeat the glories of the first Renaissance, the misery or both? That is the question, the Goliath, we all must face.

Good housekeeping

But first, we need to tidy up three issues.

What does 'Renaissance' actually mean?

History students the world over have confronted this question for over a century. 'Neither in time, extent, content, nor significance is the concept Renaissance defined. It suffers from vagueness, incompleteness, and chance ... It is an almost unusable term.'[10] Those lines were written by a Dutch historian, Johan Huizinga – in 1920. In the century since, the scholarly debate has only grown murkier. The main gripe historians have with the word 'Renaissance' is that it misleadingly makes the period sound universally pretty. That usage was begun by the Italian artist-historian Giorgio Vasari (1511–1574), in his 1550 book *The Lives of the Most Excellent Painters, Sculptors, and Architects*, to glorify recent artistic trends and distance them from prior, gothic styles. Nineteenth-century European historians picked up the term and broadened its meaning to describe a time of artistic, cultural and intellectual flourishing (a meaning that we retain today in phrases like 'Renaissance Man'). In doing so, they weren't dispassionately describing the period in which Leonardo, Michelangelo and their peers lived. Rather, they were crafting the idea that 'Renaissance Europe' had leapfrogged other civilizations – an idea that was both origin story and justification for nineteenth-century European imperialism.[11]

Today, historians are quick to point out that 'Renaissance Europe' was ugly, too. Lest we forget, less than a decade after Michelangelo finished painting his Sistine Chapel, smallpox and other European germs nearly exterminated the Aztecs, the Incas and other natives in the New World. When historians use the word 'Renaissance', therefore, they do so critically and cautiously, referring mainly to a 'rebirth' in fifteenth- and sixteenth-century Europe of certain knowledge, styles and values recovered from ancient Greece and Rome.

In this book, we begin with the term's popular meaning today – as a rare moment of mass flourishing. That notion is a good starting point, because it accurately describes the present world we all inhabit. But only if we can see both sides. Throughout these pages we emphasize how, then and now, a Renaissance age is pregnant with both goods and bads, genius and risk. By the end, our definition is clear: a Renaissance is a contest for the future at a moment when the stakes are highest.

When was the Renaissance?

History is all one piece: look closely, and threads weaving one chapter into the next can always be found. Scholars bookmark 'beginnings' and 'endings' to make the reading of our collective story manageable, and to help make the broad course of history clear, but such lines should be drawn in pencil only.

In this book, we look back mainly to a single century, from 1450 to 1550. The year 1450 is a solid starting point. Leonardo da Vinci was born in 1452, and during the period 1452–1454, a series of events took place that gave the second half of that century a very different feel from the first. At about the same time: England and France ended their Hundred Years War, a violent disruption to daily life that had dragged on since 1337; Constantinople, the ancient Roman capital that had guarded Europe's eastern frontier for over 1,100 years, finally fell to the new gunpowder cannons of the Ottoman Empire; and the warring Italian powers – Milan, Venice, Florence, Naples and the Papal States – signed into being the Italic League, a mutual non-aggression pact that allowed the whole peninsula to demobilize and invest its energies into peacetime pursuits.[12]

For similar reasons, we mark 1990 as the approximate start date for the second Renaissance. In the span of just a few years: the Cold War ended, the Berlin Wall fell, China rejoined the world economy and the commercial internet lit up. Suddenly, the world felt quite different. As we will see in Part I, the hard data shows that this period *was* different.

We loosely bookend the first Renaissance at about 1550. We must follow the evolution of ideas and events for however long it takes to clarify their meaning in the big picture. But in practice, one century gives a healthy perspective on many changes. Already by 1550, the consequences of the age, good and bad, were becoming clear – as were the wisdom and foolishness of the choices people had made along the way.

We don't predict when the second Renaissance will end. But the present 'age' is broader than this year or this decade. It's a phenomenon, a contest, that will shape the whole twenty-first century.

Why focus on Europe?

Renaissances, as we've defined them, can be found in every civilization. What took place in fifteenth- and sixteenth-century Europe has some broad parallels with the Mayan Classic Period (300–900), the early centuries of Korea's Chosŏn Dynasty (1392–1897), the Islamic Golden Age (750–1260), China's Tang Dynasty (618–907), India's Gupta Empire (320–550) and the Mughal Empire under Akbar the Great (1556–1605). As Peter Frankopan shows in his magisterial The Silk Roads, Asia and the Arab region may proudly claim to have been the source of much of humanity's progress through history.[13] We encourage others to embark on the project of looking back to those periods for more insights into our present day. This book draws perspective from a particular moment of the European experience.

Why? It's not because fifteenth-century Europe was the most advanced civilization at that time. China held that distinction, and had for centuries. As early as the twelfth century, China's then-capital, Kaifeng, was a million-person metropolis. Three hundred years before Gutenberg, Chinese block-printers were already mass-producing books cheaply enough for even modest households to consume.[14] The Ottoman Empire of the fifteenth and sixteenth centuries, by then on Europe's eastern doorstep, ran a far more sophisticated, cosmopolitan state than anything Machiavelli wrote about. And Muslims, not Christians, were by far the world's largest faith community. Europe was often regarded as a backwater, and many fifteenth-century world maps depicted it as such – on the margin.

But with the advent of the Renaissance, this suddenly began to change. Over the next few centuries, Europe caught up with, then overtook, all other civilizations on most measures of human progress and set the basic configuration for the world we live in now. It's the closest cousin, and offers the most direct lessons, to the present.

Of course, many details differ between the events of 500 years past and those of today. But do those details mean we should ignore what the past has to teach us about our own age of flourishing genius and risk? You must decide that for yourself. We think you will come to the same realization:

This is a second Renaissance.

PART I

MAKING SENSE OF A SECOND RENAISSANCE

How we got to now and what sets this age apart

2

The New World

How new maps and new media have remade the world we live in

New maps

Among the extraordinary, though quite natural circumstances of my life, the first and most unusual is that I was born in this century in which the whole world opened to us.

GIROLAMO CARDANO (1501–1576)[1]

From revelation to observation

In 1450, most of what Europe knew about the world came from the Bible. The earth was 6,000 years old. It had been 4,500 years since the Flood. The peoples of Europe, Asia and Africa were descended from Noah's three sons. This much was common knowledge, and it was reflected often in pictures of the earth, called *mappae mundi*, which placed Jerusalem at the world's centre, east (from whence the sun rose) at the top and assorted monsters along the margins. See Figure 2.1.

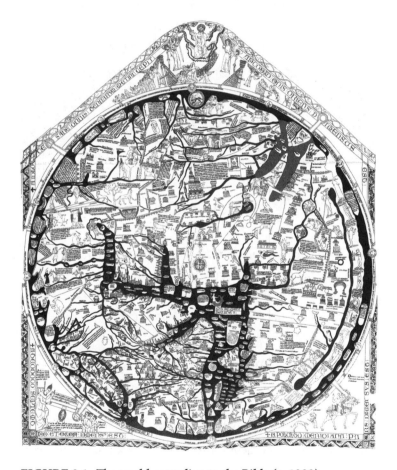

FIGURE 2.1 *The world according to the Bible (c. 1300).*
Ricardus de Bello (1285). Terrarum Orbis. *Courtesy of the Bodleian Libraries, University of Oxford.*

The most accurate map of the wider world accessible to European scholars was one drawn by Ptolemy, a first-century Greek polymath whose main cartographic work, the *Geography*, they had only recently rediscovered (in about 1400). See Figure 2.2.

Clearly, this mapmaker had a good grasp of the Mediterranean, North Africa, the Arabian Peninsula and the Near East. But beyond those lands and waters, the map's accuracy steadily diminishes. Ptolemy's Indian Ocean (bottom right) is landlocked. Africa has no southern tip, India is missing its peninsula and

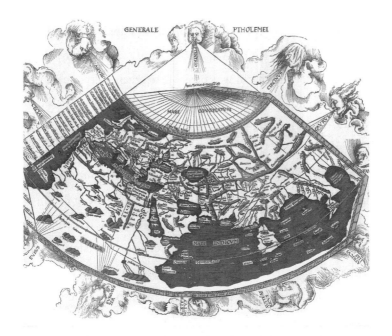

FIGURE 2.2 *The world according to Ptolemy (c. 150).*
Joannes Schott (1520), after Ptolemy (second century). The Known World. Strasbourg: Ballerman & Son. Courtesy of the Bodleian Libraries, University of Oxford.

Asia has no east coast. The Americas and the Pacific Ocean are entirely absent. And the scale is profoundly off. Ptolemy judged that his map spanned nearly half of the entire globe. In fact, it spans less than one-fifth of one hemisphere.

Europe in 1450 possessed no data to refute these glaring errors.† Seemingly impenetrable frontiers made it unlikely they ever would. Water guarded the west. Scholars knew, as Ptolemy had known, that the world *had* to be round. That much was plain to anyone who stood on Europe's west coast and admired the horizon's subtle bend, or who puzzled through the reason why the sail of an approaching ship always appeared before its hull. But they didn't know what other land masses might be out there, if any, or whether it was possible to reach them. There was, literally, no end in sight. The fear of hopeless distances, plus faith in the truths bestowed by revelation and Greek myth, kept most ships in familiar waters.

Eastward, the obstacles were far more definite: Europe's vision ended where Turkish authority began. The polyethnic, polyreligious Ottomans under Sultan Mehmed II conquered Christian Constantinople in 1453, renamed it Istanbul and thereby closed the book on the once-mighty Roman Empire. Over the next hundred years, Ottoman military victories on land

---

†Here again, Europe lagged behind other civilizations. As early as 1402, maps in the court of Korea's Chosŏn Dynasty demonstrated knowledge of Africa's southern tip, likely of Arabic origin via trade with China.

and sea shoved European powers (especially the trading empires of Venice and Genoa) out of the eastern Mediterranean, the whole Balkan Peninsula, the Black Sea, the North African coast and much of the Middle East.

But by 1500, Europe already had a very different picture of the world. New evidence accumulated by navigation and observation competed against, and began to overturn, old truths. In 1487–1488, the Portuguese pilot Bartholomew Dias found the southern tip of Africa. Ten years later, his compatriot Vasco da Gama navigated around it, then up Africa's east coast and across the Indian Ocean to the port of Calicut (or Kozhikode), the 'City of Spices'. His voyage proved Ptolemy wrong: the Indian Ocean was not landlocked after all. That news, in turn, threatened the viability of communities all along the Silk Roads between Asia and Europe – vastly lucrative overland trade routes that had been built atop the belief that no sea route existed. Of less significance to contemporaries, but of more importance to world history, in 1492, Christopher Columbus – himself in search of a new sea route to Asia – hit upon the island of Hispaniola (today's Haiti and Dominican Republic). He had found the New World.[†]

Their successes fuelled ever bolder truth- and treasure-seeking. The Portuguese continued to develop their sea route

[†]Specifically, the Caribbean; John Cabot, sent by the British, found North America in 1497.

eastward to Asia. Da Gama had sailed back to Lisbon with few significant treasures, but over the next five years, more than a dozen Portuguese expeditions carrying some 7,000 men pressed the advantage his discoveries had won. Armed with gunpowder, they conquered Hormuz in 1507 (then, as now, a choke-point for all trade through the Persian Gulf), the West Indian port of Goa in 1510 and Malacca, a spice hub, in 1511. By 1513, they had reached China's southern ports, and were running a near monopoly on trade through the Indian Ocean. Westward, the Spanish conquistador Hernán Cortés followed in Columbus' wake, landing in Hispaniola in 1504 and helping to push Spanish authority upon Cuba (1511–1518) and inland upon the Aztecs living in present-day Mexico (1518–1520). Apart from their cities full of wealth, the Aztecs boasted some of the world's most fertile cropland and had devised sophisticated irrigation to produce great quantities of maize, squash and beans. Anxious not to be left out of this new age of empire-making, in 1524, the French sent Giovanni da Verrazano to penetrate North America's east coast, and in 1534 sent Jacques Cartier on his first of three forays up the St Lawrence River.

By far the most ambitious quest was undertaken by Ferdinand Magellan (1480–1521), who in 1519, like Columbus before him, sailed westward out of Spain in search of a route to Asia. He guessed that, like Africa's, South America's southern tip would also prove navigable, and that by sailing around it he could reach the Spice Islands (Indonesia) much faster than by sailing east. He was half right. He found his southern passage, and the Straits of Magellan are named in his memory. He also discovered a new ocean on the other side and named it the 'Pacific' – for its favourable breezes.

By that choice of names, Magellan betrayed Europe's last great ignorance about world geography. Still working from Ptolemy's ancient projections, he had estimated the distance westward from Spain to Asia to be some 130° of longitude.[2] In fact, it is 230°, and Magellan's so-called Pacific makes up the difference. The world's largest, wildest ocean, it spans 130 million square kilometres – one-third of the entire globe. Five ships and 237 men sailed west from Spain. Three years of hunger, murder, mutiny and shipwreck later, a single ship carrying eighteen crew made it back and, by their circumnavigation, gave Europe definitive proof of the earth's size and shape.

Cartography's crowning achievement in this Age of Discovery was the world map by Gerard Mercator (1512–1594), published in 1569. See Figure 2.3. He incorporated decades of exploration, navigation and chart-making into his work, and the result supplanted Ptolemy as the definitive picture of the planet. With some refinements – Australia wasn't sighted until the 1600s – it remains the basic template for our own maps today.

Mercator's map did more than sum up new data. It sketched foundations for a new and (in what was still a deeply religious

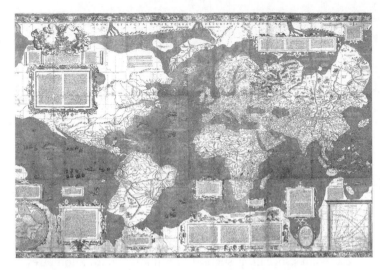

FIGURE 2.3 *The world according to Mercator (1569).*

Rumold Mercator (1569). Nova et Aucta Orbis Terrae Descriptio ad Usum Navigantium Emendate Accommodata. *Antwerp: Plantin Press. Courtesy of the Bibliothèque Nationale de France.*

age) somewhat blasphemous philosophy: that the knowledge gained from direct observation (the Book of Nature) could differ from, and even contradict, the wisdom of the Ancients and the Revelations of Scripture (the Book of God). Decorative sea monsters, religious icons and vague squiggles were replaced by a northern orientation, recognizable coastlines, and precisely drawn longitudes and latitudes. Asia and Africa were diminished to their true proportions, and Europe – which Ptolemy had set on the margins – was placed at the centre in recognition of its emerging role as chief conductor of global flows. A new world was arriving.

From ideology to market economics

A mere thirty years ago, we faced our own impenetrable frontier. It was not oceanic; it was ideological. But it presented the same contest between the power of authority to dictate truth and the power of observation to reveal alternatives.

We didn't know then what we know now – that too much central planning can doom states to economic stagnation and collapse. In the 1970s, communism seemed a permanent, valid alternative to the capitalist approach practised by democratic states. Communism was, after all, working. Communist countries generally proved able to deliver basic welfare – nutrition, education, health care – to their citizens, and the Soviet Union achieved leaps in science, not least in space exploration, which inspired fear and envy among capitalist observers.

And so, humanity was divided – politically, by the Iron Curtain; physically, by the Berlin Wall – into a contest between two mutually exclusive and nuclear-armed views of the world. On one side stood the First World: North America, Western Europe, Pacific Asia and their allies. On the other stood the Second World: the Soviets (since the Bolshevik Revolution of 1917), Eastern Europe (since it came under Soviet influence after the Second World War), China (since the 1949 founding of the People's Republic) and other communist countries. Remaining countries were labelled the Third World. Since many of them were poor, gradually this term came to refer to underdeveloped countries in general (now, such labels are considered pejorative). See Figure 2.4.

Today, this map is obsolete.

By the 1980s, the failings of centrally planned economies – clunky industries, perverted incentives, uninterested workers – had become painfully obvious, and even the biggest among them bowed to economic reality. Deng Xiaoping opened up China, and her then one-billion-person economy began to normalize trade relations with the West. Soviet President Mikhail Gorbachev pronounced his *perestroika* ('restructuring'). Economic collapse across a wide range of countries, from the Philippines to Zambia, Mexico, Poland, Chile, Bangladesh, Ghana, Korea, Morocco and

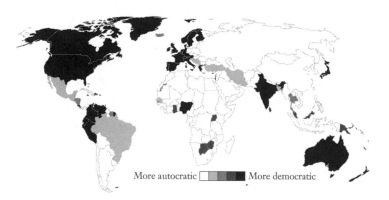

FIGURE 2.4 *The political world circa 1980.*

Source: Center for Systemic Peace (2015). 'Polity IV Project, Political Regime Characteristics and Transitions, 1800–2014'. Integrated Network for Societal Conflict Research. *Retrieved from www.systemicpeace.org/inscrdata.html.*

others, led them all in search of a better growth model. Import substitution, whereby countries raised trade walls against each other so that they could nurture their own industries at home, proved a failure: the industries could not achieve scale or excellence on the strength of domestic demand alone, nor were they strong enough to compete outside their tariff-padded walls. A growing number of countries succumbed to spiralling debt and inflation. They were forced into the arms of the World Bank and the International Monetary Fund (IMF), which insisted on the adoption of a new, export-led approach: dropping barriers to trade, letting in foreign competition and investment, protecting private property, and encouraging integration into global financial and manufacturing chains. In the span of little more than a decade, four billion more people joined the global market.[3]

Soviet President Gorbachev deemed the root cause of his country's malaise to be political, and so transmuted the capitalist wave into a democratizing one. In 1989, Poland's Solidarity movement won Poles the right to elect their own leadership. Within two years, Hungary, Bulgaria and Czechoslovakia had all chosen democratic futures, and East Germany had torn down the Berlin Wall. In December 1991, the Soviet Union itself was dissolved, Russia elected a president (Boris Yeltsin) for the first time in its history, and democracy stretched right across northern Asia.

As the Cold War thawed, populations that had been cowed into authoritarian rule by the geopolitical security concerns of one side or the other began to assert their anger against domestic concentrations of power and wealth. In 1980, military juntas ruled most of Latin America: Guatemala, Brazil, Bolivia, Argentina, Peru, Panama, Paraguay, Honduras, Chile, Uruguay, Suriname and El Salvador. By 1993, democratic revolutions had booted them all out. Two-thirds of sub-Saharan Africa's forty-six countries experienced popular power-takings during the same period – including South Africa, where many had thought it would take generations to end apartheid. All told, from 1970 to today, the ranks of formal democracies have risen from one-third to three-fifths of UN member states.[4] See Figure 2.5.

Of course, political differences remain. If 'democracy' means (1) majority rule determined by free and fair elections, (2) protection for minorities, (3) respect for basic human rights and (4) the legal equality of citizens, then less than half of the world's population lives inside one.[5] And in many places, democracy is under threat. The Russian parliament's once boisterous lower house (the Duma) is now little more than a rubber stamp for Vladimir Putin's post-post-Cold War policy agenda. Media freedoms have taken a beating in Latin America, Turkey, Hungary, the Middle East, northern Africa, while in the United States those outlets who criticize the Trump Administration are labeled 'fake news'. In developed democracies, voter participation rates are in long-term decline, and civil liberties

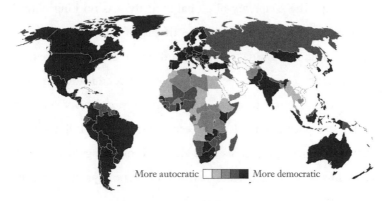

FIGURE 2.5 *The political world circa 2015.*
Source: Center for Systemic Peace (2015). 'Polity IV Project, Political Regime Characteristics and Transitions, 1800-2014'. Integrated Network for Societal Conflict Research. *Retrieved from www.systemicpeace.org/inscrdata.html.*

have been clawed back in the name of public security. (Ever since Edward Snowden blew the whistle on surveillance activities by the National Security Agency (NSA) in 2013, this once hushed trade-off has been loudly debated, but it has not been reversed.) On the other hand, the Arab Spring revolutions from 2010 onward across the Arab world, the dissolution of Myanmar's military junta in 2011, stirrings of political reform in Cuba, Hong Kong's 'umbrella revolution' pro-democracy demonstrations in 2014, and even the evolving rhetoric of the Chinese Communist Party make it clear that 'democracy', in some form, is a prerequisite to 'legitimacy' everywhere in today's world.

Through the 1990s, as the concept of 'rule by the people' spread, economic performance became the litmus test of political leadership. The *realpolitik* of global security was no longer top-of-mind among voters once the threat of the Soviet Union and communist China receded, and more mundane welfare considerations took centre stage: employment, education, health and nutrition, infrastructure and technology, currency stability and the environment. 'It's the economy, stupid', Bill Clinton famously pronounced in his 1992 electoral contest against George H. W. Bush – a sitting president whose foreign policy achievements were unassailable and yet, suddenly, irrelevant.

The growing global consensus that put economic growth first transcended many political differences that remained between states. The World Trade Organization (WTO), symbol of that consensus since its founding in 1995, now counts 161 members, including every major world economy (the last big holdout, Russia, joined in 2012).[6] Beyond opening our doors to one another, via the WTO we have also rearranged our furniture – harmonizing our domestic rules and institutions – to reduce further the otherness of operating in one another's economies.

The momentum of global trade negotiations has stalled. In the US and large parts of Europe, 'pro-trade' suddenly means 'anti-middle class'. But the past twenty-five years of WTO negotiations and dispute settlement have already broken down most trade walls. In advanced economies, average tariffs on imports are near zero. The Trans-Pacific Partnership (TPP) between the United States and eleven other states around the

Pacific Rim may be dead in the water, but existing regional clubs – the European Union (rededicated in 1993), the North American Free Trade Agreement (NAFTA, since 1994), the Free Trade Area of the Association of Southeast Asian Nations (ASEAN, 1992), the Southern Common Market (MERCOSUR, 1991) and the Southern African Development Community (SADC, 1992) – have already driven deep political and economic harmonization among close neighbours. So deep, it is proving difficult for protectionists to uproot what's been done. Brexiteers who are negotiating the United Kingdom's divorce from the EU find themselves acceding to a wide swath of EU regulations in order to retain market access for British goods. And Trump, who campaigned in the US on the promise to tear up 'bad deals' left and right, faces strong opposition at every step from members of his own party. They know that protectionism, just like free trade, will create both winners and losers among their constituents.

Only one country – North Korea – still rejects the notion of a global market. Even there, the idea is making inroads. Pyongyang's elite now drink some 2,500 tons' worth of imported coffee per year (up from 0 in 1998), while chatting on 2.5 million smartphones (up from 0 in 2009).[7] From well under 50 per cent in the 1980s, now almost the entire human population is linked by trade.

Democratic rhetoric and market economics have circumnavigated the globe.

New media

Gutenberg

The newness of the Renaissance world went beyond physical space; it extended to the realm of thought. In parallel with the forging of new relationships over land and sea, ideas themselves transformed—as did the paths over which ideas flowed.

The human eye has trouble recognizing even familiar faces 100 feet away; under typical circumstances, the human ear cannot pick up conversations beyond a similar distance. To reach any farther, our contact with one another must travel through some medium other than air. In about 1450, Johann Gutenberg (c. 1395–1468), a German entrepreneur in the city of Mainz, offered one that would become famous. It was a clever combination of innovations: a hand-held mould that made it possible to cast thousands of little metal letters (or 'type') quickly; a frame into which those thousands of letters could be arranged to spell out words and sentences; and a formula for an oil-based ink that both adhered to the type and transferred well when squeezed against a sheet of paper. To this mix he added two common local ingredients: a press (familiar technology in Europe since ancient times, albeit for squeezing olives and grapes) and paper. Paper had arrived in Europe three centuries earlier, via Moorish inhabitants in Spain who themselves had lifted the idea from the Chinese. It was cheaper than parchment (which was made from animal skin), and by Gutenberg's time was available from half a dozen mills in Germany.

The result was the world's first genuine printing press, and it set off a communications revolution.[†] A person born in the mid-1450s, at the time the world's first major printed book (Gutenberg's Bible) appeared, could on his fiftieth birthday look back on a short lifetime during which perhaps fifteen to twenty million books had been printed – easily more volumes than all the scribes of Europe had generated since ancient Roman times.[8] He or she probably had a hard time remembering a world without this suddenly ubiquitous object – a world where the only means of communicating information were face-to-face oral encounters and handwritten manuscripts; where a 'well-educated' person had read perhaps a dozen of the latter; and where reading any more than that meant making a long pilgrimage to the Papal library at Avignon (pre-Gutenberg, one of Europe's largest libraries, with over 2,000 volumes) or to one of Christendom's great monasteries. But no longer. In a span of fifty years, the printing press spread into a network of more than

---

[†]The prize for the first use of movable type for printing properly belongs to Bi Sheng (990–1051), who developed such a system in China around 1040 AD. Korea's Goryeo Dynasty also developed movable type, around 1230. Both versions failed to take off. Given the complexity of Asian character sets, they were too unwieldy and too expensive to displace manually carved woodblocks. Gutenberg appears to have discovered movable type independently.

FIGURE 2.6 *Europe's print network, 1500.*
Source: Greg Prickman (2008). 'The Atlas of Early Printing'. University of Iowa
Libraries. *Retrieved from atlas.lib.uiowa.edu.*

250 hubs across Europe (see Figure 2.6), and the sum total of
over 1,500 years of recorded European culture doubled. Over
the following twenty-five years, it doubled again. Information
growth went from gradual to exponential.

Impacts

This new medium, print, inexorably made the old obsolete.

It upended the economics of book-making, converting what
had once been a priceless artefact into a cheap commodity. The
German writer Sebastian Brant (1457–1521) commented in 1498:

'By printing, one man alone can produce in a single day as much as he could have done in a thousand days of writing in the past.'[9] He wasn't exaggerating. In 1483, Ripoli Press charged three florins per *quinterno* (five sheets of paper folded in two like a notebook) to set up and do a print-run of Plato's *Dialogues*. A scribe charged less – say one florin – but only produced one copy. In less time, Ripoli Press churned out 1,025.[10]

Print greatly standardized learning. Previously, every single book had been a unique object. Different fonts, pictures and page numbers, intentional and unintentional insertions, deletions and other idiosyncrasies meant that no two copies of any title were completely alike. Print didn't eliminate such quirks completely, but it did pare them down. Now, when people learned their Cicero, they were more likely to read the same speech, and if somehow a copy were destroyed, scholars had plenty of reliable backups. The consequences were profound, not least for science and the emerging fields of botany, astronomy, anatomy and medicine. Printing-press-compatible woodcuts and engravings replaced hand-drawn illustrations, and for the first time it was possible to put nearly identical, detailed images, diagrams and maps before scattered scholars and navigators. Data-rich pictures like those that appear throughout Andreas Vesalius's *De humani corporis fabrica libri septem* (1555), detailing the muscular structure of the human body, would simply not have been feasible in a pre-Gutenberg version. See Figure 2.7.

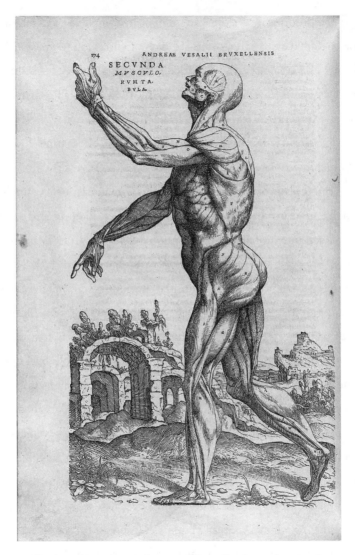

FIGURE 2.7 *Printing made it possible to spread complex visual information.*

Andreas Vesalius (1543). De humani corporis fabrica libri septem. *Basil: Johann Oporinus. Courtesy of US National Library of Medicine.*

Print improved access. Pre-print, knowledge was more of a walled garden. Most texts were in Latin (a hurdle that only educated elites could climb over), and most expertise was accessible only through oral instruction in universities and apprenticeships. The new vernacular-and-picture-laden books made knowledge 'common', extended it to apprentices, shopkeepers and clerks, and raised popular interest in learning how to read.[†] Meanwhile, the copious publication of books on history, philosophy and the natural world empowered scholars to bypass academic gatekeepers. 'Why should old men be preferred to their juniors, now that it is possible for the young by diligent study to acquire the same knowledge?' wondered the monk Giacomo Filippo Foresti (1434–1520) in 1483.[11] Many youth wondered exactly the same thing. One of the most important astronomers of the sixteenth century, Tycho Brahe (1546–1601), taught himself much of his craft from books published by Copernicus and others.

Print expanded the geographic range over which knowledge could be shared. While much of the fifteenth and sixteenth centuries was about Europe discovering and extracting the natural and human resources of other continents, Europe itself did add

---

[†]On the flip side, it also meant that knowledge began to get stuck in whatever language it was produced in. Translators became a necessary but insufficient bridge – something that is even truer today, because dictionaries are much thicker. English, for example, has five times as many words now.

one big ingredient into the mix: Western knowledge and ideas. Books were cheap and light, and they travelled far. *Indulgentiae ecclesiarum urbis*, a guidebook to Rome (a key pilgrimage site in Western Christendom), had by 1523 been sold in forty-four Latin editions and twenty vernacular editions across Europe and the Mediterranean.[12] Printed illustrations from Antwerp could by the 1500s be found everywhere Europeans sailed, including India, China, Japan, Mexico and Peru, and exposed local artists to European forms and styles.[13] Bible-bearing missionaries exported European and Judeo-Christian ideas about sovereignty, property, God, sin and salvation, and 'Man's' relationship with nature to their New World colonies and Asian trading partners.[14]

Print also expanded the range of *content* available for public consumption, and the public's participation in its creation. The first books to be typeset and printed were religious tomes. Then came Latin writers (Cicero, Virgil, Livy, Horace), followed by earlier Greek authors (first in Greek, and later in Latin), followed by the same works all over again – this time, in the vernacular (mainly French, English and Italian). Ancient Greek writings had survived the Middle Ages only in badly scattered, often mangled translations. But in the fifteenth century, whole Greek texts began to reappear in Western libraries. Scholars sojourned to Constantinople (then, still under Greek rule) and recovered them from the source. When Constantinople fell to the Turks, this trickle became a flood. Greek artists and scholars, disgruntled at

Ottoman rule, migrated westward to Italy with their dog-eared copies of Plato and Ptolemy under arm. Suddenly, the classical Greek heritage was restored: whole, in native clarity and brought to life by native interpreters. Western European intellectuals were hungry to mine this treasure trove for ancient achievements in philosophy, mathematics, astronomy, biology and architecture. Through print, the past was rediscovered and its significance interpreted for current and future generations.

But the 'classics', as ancient Greek and Latin texts eventually came to be called, could not by themselves keep the swelling number of Europe's print houses busy. The very purpose of books expanded, from storing past wisdom and spreading religious beliefs to propagating new ideas and experiences. A new format emerged – the pamphlet – and it widened the possibilities for self-expression. Brief, quick and cheap, printed pamphlets were the tweets of a half-millennium ago. Tradesmen, clerks, artisans and other professionals and preachers published some 4,000 different leaflets between 1500 and 1530.[15] Pamphlets also enabled scholars to quickly pin their name to a discovery or refute a rival's results. The Great Conjunction of Jupiter and Saturn in 1524 by itself generated some 160 pamphlets by sixty authors (most of them fuelling hysteria that the end was nigh).[16] Other pamphlets sought to race ahead of plagues or political crises, and supply a worried public with the facts (and fiction) about who would get struck down and who would be spared. Martin Luther accidentally set off the Protestant Reformation when his blistering critique of the Catholic Church, nailed to the door of his local church in 1517, was reprinted and spread Europe-wide. (For more, see Chapter 8.)

None of these impacts were instant; society took time to adapt to its new context. Scribes remained common for decades, and a century after the invention of print, conservatives were still pointing out the technology's faults. It could, for example, propagate mistakes (such as the so-called Wicked Bible, published in London by Robert Barker in 1631, whose seventh commandment read, 'Thou shalt commit adultery'). But printing proved too useful, too quickly, to be stopped. The chief of the Vatican Library, Andrea de Bussi, reflected in 1470: 'One can hardly report inventions of like importance for mankind, whether in ancient or modern times.'[17]

Zuckerberg

Today, we can. The advent of 'digital' as a new medium for capturing, communicating and exchanging data is a second Gutenberg moment. Digitization renders the analog world we live in – books, speeches, football games and taps on a touchscreen – as a sequence of 0s and 1s. Like Morse code, it's tedious for humans ('tedious' translates into '011101000110010 1011001000110100101101111011101010101110011'), but easy for computers because the distinction between 0 and 1, 'on' and 'off', is clear. We lose some information in the conversion (a smooth analog sound wave becomes a stepped ziggurat in digital), but the trade-off is that we gain the processing power of machines. And processing power is something we know how to grow quickly. In 1965, Intel's co-founder, Gordon Moore, noted that the number of transistors his company could fit onto a computer chip (and hence, the chip's processing power) doubled every two years or so. 'Moore's Law', as it became known, has held true ever since.

It's perhaps the most important empirical observation of our time. One of the defining features of the first Gutenberg moment was speed: within the span of a single lifetime, a new medium for culture and communication was born and became ubiquitous. So it is with our own. Consider the physical infrastructure at its base. In the fifteenth century, that infrastructure was printing presses; today, it is fibre-optic cables, overland and undersea. The first intercontinental fibre was laid in 1988. Since then, as the computing power to pump data through them has grown, their once sparse threads have become a dense weave. And the population of users connected to that infrastructure has multiplied seven-fold since the turn of the millennium, from 400 million to over three billion people.[18]

This is the fastest mass adoption of any technology, ever. At least, it was, until we miniaturized digital devices and made them mobile. As recently as 1998, only 20 per cent of people in the developed world and 1 per cent in the developing world had a cell phone.[19] Now, in the former, mobile subscribers outnumber people; in the latter, penetration has passed 90 per cent.[20] See Figure 2.8.

Nearly one-third of mobile users can now also get online with their phone.[21] The only thing in human culture growing faster than

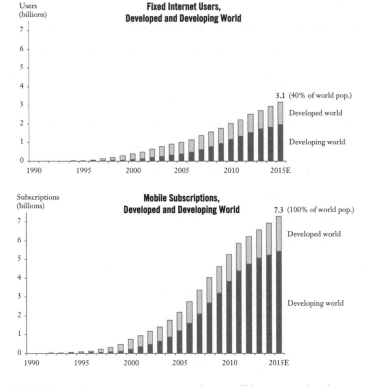

FIGURE 2.8 *In just twenty years, almost all humanity has been connected, by voice or data.*

Source: World Bank Databank (2015). World Development Indicators. *Retrieved from data.worldbank.org.*

digital mobile use right now is data itself – in large part because every year we produce billions more, better devices to capture and share information. These devices include not only smartphones, but also networked automobiles, dishwashers, MRI machines and giant radio telescopes. In 2011, there were as many networked devices on the planet as people. By 2015, they outnumbered us three to one. With them, humanity created, copied and shared about 44 zettabytes of data in a single year. That is a very large number – a '44' with 21 zeroes behind it. To put it into vague perspective, it would fill a stack of 128-gigabyte smartphones 250,000 kilometres high – two-thirds of the way to the moon. And it's doubling in height every two years. As recently as 2005, that annual stack of data reached 'only' from Miami to London.[22]

Fresh Impacts

The digital medium has, like print before it, upended the economics of how we all capture and share data. Thanks to Moore's Law and the rapid advances in computing power that go with it, we've pushed the digital interface right up to the human edge – up to everyone's ears and mouths, in our faces and at our fingertips – so that we can capture and share all our thoughts and speech in digital form and give them digital properties, namely: they can be copied perfectly an infinite number of times at near-zero cost; they can be consumed, edited and reworked, simultaneously or serially, hundreds or thousands or millions of times; they can be compressed, stored, backed up and retrieved on demand; and they can be amplified and repeated over any distance at light speed with near-zero signal loss. These properties have rendered distance, time and the costs of both largely irrelevant to the distribution and exchange of ideas.

As recently as 2001, the average long-distance phone call between, say, the United States and the United Kingdom cost up to $1.75 per minute, and we rationed those minutes accordingly. Today, thanks to digital services like Skype, the cost has fallen by a factor of 100, and we've largely ceased to care about it. International call volumes have almost quadrupled since 2001, from 150 billion to about 600 billion minutes.[23] The only relevance distance has to a phone call any more is the hassle of coordinating time zones – which is one reason why asynchronous modes of contact like WhatsApp and Facebook Messenger have taken off.

The other once-luxury, now-commodity is online data storage and processing – the cloud. Google now gives away, to each of its nearly one billion cloud users, online storage worth about $15,000 per person at 1995 prices. In other words, what would have cost a combined $15 trillion just twenty years ago is now free.[24] Not only a large share of all public knowledge, but also our private libraries – of letters, photos, music and corporate databases – are available to us anywhere, anytime. 'Cloud' is a catchy, but misleading, metaphor; it's more like a skin – always at our fingertips, inseparable from our identity.

Books, and the ideas they contained, were carried along every land and sea route Europe's new maps revealed; so it is today with digital data. The selfie taken by Ellen DeGeneres with seven other celebrities at the 2014 Oscars generated two terabytes of traffic in just twelve hours as it was downloaded to twenty-six million devices worldwide. In 2013, global data traffic broke the one exabyte per day barrier – more per day than total *annual* traffic in 2003. Traffic in 2014 was another 1.5 times greater.[25] As the online population swells (up to five billion people in 2017), and as each connected person consumes more content (especially video), total data traffic will continue to soar, and spread.[26]

Meanwhile, the busiest crossroads has shifted from the United States to Western Europe, which has become the prime hub for data exchange with Eastern Europe, the Middle East and Africa.[27] See Figure 2.9. A decade ago, weak physical infrastructure excluded many developing countries from the digital age. Now, smart mobile devices have helped them leapfrog those limits. By 2015, a greater share of humanity (95 per cent) had access to at least 2G cellular coverage than to electricity (82 per cent).[28†]

The digital medium has also helped *standardize* communication – most notably, through the sharing of video. Video-sharing only became practical after the mass adoption

†Where electricity is not supplied through a grid, internet-connected phones are charged at local stores with generators, at work or elsewhere. Phone charging is one of the myriad of micro-businesses that exist in poor communities.

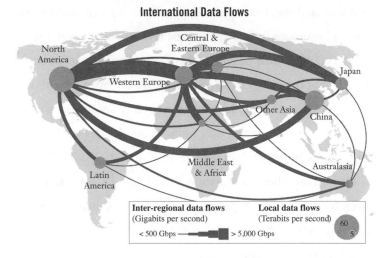

FIGURE 2.9 *Data now flows thickly between all continents.*
Source: James Manyika, Jacques Bughin, et al. (2014). Global Flows in a Digital Age.
New York: McKinsey Global Institute; Cisco (2015). Visual Networking Index.
Retrieved from www.cisco.com; plus authors' analysis.

of fixed broadband (which, by 2015, connected 11 per cent of households globally).[29] Video is high bandwidth for a reason: it captures complexity better, engages our brains more completely and reduces data loss compared with static and audio-only forms. These strengths may not be evident when you're making a routine call to the in-laws, but they shine through if, say, you're trying to explain the 'Viability of Bioprinted Cellular Constructs Using A Three Dispenser Cartesian Printer' – as a 2015 article in *JoVE*, the *Journal of Visualized Experiments*, aims to do.[30]

Digitization has freed speech. Twenty years ago, we divided communication into 'private' (one-to-one) and 'public' (one-to-many and many-to-many) forms. While cheap means of mass communication existed for the former (telephone, postal systems), the latter always involved very high distribution costs – through channels such as newspapers, books, cassettes and electromagnetic signals (television, radio). Typically, only corporate or state entities (publishing houses, media companies, and television and radio stations) could afford to build such channels, and they restricted access to only those communications that served their purposes.

Today, this distinction is a dim memory. Public distribution is now cheap, too. We, much like Tycho Brahe before us, can ask ourselves: Why should old voices be preferred to the new, now that it is possible for everyone to speak to their audience directly? This altogether valid question has thrown the whole of traditional media into a crisis. Newspaper journalism is no longer about selecting 'All the News That's Fit to Print'; now it's about curating content and generating buzz around an editorial viewpoint, in the hopes of getting added to readers' own timelines and newsfeeds. 'Fake news' portals, unencumbered by nuance and fact-checking, often prove better at this game than classical news organizations.

The role of schools and teachers is also changing. A good teacher's job is no longer to hand out information. Students in well-connected societies already have the world's knowledge at hand; uploading it to their brains has only marginal social benefit. Today, the teacher's job is to help students learn how to retrieve that information, critique it, combine it and add to it with their own research and opinion.

For those who choose to add their own voice to the global chorus of information and ideas, our Gutenberg moment offers many ways to do so. Print gave rise to the novel, the essay and the pamphlet; digitization has given rise to blogs, Snapchat channels, newsfeeds, tweets and Pinterest boards, and an endless variety of virtual goods such as apps and eBooks. In its first decade, the internet's usefulness consisted chiefly of disseminating information quickly and cheaply. Now (enabled by the spread of broadband and mobile), it invites users into content collaborations (such as *Quora* for facts, *GitHub* for software coding or *Thingiverse* for 3D print designs), news and opinion portals (such as *The Huffington Post* or *Medium*) or science projects such as the *Open Tree of Life*. All these new forms share one common characteristic: they involve a switch from audience to participant – from consumer to producer and distributor of content.

Finally, we are building a new layer of group intelligence. We can convene, sense, speak and act as groups with greater ease, power and speed. We can help one another find lost children or get help in a crisis. We can know more about what our fellow citizens are thinking and feeling. If Facebook were a nation, it would be the most populous on Earth, with over 1.5 billion active users each month.[31] And despite being dispersed around the globe, they are all, on average, less than four degrees of separation apart.[32] On Facebook, even if we've never met, a friend of your friend knows a friend of my friend.

This new group intelligence has been pivotal in many of the most talked-about events of the twenty-first century: the Arab Spring, the Occupy movement, public relief efforts in response to Hurricane Sandy, the Paris Climate Accord and the success of populist political campaigns in the United States and Europe. The wide range of these activities highlights how the new digital medium can bring both positive and negative outcomes. Societies and citizens are still fumbling to learn how to operate and manage this layer of consciousness. It has helped give rise to the Islamic State of Iraq and the Levant (ISIS/ISIL) – and to new Arab secular movements that reject not just religious violence, but religious governance.

It's difficult, but already it is transforming us. The 'will of the people', the 'social contract' and the 'pulse of the nation': these once-abstract terms from the Philosophy Department are becoming more concrete, measurable and parts of our culture and politics. Their impact can be seen each time old authorities— be they political parties or the media—are bypassed by new movements. Populist alternatives are challenging the authority of the status quo from every side of the political spectrum: conservative (in the form of Donald Trump or Brexit), leftist (Jeremy Corbyn) or centrist (French President Emmanuel

Macron). What they all have in common is the use of new media to mobilise against prevailing power structures.

* * *

There will be a day, not far distant, when you will be able to conduct business, study, explore the world and its cultures, call up any great entertainment, make friends, attend neighborhood markets, and show pictures to distant relatives – without leaving your desk or armchair.

Bill Gates, 1995.[33]

What is striking is not how right Bill Gates was, but how hard it is for us to remember the world in which none of that was possible. The digital medium has spread so rapidly, and so pervades our daily lives, that already we can scarcely believe it once took a trip to the public library to learn that the capital of Mozambique is _____, or that the only way to show our friends back home our vacation photos was to develop an extra set of prints and mail them. As with the printing press, we are again turning upside down how we acquire and exchange knowledge, and how we convene communities. And as before, our communities are simultaneously knitting together through shared ideas, and tearing apart the wider fabric of shared society.

It's a new world. And it's changing all of us.

3

New Tangles

How all human connections have become denser and more complex

What happens when you gather the four corners of a map together? You change how every point on that surface relates to every other. What once were margins suddenly become new ports in a sphere of possibilities. The centre, once fixed, becomes relative. Distances that previously tapered off into the void become bounded and knowable.

Columbus, Magellan, da Gama, Gutenberg – they did this to their world. And we're doing it to ours. The evidence goes beyond the pervasive digital domain. Every way that humanity connects – via trade, money, communication and travel – offers proof that we now live in a new world.

Trade

Slaying sea monsters

Trade is a narrow – and therefore flawed – proxy for global connectedness, but it's a good leading indicator. Historically, profit-seeking businesses and entrepreneurs are among the first to venture through new cracks in the barriers that divide peoples. When Christopher Columbus 'discovered' America, when Vasco da Gama reached India via the southern tip of Africa, when Magellan's crew successfully sailed into Asia from the *wrong direction*, a big part of their mission was trade – specifically, to find alternatives to the Ottoman-controlled overland routes to the East.

Prior to these voyages of discovery, most trade was regional, and the long-distance intercontinental trade that did take place was mainly overland or across inland seas. Europe was a quaint peninsula on the sidelines of the world. 'Europe', as a continental label, didn't even exist. Its inhabitants were a disunited, often warring, collection of Venetians, Aragonese, Bavarians, Florentines and other populations who produced and consumed among themselves with little consequence for other regions. Trade with the known world (Asia, the Middle East and Africa) amounted to at most 2 per cent of the European economy.[1] Europeans had to pay for their imports of porcelain, silk and spices with hard cash – gold and silver – since they didn't make enough products deemed valuable by other civilizations.

The new maps changed all that. The world's precious resources, as then understood (slaves, spices, sugar and gold), were put into global motion for the first time. Europe – the term gradually began to mean something – choreographed these increasingly large and intercontinental flows. In the early 1500s, Atlantic slave traders started up the horrific business of shipping 10,000 to 15,000 Africans annually from their native homes to colonies in North and South America. There, the slaves worked plantations of sugarcane, coffee and (after 1560) tobacco, producing commodities for European consumption on the other side of the ocean.[2] Slaves also mined New World gold and silver. Spain and Portugal extracted 150 metric tons of gold from the Americas (especially South America) in the sixteenth century – equivalent to all of Europe's gold output over the same period.[3] Some they sent home to pay off debts and finance wars, but the bulk they shipped to Asia to buy more Oriental luxuries: porcelains, silks, tea, coffee and especially pepper (which for the first half of the 1500s made up 85 per cent of all Portugal's trade through the Indian Ocean).[4]

Ocean freight volumes were modest throughout global shipping's first hundred years. The Portuguese sent some seven ships through the Indian Ocean to trade with Asia per year, each carrying 400–2,000 tons of trade goods and bullion. The Spanish had more traffic with their New World colonies; by 1520, they were sending two ships per week across the Atlantic. Still, the sea monsters had been slain, distances were demystified and ventures across the high seas became routine (if still dangerous). Ocean-going trade began to link the world's continents, cultures, resources and languages, and international finance and large-scale credit emerged to fund ever more far-flung commercial expeditions. The economic centre of gravity for the whole world shifted from the Middle East, which since ancient Babylon had been humanity's crossroads, to Europe. 'The discovery of America, and that of a passage to the East Indies by the Cape of Good Hope, are the two greatest and most important events recorded in the history of mankind', Adam Smith observed some 300 years later in his *Wealth of Nations* (1776).

On land, the wall between West and East proved more porous than the spectre of the marauding Turk had suggested. The presence of two civilizations on each other's border, neither in a position to conquer the other, forced both sides to evolve more sophisticated commercial, diplomatic and cultural transactions. The Genoese lost access to the Black Sea; the Venetians lost the islands and ports of the Aegean and Eastern Mediterranean. But market demand for the goods supplied along those routes didn't go away. Enterprising merchant houses, diplomats and lawyers together hammered out innovations in banking, credit, accounting and currency exchange to keep the Silk Roads open for business. Meanwhile, in 1517, the Ottomans conquered Egypt (which connects to the Indian Ocean via the Persian Gulf), and they too began to develop seaborne shipping links with Asia.[5]

Tearing down walls

Today, once again, the precious resources of once-isolated lands have been put into global motion.

The walls that divided 'us' from 'them' in the Cold War era meant that global exports of physical goods (measured as a share of world gross domestic product (GDP)) were no higher in 1973 (12 per cent) than they had been in 1913 before the outbreak of the First World War.[6] No higher, despite the many big, new catalysts of cross-border trade introduced in those intervening sixty years, including the invention of wide-body passenger and cargo jets and a commercial airline industry, intermodal container shipping, mass domestic and international telephony, an international gold standard to eliminate exchange rate risk from international money movements and the multinational corporation.

Once the walls came down, the flow of merchandise became a cascade – far greater in volume and variety than during the previous half-century, and mutually reinforcing as new markets and production centres connected into the global economy.

New volumes

The global goods trade, as a share of total economic activity, stayed flat through the 1980s. Then, suddenly, it started to blossom. In 1990, traded goods accounted for only one-seventh of global GDP. By 2014, it was a full quarter. One out of every four dollars earned, worldwide, now comes from selling merchandise to other countries. And the value of that merchandise has risen by over 500 per cent, from $3.5 trillion in 1990 to more than $20 trillion today – despite the worldwide recession caused by the 2008 financial crisis and rising anti-trade policies and rhetoric.[7]

Trade in services is historically much lower – it's harder to export, say, haircuts than Harley-Davidsons – but here, too, volumes have grown dramatically. Cross-border service flows have doubled in relative terms since 1990, from 3 per cent to over 6 per cent of global GDP, and sextupled in value, from $0.8 trillion to $4.7 trillion.[8]

New variety

Beyond volumes, the variety of global trade connections has grown, too.

This variety is, first, geographic. In 1990, a majority of trade was confined to the developed world. Fully 60 per cent of the global exchange in goods was made up of rich countries exporting to one other. Developing countries trading among themselves made up just 6 per cent. But now those respective shares are approaching equality. Trade everywhere has grown, but it has grown twice as fast along the new trade routes that have opened between emerging markets.

Rankings of the world's container ports reflect this rebalancing. In 1990, all the world's top ten ports by annual volume were in developed economies. By 2014, fourteen of the top twenty-five were in the developing world, and China by itself boasted seven of the top ten. The world's busiest container port since 2011, Shanghai, did not appear in the top twenty-five in 1990.[9]

The trade *mix* has also become more varied. The single biggest chunk of the global goods trade was, and remains, commodities – oil, gas, coffee, wheat, iron and other raw resources. But among *manufactured* goods, what gets traded now is far more diverse than just a quarter-century ago. A page from the July 1991 journal of the International Civil Aviation Organization heralded the delivery of Air China's first Boeing 747, which 'is used to transport textiles, apparel and other goods from Beijing to Los Angeles, San Francisco, London, Paris and Hong Kong. On return flights, the freighter's payload includes computers and other electronics items'.[10]

Today, we can all look back to such vignettes with amused incredulity. The simple mercantilist approach that developed economies once took to the developing world – leveraging their cheap labour and abundant resources – is obsolete. Emerging economies no longer simply supply inputs and markets; their home-grown champions now compete globally for capital, for customers, for talent. In 2012, China overtook the United States to become the world's largest manufacturer. Brazil, India, Indonesia, Mexico and Russia all rank among the top fifteen.[11] In the past quarter-century: Vietnam dismantled central planning in its agricultural sector and went from being a rice importer to one of the world's biggest rice exporters; Bangladesh built from scratch a $1.5 billion apparel export industry;[12] New Zealand's small dairy farmers consolidated and displaced the whole of the European Union as the world's largest dairy exporter, accounting for one-third of the traded market;[13] India built a $100 billion IT export industry,[14] which now performs 70 per cent of all outsourced market research and data analysis globally;[15] and the list goes on.

China, of course, is the stand-out case. From near-total isolation thirty years ago, China's economy now trades with over 230 countries and regions – more than any other country in the world. Its share of world exports has grown six-fold since 1990, from 2 per cent to 12 per cent of the global total – again, more than any other country.[16] The dollar value of its exports has grown almost forty-fold, from just $62 billion to over $2.3 trillion in 2014.[17] The mix has shifted from light manufacturing (clothes, shoes, textiles and furniture) to big-value machinery and electronics. And exports are only half the story. China's imports have kept pace, growing from $20 billion in 1980 to $2 trillion in 2014 – mainly advanced machinery and power-generation equipment, followed by energy and raw materials.[18] China is the single largest customer of all the big economies in its region (such as Japan, Australia, South Korea and Taiwan) and of the biggest Latin American and African economies (Brazil and Nigeria). By itself, China now accounts for nearly one-third of all developing-world trade.[19]

Supply chains are quickly adapting to these new capabilities and threats. In 1992, Nokia launched the world's first mass-produced mobile phone, the Nokia 1011. It was assembled mainly in the UK and Finland (close to its European launch customers), with components sourced from South Korea. Compare that with Apple's iPhone now. Its over 700 suppliers represent thirty-plus countries on five continents.[20] This rising logistics complexity is partly due to the growing complexity of products themselves (the 1011 didn't have a camera, let alone a touch screen). But it is also due to the rising capabilities of the emerging world to make and buy advanced products, plus the growth of communication and transportation technologies that make it possible to stitch together many different countries' contributions to supply and demand. In the 1990s and the 2000s, we called this 'offshoring', and it mostly meant sending manual and repetitive parts of the value chain (such as assembly and customer help) off to low-cost countries.

Now this term is passé; it implies an idea of 'home and away' that management needs to purge if it is to compete in today's markets. Products are 'made in the world' – and some, like the iPhone, are bought in the world, too. Business breaks apart the entire value chain and locates each piece for strategic reasons: offshoring some, re-shoring and near-shoring others. Cost matters, but it does not dominate the decision. In the twenty-first century, it can be just as profitable to make components for US automobiles in Tennessee as in Guangzhou – once time, overheads, responsiveness and political risks are factored in. See Figure 3.1.

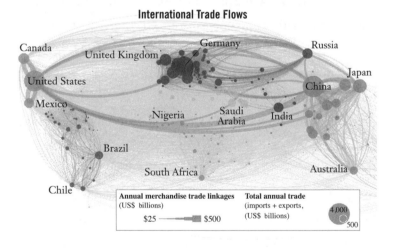

FIGURE 3.1 *Trade has become a genuinely global phenomenon.*

Image credit: Professor Rahul C. Basole and Hyunwoo Park, for Ghemawat, Pankaj and Steven A. Altman (2014). DHL Global Connectedness Index 2014. Retrieved from www.dhl.com/gci; plus authors' legend and labels.

Finance

From Venice to Antwerp

The new maps and media have also transformed financial connections. Finance is always a good place to look for evidence of social change, because it plays a fundamental role in society. We don't always recognize that role: 'finance' is one of those concepts that get used so much, we have a hard time sorting out what it's really about.

Strip away the sky-high bonuses and buildings, and what's left is an industry that serves a basic, essential function in an economy: simply, to match idle money to activities that need it so that those activities can happen. That's the aspect of finance that really matters. During the first Renaissance, this function changed in two ways, both of which sound familiar: the geography of capital-raising shifted and expanded – from a Venice-dominated local affair into an Antwerp-centred continent-wide market activity – and the participants in that market widened beyond merchant-traders to include everyone from princes to peasants. Together, these changes caused the volume of financial flows to ramp up, and tied the fortunes of the whole European continent closer together.[21]

Beginning in the late fifteenth century, Europe's economic centre of gravity shifted from the Mediterranean towards the Atlantic, and Italian banking houses and methods shifted with it. Partly, this was because the Italians *pushed* into the new growth centres: the Medici, for example, moved their main branch from Florence to Antwerp. And partly it was because the emerging merchant houses in Germany and the Netherlands *pulled* Italian expertise into their own accounting, contracting and finance practices.

With diffusion came innovation – and deregulation. The main Italian financial instrument was the *bill of exchange* – essentially, an IOU between buyers and sellers of physically traded goods. An Italian pepper buyer in 1450 didn't pay his Mediterranean supplier right away. Instead, he gave that supplier an IOU, and paid it off only after he had transported and resold the spice to continental buyers. IOUs were a convenient form of credit, with one crucial limitation: they could not be transferred to third parties. The Italians saw them as private promises made between two people who trusted each other enough to conduct business on account rather than in cash.

But in coastal Antwerp, the new capital of European commerce in the sixteenth century, traders chafed at this constraint. Pepper from India, silver from the New World, cloth from England and metals from Germany all passed through the port city. The buyers and sellers of these commodities spanned the whole of Europe; at any one time they owed, and were owed, payment on dozens or sometimes hundreds of unique IOUs with unique due dates. To keep commerce flowing smoothly, they needed a more flexible credit instrument to help net out their positions. So, by about 1520, they made the bill of exchange transferable. (The hard part was beefing up the legal system so that default risk could be transferred, too.[22])

Very quickly, an 'international republic of money' arose – in total value, hundreds of times larger than the physical trade it financed.[23] Now, instead of haggling with local buyers and suppliers, a trader could raise the money needed to pay for his next Indian pepper expedition by selling IOUs (bills of exchange) on the Antwerp bourse. The marvellous liquidity of public capital markets gave the trader an easy way to raise money, hedge risk and discover the current market price for his goods. The bills he had sold changed hands many times before any of his ships reached port: twenty times was common; a hundred times was not unusual. Sometimes, the motive was to realize profits or cut losses (pepper prices were notoriously volatile); sometimes, whoever held the bill needed cash fast for some other use. Bills written by the best-reputed merchant houses (such as the Fuggers) passed from hand to hand almost like today's paper currency.[24]

The upshot of all this new market activity was broader participation and continental integration in finance. Some 5,000 merchants from every European nation were represented on the Antwerp bourse. As one such merchant put it, 'A confused sound of all languages was heard there, and one saw a parti-colored medley of all possible styles of dress; in short, the Antwerp Bourse seemed a small world wherein all parts of the great world were united.'[25]

Individuals no longer had to engage in trade to profit from it. Anyone who liked the terms being offered and the trader's reputation could trade in bills of exchange. Non-merchants – institutions, trustees and small investors – all became active short-term players. With so many players taking part, the pool of available capital swelled and an ever-growing number of trading ventures could set sail. Other ventures also drew from the pot. Municipal governments from Calais to Oslo mortgaged state rents and lands on the bourse to raise big sums for agriculture, housing, mining and transportation projects.

Bourses helped to integrate physical markets in Europe, too. As capital markets pushed down the costs and risks of financing trade, transportation costs and delays mattered less. Soon, Spanish and Portuguese bakers found that wheat grown as far away as the northern Baltic could be cheaper than more local grain. Similarly, French and Portuguese salt began to muscle its way into Baltic producers' home markets.

The new market for finance stitched the economic fortunes of the continent more closely together. This presented new risks, but it also helped more people seize more of the opportunities that the age presented.

From Wall Street to Dubai

Deeper integration, wider participation, sharply increasing scale and risks: this is the story of contemporary finance as well.

How did we reach a place where, in 2007, popping a US real estate bubble precipitated a global economic meltdown? In 1990, raising and investing capital abroad was an activity confined mainly to the club of rich-world countries. The United States and Western Europe were the centres of cross-border finance activity. As late as 1999, the former was partner to 50 per cent, by value, of all international deals;[26] nine-tenths of all cross-border money flowed between developed countries.[27] Flows into and out of emerging markets were small. The developed world had scant information about emerging market opportunities; emerging markets had scant infrastructure and expertise to improve the situation.

During the first Renaissance, both push and pull factors spread Italian credit practices across the European continent. Since 1990, similar drivers have spread capital market activity across much of the planet. The most obvious factor pulling developed world capital into emerging markets has been, again, a shift in the locus of economic growth. As developed-world growth stagnated, investors were lured into the capital-hungry economies of rapidly developing countries. In just a few years, these economies implemented major reforms designed to make themselves more attractive to foreign money. In addition to opening their economies to trade, they brought international creditors and investment bankers into their economic policy shops, adopted more familiar fiscal and monetary policies, made it easier to move money in and out of the country, and put valuable state assets up for sale to private investors. Meanwhile, in the advanced economies, declining interest rates and tepid economic growth pushed investors out of their comfortable confines.

Diffusion was, once again, accompanied by financial innovation that caused a sudden leap in the scale of market activity. The main innovations – 'securitization' and 'credit derivatives' – were likewise about making debts and risk more easily transferable. By securitization, a lender mixed together the various IOUs he held (in modern parlance, bonds and mortgages). 'Quants', a new shorthand for physics and maths graduates who in previous years might have gone into rocket science instead, measured the mix carefully to reduce its total risk while preserving its outsized returns. The lender then sold shots of the resulting cocktail to other investors. In that way, he or she cleared the debts off the books and was free to lend some more. Credit derivatives emerged as a kind of insurance policy, bought by a lender against the risk that some of the more iffy IOUs he held would never be paid off. He bought credit derivatives from third parties willing to take on that risk (for a fee); if the borrower did eventually default, the third party would cover the lender's loss. Again, clearing this risk off his books freed the lender to lend more.

One important consequence of these two innovations was the emergence of the subprime mortgage market in the mid-1990s. Until the mid-1990s, a borrower was either 'prime', meaning he got a loan at the going rate, or 'subprime', which generally meant he did not get a loan at all. In the mid-1990s, lenders armed with these new powers to offload debt and risk (and with ever cheaper, more powerful computers to help do the maths) began to offer loans to subprime borrowers – at high interest rates. Subprime originations grew from \$65 billion in 1995 to \$332 billion in 2003.[28]

Deregulation also played its part. In 1986, reforms undertaken by Margaret Thatcher in the UK eliminated fixed trading commissions and introduced electronic trading. Over the subsequent decade, European economic and monetary union made it easier and easier for capital to flow around Europe. In 1996, the US Federal Reserve started letting financial institutions use credit derivatives to reduce their reserve requirements (again, so that they could lend more). In 1999, the US Financial Services Modernization Act repealed the 1933 Glass–Steagall Act and let banks, securities firms and insurance companies compete in one another's industries.

New volumes

Suddenly, cross-border financial flows took off. Between 1990 and 2007, global cross-border flows grew from about $1 trillion to over $12 trillion *per year* – an average 16 per cent annual jump every year for nearly two decades.[29] The 2007–2008 financial crisis scared away or broke up a lot of this activity (mostly among advanced economies), but some $4.5 trillion of debt and equity still crosses borders annually.[30]

New variety

Not only are financial flows much greater, but they move through many more places than twenty-five years ago.

Western Europe has built deeper linkages with emerging markets – Africa, the Middle East, Russia and Eastern Europe, and other parts of Asia. And big new links have been forged directly between emerging economies. Latin America now has investment links with emerging Asia that are as important as its links with Western Europe. Foreign direct investment (FDI) into developing countries has risen from less than one-fifth to almost three-fifths of global FDI since 1990.[31] (FDI matters because it's generally long-term and forges a link between sender and receiver over which technologies and management skills can be shared.) And while debt, equity and other forms of investment into advanced economies remain sluggish, flows to China, South Asia, Latin America and Africa have already regained their pre-crisis importance.

The world's capital has been stitched together into a bigger, more complex and more global network of investments. See Figure 3.2.

You don't have to look at a map of the world to witness this new global integration of finance. You can see it in your own personal portfolio – or you could, if reporting by financial institutions were less opaque. Your pension (in the United States, your 401k) may be invested in a wind farm in Yorkshire, a gold mine in Mongolia, real estate in Rio – or, quite possibly, all three. The home loan you took out a few years ago could well be owned today by a company

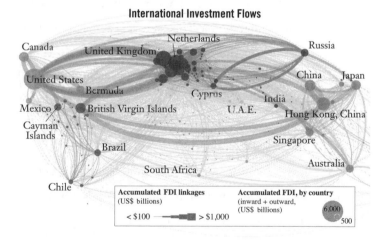

FIGURE 3.2 *Cross-border finance tangles the world's balance sheets together.*

Image credit: Professor Rahul C. Basole and Hyunwoo Park, for Ghemawat, Pankaj and Steven A. Altman (2014). DHL Global Connectedness Index 2014. Retrieved from www.dhl.com/gci; plus authors' legend and labels.

in the Cayman Islands. The monthly payments you make on your credit card debt, student loan and car loan are being passed on to bondholders in London, Dubai, Tokyo, Johannesburg and elsewhere.

The scale and complexity of our financial interconnectedness breed new risks, but also bring opportunities. Across the planet, it is more likely that projects in need of money will get it. It's estimated that over 700 booming cities across the developing world will need a combined $40 trillion of new infrastructure by 2030 – roads, ports, power stations, water and telecom utilities, schools, hospitals and the like.[32] Few will be able to pay the upfront costs themselves. And the help flows both ways. In aggregate terms, developing countries have become net capital *exporters* to the developed world.[33] That can be good news for a developed country like Canada – blessed with abundant natural resources but a small population. Canada aims to invest an estimated $650 billion by 2020 into its energy sector alone;[34] it won't find that much idle capital among its thirty-five million citizens.

Finance is risky, and its main actors quite often lose sight of their real role in society, but as an industry it has never been better placed to underwrite human achievement.

* * *

To sum up all the above, trade is now twice as important to global economic well-being as it was twenty-five years ago. The combined value of annual cross-border goods, services and money flows has risen from just over 20 per cent of global GDP in 1990 to nearly 40 per cent today (in money terms, from about $5 trillion to almost $30 trillion per year). And the developing world's share of that total has tripled.[35] Once again, the world's economic resources have been put into global motion. And once again, livelihoods both depend upon and are threatened by these new flows.

People

What about the world's most precious resource – people? When the maps of the world are redrawn, individuals are put into new relationships with one another. Old margins become new gateways. Spectators become participants — and vice versa. To travel is the oldest human impulse: when the world opens, the flow of people – of *us* – reflects how.

Short-term travel

For people with sufficient talent or means to move around during the first Renaissance, there were suddenly many more must-go-to places. To the established crossroads for business (Venice, Paris), higher learning (Padua, Bologna) and culture (Florence) were added Antwerp (trade and industry) and the great Atlantic and Asian gateways: Lisbon, Seville, Amsterdam and (later, by 1600) London, among others. The Catholic Church resurrected Rome from a long period of neglect, and once again all roads led to it. Venice, the seaside middleman between European and Eastern trade, became even more cosmopolitan than before. There, Christians and Jews from all over Europe and the Levant rubbed shoulders daily with one another, with Ottoman Turks, and with a smaller number of itinerant and permanent trade representatives from Africa and the Far East. The city itself evolved into an unusual blend of Byzantine, Islamic and Italian architecture in sympathy with its complex demographics.

Crossroad cities boasted diverse, crowded cultures and an ever stronger flux of new people, goods and ideas. Those three conditions – diversity, crowds and change – came together in ports, at markets, in churches, at court, in the houses of the wealthy and in universities (where exchange was simplified by a common academic language, Latin). By the early sixteenth century, over 40 per cent of students at Krakow's famous Jagiellonian University were foreigners, from as far away as Scandinavia and Scotland; Italy's Padua graduated hundreds of Germans per year. Pilgrimages to such cities became a must for the sixteenth-century elite: to acquire the new knowledge, skills and networks necessary to succeed in a rapidly changing world; to access new pools of patronage for professional development and escapades; and to learn new languages, particularly Greek but also Arabic and Hebrew, in order to participate in the most learned discussions of the age.

Today, the crossroads are again teeming with travellers. New York, London, Tokyo, Paris, Singapore, Los Angeles, Brussels, Beijing, Sao Paolo: try to find a global leader in any field, anywhere, who has not visited at least one such hub. You can't. Others are following in their footsteps. Between 1990 and 2015 the worldwide total of international tourist arrivals (defined as visits of at least one night) rose from 440 million to 1.4 billion visits, with China now the biggest source of travellers.[36] Air traffic presents similarly stark evidence. Total passenger trips have leapt from some 500 million in 1990 to over 3.2 billion in 2015.[37] And since 2011, international flights have outnumbered domestic.[38]

Many factors have driven this growth. One is the invention of low-cost carriers (Southwest Airlines, EasyJet, RyanAir, Peach and others) in North America, Europe and Asia, which broadened considerably the community of airborne commuters. But a bigger factor is the emergence of new hubs on the once-margins of the world, plugging those populations into the global circulation of jet-setters.

Their emergence is plain to see in rankings of the world's busiest airports. In 1990, only two of the world's top twenty-five busiest airports (by total annual passengers) stood outside North America, and those were the major European hubs: London-

Heathrow and Frankfurt. Today, sixteen do – including Beijing at #2.[39] The shift is also clear in the declining weight of the top twenty-five. Back in 1990, they made up more than 50 per cent of global traffic. Today, it's less than one-quarter, because there are so many new routes and nodes through which passengers flow – especially in China, where air traffic has grown twenty-fold.[40]

Twenty years ago, three-quarters of fliers were from North America and Europe. Today, North American, European and Asian travellers each make up one-quarter of those who travel the skies. The term *jet set* still implies the activities of a small elite, but within the next twenty years, billions more people will join the club. The big aircraft makers, Boeing and Airbus, figure that between 2015 and 2034 the fastest passenger growth in the aviation world will be in Africa (albeit from a low base), followed by Latin America, Asia, then the Middle East. Links between Africa and Latin America will be the fastest-growing interregional routes. In absolute numbers, Asian traffic will soon dominate the departure lounges. If aircraft makers' predictions hold, by 2034, Asian passenger traffic will outnumber North American and European numbers put together.[41]

Long-term migration

Maligned by xenophobes, Long-term travellers, or migrants, are exceptional people. To migrate is to defeat the geographic, cultural and socio-economic distances that otherwise separate us from others. For migrants themselves, and for their sending and receiving societies, the test is profound. Migrant journeys – whether from the country to the city (urbanization) or from home to abroad – are often heroic stories of courage in the face of great odds.

The first Renaissance bore witness to a marked increase in migrant flows, and so does the second.

Urbanization

In the pre-Columbus world, on average only about 10 per cent of Europe (with wide country-by-country variation) lived in towns of 5,000 people or more. Trading nations like Italy topped the urbanization charts (15–16 per cent); countries stuck on Europe's margins (such as Spain, Portugal, the British Isles) scored in the low single digits.[42] But with the new maps, the margins became gateways, and their cities caught up quickly. Within 100 years, Portugal's urban share of its population had quintupled from 3 per cent to 14 per cent.[43] British urbanization doubled (from 2 per cent to 4 per cent), as did Spain's (from 6 per cent to 11 per cent). Seville, which became Spain's international trading hub for New World goods, saw its population soar from around 60,000–70,000 residents in 1500 to as many as 150,000 by 1588. Tens of thousands more passed through on their way to the Americas.[44] Existing hubs also enjoyed an influx of new people. Cities offered more certain incomes, the protection of urban fortifications (conflicts like the Italian Wars of 1494–1559 were best weathered behind stout walls), and a richer social and intellectual life than rural villages afforded. Most importantly, a move to a city – especially a trading city – was a move closer to knowledge, markets and opportunity. In 1500, only five European cities could boast populations over 100,000; by 1600, a dozen did so.

Back in 1990, the most urbanized countries all belonged to the developed world. About three-quarters of North America and Oceania, and 70 per cent of Europe, Latin America and the Caribbean, lived in cities. But in Asia and Africa, on the margins of the world economy, a minority of people (30 per cent) called a city home.

Those continents are margins no more, and today over half of Asians and 40 per cent of Africans live in cities. In absolute numbers, over the past twenty-five years their urban populations have doubled. Put another way: across Asia and Africa, the present generation has, by itself, duplicated the previous *5,000 years'* worth of urban population growth.[45]

As a result, in 2008, humanity as a whole quietly passed a significant milestone: for the first time in our species' history, a majority of us dwelt in cities. Barring a cataclysm, we will never see the other side of that threshold again. We are an urban animal now, and although our habitat trends vary locally, in net global terms *all* future population growth will be in cities. By 2050, humanity's urban population may grow by another 2.5 billion people; our rural population is expected to *shrink* by 150 million.[46] The city is the centre of things, and as a species we are rushing to be there.

New crossroads are again emerging. Mega-cities like Tokyo, New York, London, Toronto, Paris, Delhi, São Paulo, Mumbai, Mexico City, Shanghai and Dhaka command the world's headlines, but the real story – at least so far as urban growth is concerned – will play out in the more than 700 developing-world cities with populations that exceed 500,000 today, and the more than 350 new cities that will reach that threshold by 2030. They will add 1.3 billion inhabitants through 2030 – compared with an increase of just 100 million dwellers in existing big cities.[47]

We know these new crossroads only vaguely, if at all. They include some 150 regional hubs of five to ten million inhabitants, like China's Changsha, Brazil's Joinville and Mexico's Veracruz; a few hundred midsize-growth cities of one to five million, like India's Ahmedabad and Russia's Sochi – often built around local natural resources or industrial clusters; and thousands of smaller boomtowns few of us could find on a map, such as Hengshan, Leibo, Kuchaman City, Konch, Caxias, Timon, Escobedo and Abasolo.

China leads the urbanization story. Between 1982 and 1986, the dismantling of state-planned agriculture released surplus workers from their rural posts. China's urban population catapulted from about 200 million to almost 400 million people in four short, hectic years of transformation.[48] China's next urban boom began after 1992: Deng Xiaoping embarked on his historic Southern Tour of China's southeast coastal region (during which he may have proclaimed, 'To get rich is glorious'), solidified pro-market reforms as Communist Party dogma, and prompted an export-driven expansion that lured rural labour to the coast. Shenzhen, on China's Pearl River Delta, became the modern-day Seville. A fishing village of some 10,000 people during the 1970s, it was anointed a Special Economic Zone in 1979 and reached 2.5 million inhabitants over the next decade. After the Southern Tour, growth leapt into a new gear: by the year 2000, Shenzhen's population topped eight million and by 2015, ten million (or fifteen million, counting migrant labourers).[49] The story was repeated in dozens of other places, so that today over half of China's population – nearly 800 million people – live in its cities.[50] In one generation, almost half a billion people – equal to the present population of the European Union – relocated.

Africa will write the next chapter of population growth and urbanization. From now until 2030, Africa, not China, will experience the world's biggest and fastest urban expansion. While China's total population will stay flat at around 1.3 to 1.4 billion, Africa's is expected to swell from about 1 billion people today to over 1.6 billion. As many as four-fifths of those newcomers will be born into cities, pushing the urban share of Africa's population up to 50 per cent by 2030. Cairo, today Africa's most populous city, will grow from eighteen to twenty-four million. But by then it may be overtaken by Lagos or Kinshasa (both on pace to double in size from about twelve million today).[51]

* * *

Urbanization brings many benefits. By physically squeezing humanity closer together, it improves the efficiency with which we use our world's land, energy, water and other resources. It increases the density of our societal relations and interactions, and brings us all closer to physical and digital infrastructure that links us globally. And cities concentrate human resources. Financial capital, production, markets, talent, information and knowledge creation: all these pieces are easier to find and accumulate inside cities. With the right supporting conditions, this can have big, positive consequences for human achievements. But it carries new risks, too.

Crossing borders

The first Renaissance was also an age of massive, and mostly forced, movement of people from one country to another.

This circulation began within Europe itself. In the east, the Turkish conquest of Constantinople prompted thousands of Greeks to flee westward to the Italian cities of Venice, Florence and Rome. In the west, in 1492, the Catholic monarchs Ferdinand and Isabella managed to subdue the last remnants of the once great Muslim territory of al-Andalus. Muslims from North Africa had occupied large parts of what is now Spain and Portugal since 711; now, they were unwelcome guests in their former home. Ferdinand and Isabella escalated their Inquisition, which had begun in 1478: trials and harassment that eventually evicted tens of thousands of Jews and Muslims in the name of national unity and Catholic purity.[†] Beginning in the 1520s, the rest of Europe experienced another flow of displaced people – this time, as the result of Luther's Reformation. That violent division of Christendom into Catholics and Protestants produced migration on a scale that Europe had not seen since the fall of the western Roman Empire in the fifth century, and would not see again until the First World War.[52]

The most infamous mass migration was the Atlantic slave trade, which began within a few years of Columbus' discovery of the New World and which transplanted over eleven million Africans to the Americas by the mid-nineteenth century. As with the seaborne goods trade, this grim business started off modestly. Some 400,000 Africans had been delivered by the year

---

[†] The Ottoman ruler Sultan Bayezid II sent his own fleet to resettle Jews from Iberia into his empire. He later remarked how the Catholics' anti-immigrant stance had 'beggared their own country and enriched mine'.

1600, forced to join some 250,000 Europeans in their New World colonies.[53] But the inhumanity had begun, and would balloon in the centuries to come.

This forced migration was driven mainly by economics. Europe hoped to extract enormous wealth from its new colonies through plantations of cotton, coffee, sugar, tobacco and indigo, and mines of gold and silver. France and Britain claimed new arable territories in North America; Spain and Portugal had new territories stretching south from today's California to Chile. Europe and the Mediterranean presented ready markets for their produce. All that was missing was manpower. The solution in the fifteenth and sixteenth centuries was the slave trade. Europe hunted and captured people from the freshly mapped African coast and relocated them across the ocean to supply labour for the Americas. (Local slaves might have been cheaper, but European disease was eradicating the indigenous labour pool. See Chapter 4.)

The ethics of migration have been totally transformed over the past 500 years. As Ian and others point out in *Exceptional People*, while one class of migrants, notably refugees, may abandon home because circumstances leave them little choice, today's *economic* migrants typically enjoy far more freedom in their decisions to move. They can obtain higher wages and a better quality of life (for themselves and for those who depend on them back home), and in exchange they contribute to the growth and dynamism of a foreign economy.

Once again, the opening up of new resource- and consumer markets has spurred a transplant of labour. In 1975, two-thirds of the world's labour force toiled behind the walls of closed or highly protected economies. Today, most of us work in countries still committed, at least formally, to an open trading system. These political and economic transformations have forced states to rethink to whom they grant the privilege of movement. Historical and colonial ties, or racial and national discrimination, still cast a long shadow over immigrant admission policies, sadly. Increasingly, however, immigrants' capacities to contribute skills, ideas or financial capital to their host country matter more.

How large the present-day transplant of labour is depends on how you look at it. In absolute terms, the total number of people living abroad has grown by two-thirds in a single generation, from 150 million in 1990 to almost 250 million today.[54] On the other hand, humanity has swelled by almost 50 per cent over the same period. As a share of the world's population, therefore, the global stock of migrants has remained pretty flat – about 3 per cent – since the 1980s.[55] That should surprise us a bit, given the rising tide of anti-immigrant sentiment in many destination countries.

Cut through the scare-mongering, and the fact is that migration throughout this brave New World of ours is, once again, off to a modest start. Persistent restrictions on cross-border work and living mean that, among all things that can move around this earth, people still have the hardest time.

And yet, they find a way. In 2004, the European Union began an expansion to include countries in Central Europe, Eastern Europe and the Baltics. EU expansion granted those populations mobility rights they had long desired but been denied. By 2015, over fourteen million EU citizens were living in an EU country outside the country of their birth.[56] Globally, some seventeen million people migrate to a new country each year, in a variety of visa categories.[57] Year by year, migrants are tying every region of the world together at the family level. See Figure 3.3.

The rest of us are lucky they do. The United States is home to nearly fifty million legal immigrants from virtually every

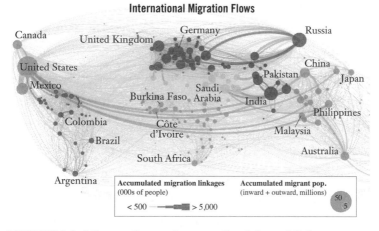

International Migration Flows

FIGURE 3.3 *Migrant flows criss-cross the globe and link every region.*

Image credit: Professor Rahul C. Basole and Hyunwoo Park, for Ghemawat, Pankaj and Steven A. Altman (2014). DHL Global Connectedness Index 2014. Retrieved from www.dhl.com/gci; plus authors' legend and labels.

other country of the world – and, it's estimated, eleven million more who are undocumented.[58] Many societies are divided by intense political debates about the merits and costs of letting people move more freely. But among economists, there is virtual consensus: migrants are a major source of innovation and future jobs, and a freer flow of migrants would boost economic growth, stimulate innovation and cut poverty.

Unskilled and semi-skilled immigrants on average contribute more to their employers and to governments than native workers, as they tend to be paid lower wages and receive fewer benefits. These immigrants supply the world's better-off with low-priced healthcare, child- and senior care, and (through their back-breaking work in seasonal agriculture) cheaper fruits and vegetables. They staff manual jobs that fewer and fewer long-term residents – especially the growing share who have gained a university education and expect to be rewarded for it – are willing to take. And they pay taxes. (A major study of the UK experience found that, in the first decade of the twenty-first century, immigrants paid in, via taxes and other public goods, some $150 billion more than they took out via state benefits. Natives, by contrast, withdrew a net $1 trillion.[59]) Because immigrants tend to be younger and are more likely to get a job than the average citizen, they also help to ease the aging of host countries' populations. This is a critical concern for most developed economies, since the older their populations get, the heavier the burden imposed by welfare services upon the remaining wage earners becomes. (In Europe, the aging problem is severe: it has been estimated that just to maintain welfare programmes at present levels would require 1.4 billion more wage-earning immigrants to arrive between now and 2050. The more likely outcome is modestly rising immigration coupled with steadily declining welfare.)

Other immigrants offer scarce labour. In the United States, two-thirds of the country's science and engineering workforce are immigrants, and 10 per cent of IT jobs go unfilled because no one with the right qualifications shows up to take them. In the UK, around 12 per cent of the whole workforce are immigrants, but they fill *half* of all new jobs – either because the skills they supply are unavailable domestically or because they're doing jobs that nobody else wants.[60]

Perhaps most importantly, immigrants spice things up. They carry with them their culture, language and ideas, and they connect their host country to useful networks back home. Plus, they bring to their work the same courage and ingenuity they demonstrated by moving to a new country. The founders of Google (Alphabet), Intel, PayPal and Tesla were all immigrants. In 2005, immigrants headed up 52 per cent of all Silicon Valley start-ups and 25 per cent of *all* US technology and engineering firms founded in the previous ten years. Immigrant-American Nobel laureates, National Academy of Science members and

Oscar-winning directors outnumber their native-born peers three to one.[61]

Some economists figure that returning to a pre-First World War immigration regime (when labour moved freely about the world) would contribute $40 trillion – 2.6 times present-day US GDP – to the global economy over the next twenty-five years, and more or less end poverty at the same time.[62] 'All foreigners have the unrestricted right of entrance and residence', Britain's secretary of state, Lord Granville, pronounced – in 1872. Then, the world's great power demanded no passports and imposed no quotas at the border. That right-to-migrate regime is not likely to return any time soon – in the present political environment, it's hard to believe that it ever existed. But whether our politics support immigrants or not, an ever-growing number are going to try to find their way across borders.[63]

The first driver of emigration is financial: the average developing-country émigré can multiply his salary five-fold by moving to the United States. A second driver is global development and population growth. Sub-Saharan Africa and South and East Asia are emerging from their poverty traps and will soon boast the world's largest (and increasingly capable) workforces. A third driver is desperation. Disaster and persecution force individuals to abandon homes that can no longer offer safety or shelter. In 2015 alone, millions of refugees fleeing civil war in Syria poured into neighbouring Lebanon, Jordan and Turkey. A million more fled to Europe. There, they joined people escaping conflicts in Libya, Eritrea, Iraq and Afghanistan to create the continent's greatest refugee crisis since the Second World War.[64]

* * *

The first Renaissance gave humanity its first glimpse of its global self: diverse, strong and vulnerable. Now, after decades of walling each other off, we are coming to see it again. As the ranks of travellers and migrants swell from the few to the many, we will all be changed by the labour, culture, language, networks, needs and ideas they spread around the world.

Technology

New ships

New globe-spanning flows do not simply happen. In the first Renaissance, new maps presented both problems and opportunities. European sovereigns, bankers and adventurers focused significant resources and took big risks – hoping to overcome the challenges of long-distance trade and exploration in order to capture the benefits. Ship design innovation blossomed (possibly thanks to borrowings from China).[65] New sails (certainly borrowed from the Ottomans) and new rudders improved speed and manoeuvrability. Ships also got bigger.

Bigger ships were better suited to the open sea and earned more profit (since cargo capacity scaled up faster than crew costs). By 1600, the capacity of the average ship had swelled from 300 to over 1,000 tons.[66] Europe also continued to invent new applications for Chinese gunpowder, and the galleon emerged as a heavily armed escort for Europe's trading fleets.

New tools and techniques revolutionized navigation. Columbus crossed the Atlantic with no reliable way of knowing his ships' latitude or longitude. He sailed due west and hoped for the best, and when he first sighted Hispaniola he mistook it for Japan (he was off by 6,000 miles).† Astronomers and mathematicians took on the challenge, and within a few decades any sailor could look up his latitude in a book of tables by measuring the height of the sun (or, at night, the North Star) with a new astrolabe.† (Again, Islamic collaboration was key. In the 1400s, Ottomans brought to Europe the Arabic number system – replacing the abacus – and higher algebra, without which no tables could have been written.[67]) In 1533,

---

†It was Amerigo Vespucci, who travelled to the Americas in 1499 and published *Novus Orbis* (*The New World*) about his voyages, who popularized the *Aha!* insight that this landmass was a whole new continent. Mapmakers therefore named it after him.

†Longitude took much longer. Without radar, GPS or satellite, the simplest way to know your longitude at sea is to compare the ship's local time with the local time at a known longitude, then add/subtract 15° per hour of difference. Unfortunately, a clock that could keep time at sea wouldn't be invented until 1763.

Reinerus Gemma invented triangulation, which greatly improved navigation on land.[68] Better navigation led to better maps, culminating with Mercator's 1569 picture of the known world.

The technology of business also changed. As trade volumes grew, new service industries emerged to support trade and make it easier. Ocean and overland transportation evolved from a wholly in-house activity – every merchant had to arrange his own ship or wagon train and crew – to an outsourced function run by specialized courier companies. They organized or bought shipping capacity and then resold it as a packaged solution to traders. Merchants could focus on their core business and reduce their risk by locking in fixed freight rates, and smaller traders found it easier to start up. Instead of chartering a whole ship, now they could buy cargo space piecemeal from service providers.[69]

Commission agents likewise created a new market in sales and purchasing services. Large merchant houses maintained networks of permanent representatives in major cities who did business and handled information on their behalf – infrastructure that lesser firms couldn't afford. Then commission agents stepped in. By contracting themselves to many clients on pay-per-use terms, they turned that large fixed cost into a small service fee. Together, these new service industries made it possible for even small firms to trade with multiple distant markets.[70]

Newer ships

New technologies are playing the same role today – enabling greater volumes and variety of goods, services and people to circulate. In the sky, aerospace improvements have extended the range that aircraft can fly and lowered their operating and environmental costs. Now, no two cities on the globe are more than a day apart, and more of us can afford to fly between them. In the United States, the cost of flying has fallen by as much as 40 per cent over the past thirty years.[71]

On land, the emerging 'Internet of Things' – tagging everything from cars to Coke machines with little chips and computers that can link to data networks – means that more and more objects in the physical world are adopting digital properties. Orchestrated by computers and drones such objects can start to move about in volumes, at speeds and with efficiency far beyond human capabilities. Today, they number fifteen billion; by 2020, there will be fifty billion such objects in the world.[72] In Seoul, Korea, for example, the entire public transportation system – every bus, taxi, train and public bicycle – is now networked.[73] The expectation is that travel times will quicken and road congestion will fall as every user and 'device' on the network starts to make computer-aided traffic management choices.

The Internet of Things will transform the volume and variety of physical flows on land. We know this, because it has already helped to do so at sea. So far, that is where new technologies have done the most to enable new global flows. 'Containerization' has digitized shipping by putting everything from cars to crayons into identical, traceable boxes. This revolution began in 1956 with the advent of the container ship, and by the early 1990s, all the world's major ports had been converted to handle them. Today, containers carry 90 per cent of all non-bulk cargo.[74] The simple box is so powerful because it slashes shipping's biggest bottleneck: getting things on and off. Every container can be handled the same way (meaning machines can take over most of the labour) and be swapped quickly and easily from ship to airplane to train to truck. In 1990, the world shipped twenty-five million containers. Today's volumes are pushing close to 150 million per year.[75]

This story is widely told. Less told is how the *routes* these boxes travel have changed. The ships themselves tell it best. Once again, as new maps presented new opportunities, ships got bigger. The same economics that ruled the first Renaissance rule today: cargo capacity scales up faster than cost. But in 1984, the capacity of container ships topped out at about 5,000 TEUs (Twenty-foot Equivalent Units, or the size of a standard container), and remained stuck at that threshold for the next twelve years.

It had nothing to do with the technology of shipbuilding. Rather, it was because a 5,000-TEU ship was the biggest that could squeeze through the locks of the Panama Canal (such ships are labelled 'Panamax'), and no one wanted to buy a container ship that could not serve global shipping's most important route: the canal link between the Americas' Atlantic and Pacific coasts.

In 1996, however, one of the biggest shipping companies in the world, Maersk of Denmark, decided to challenge that orthodoxy. It took delivery of the 6,400-TEU 'post-Panamax' ship *Regina*. The economic centre of gravity, Maersk reasoned, was shifting. The Panama Canal was irrelevant to the fastest-growing trade routes: the Pacific routes connecting the Far East (China, Korea, Japan), the Asian Tigers (Hong Kong, Singapore, Taiwan), and the west coasts of North and South America; the Atlantic routes connecting Europe to South America; and the Indian Ocean routes connecting Europe to the Middle East and Asia (via the Suez Canal).

Once that taboo had been broken, container ship design leapt forwards. In 1998, ships broke the 7,000-TEU barrier. In 1999, they broke 8,000. In 2003, the first 9,000-TEU ships hit the water, and in 2005, 10,000-TEU ships appeared – 61 kilometres' worth of boxes on a single ship. At the time, a 10,000-TEU ship was an important milestone because it approached 'Suezmax', the size constraints of the Suez Canal. The Suez Canal, in Egypt, is a critical sea link between the Mediterranean and the Indian Ocean; it connects Europe directly with the Middle East and Asia, bypassing Vasco da Gama's long voyage around Africa's southern tip. In 2009, it was deepened to handle up to 18,000 TEUs; in 2015, a second, parallel channel was dug, effectively doubling the canal's capacity. But the Suez, too, is less important than it once was, and the latest container ships (such as the 19,200-TEU *MSC Oscar*, christened in 2015) are already pushing its maximum capacity.

It's a reflection of how much has changed. Absurd just two decades ago, today it makes sense to build a behemoth (400 metres long, 59 metres wide) that will never pass through the Panama Canal (not even the new, larger Panama locks opened in 2016) and can barely scrape through the Suez. As global trade volumes recover, it may soon make sense to build even bigger, 'Malacca-max' container ships that can pass through neither. The Malacca Strait – global shipping's third pincer point, which connects the Pacific, China and the Far East to the Indian Ocean – is where future volumes will be. The logic that today tells shipping companies to pass through the Suez Canal, bypassing Africa, will compete more and more with a logic that says it pays to go the long way around. Marginal no more, African ports such as Durban, Mombasa and Dar es Salaam are important waypoints on growing trade lanes between Africa and Oceania, between Africa and South America, and between West and East Africa.

Finally, as with the rise of new trade intermediaries in the Renaissance, global flows today are being enabled by a variety of new pay-for-service platforms – in advertising, payment processing, warehousing, data crunching, professional services and capital-raising – that make big business infrastructure available to small firms in small increments, and help many more merchants pile into global markets. These platforms have made viable: global niche markets for everything from bacon-flavoured soap to Japanese Zen garden designers; micro-scale transaction models like micro-lending, micro-payments and micro-work; high-frequency trading on Wall Street; and global vacancy searches for job seekers. The arrival of 3D printing means that even manufacturing is becoming a pay-per-use service. Across a growing range of products, the expensive, customized moulds and dies needed to form plastics and shape steel can be replaced by cheap digital blueprints. A robot can then assemble the physical version, one layer at a time, when and where it is wanted. Engineers can take advantage of this technology to craft objects too complex for traditional manufacturing, like parts for a SpaceX rocket engine, but so can millions of designers who lack the funds or scale to prototype their ideas in a factory. As this 'maker movement' spreads, it may eliminate many physical flows from producer to consumer, but it will also enable new digital flows from artisan to everyone.

Beyond 'connected'

We've drawn together the corners of a 1980s-era map that had put the West on the left, the East on the right and marginalized the rest, and completely recast relations among states, organizations and people. We've transformed the fringes – Guangzhou, China; Santos, Brazil; Durban, South Africa – into hubs where global flows of goods, capital, people and ideas meet and are exchanged. We've de-centred, so that what gets decided in Beijing, in Brussels or in cyberspace can change our lives as surely as decisions taken in our own capital. The whole world beckons, and we've pushed technology to speed us up until we can – and do – sense it all.

In the 1990s, the world was 'connected'. That one word captured best our rising relatedness to one another and the new possibilities opening to us. Today, the descriptor is no longer adequate. It fails to convey the implications of twenty-plus years of political, economic and social adaptation to a new global context. We are *entangled* now, and our present entanglement goes beyond the connectedness of the 1990s in three important ways.

Stuck together

First, it is less optional. 'To connect' suggests choice – that we can cherry-pick only those links that serve our interests best. But we cannot so easily untangle ourselves. Not only goods, but *bads* flow in new variety and volume. The first Renaissance saw the slave trade blossom. In the second the illicit economy is booming. It is estimated to surpass $10 trillion.[76] Probably 20 per cent of all global trade is illegal.[77] Money launderers, human traffickers, illegal arms sellers, hazardous waste smugglers and pirates (online and on the seas) are all enjoying growth at our expense.

Many more of the bads that bind us are perfectly legal. Global capital markets help fuel growth and fund technology transfers, but are also fickle. When their mood swings, whole regions suddenly get depressed. Likewise, when China's economy slows down, employers around the world are forced to cut jobs and investments. The world's shipping fleet exchanges some three to five million km^3 of ballast water between the world's oceans each year. Doing so thrusts alien species into one another's ecosystems, crowding out native species and destroying their habitats. (In the United States alone, bioinvasion causes losses north of $120 billion per year.[78]) Our collective carbon emissions are projected to raise global temperatures by between two and four degrees Celsius by 2100.[79] And we can all relate to Martin Luther's experience of having his own views spread farther and faster than intended, as happens on social media today.

Knotted

A 'tangled' world sounds messier than a 'connected' one, and it is. Many old knots remain, and many new ones are created as the threads between us multiply. In the Renaissance, one stubborn old knot was ignorance. Superstition and inexperience continued to dampen ocean-bound journeys for at least a century after such voyages first began. And most advanced knowledge was still trapped in Latin. Those who could not read it (the vast majority) had a difficult time observing, let alone participating in, new discoveries.

But many people *were* able to start reading vernacular literature, and this compounded a different knot: identity. Print helped harden national identities. In oral language, there were hundreds of 'Englishes' – dialects that were mutually incomprehensible. In print, there were only a few. Through this more uniform field of communication, English, French, Spanish, Italian and German speakers gradually became aware that they each belonged to a far broader community, millions strong, than they had ever imagined: a nation.[80] National identity would inspire some of the sixteenth century's most brilliant literature – in English, William Shakespeare (1564–1615); in Spanish, Miguel de Cervantes (1547–1616). It also began to inspire national*ism* – the idea that my nation is in contest with your nation – and gave people a new, wider lens through which to disregard, distrust or do violence against 'the other'. Religious identities also hardened over the period (and forced many of the refugee movements cited earlier).

Today, ignorance still frustrates the connective forces that would otherwise link humanity more smoothly. One root problem remains ignorance of one another's native speech. Like Latin before it, English is a common language that connects the learned. It is a powerful enabler of international politics, business and scholarship. But also like Latin, most people (roughly 75 per cent) don't speak it, and so have a harder time taking advantage of many opportunities that our global entanglement presents. The internet is the best example. Non-English internet content is rising, but in 2015, English still accounted for over half (55 per cent) of all websites.[81] (The next most popular language, Russian, accounts for only 6 per cent.) It's a wall that works both ways. Nearly a quarter of all Internet *users* speak Mandarin Chinese.[82] Those of us who don't will have a hard time sharing in their conversations, interests or understanding of the world.

Identity, too, is a persistent knot, in its nationalist, religious and other forms. The trend over the past fifty years has been for countries to break apart, not come together, as minority groups decide that they're better off imagining a smaller, more uniform society whose destiny they can better shape.

Europe's ambitious project of political union had been the big anomoly to this trend. Now the strains of this age are exposing the cracks in the notion of a pan-European identity—just as Martin Luther's Reformation exposed the cracks in a pan-European religion.

Independence movements can realize one of humanity's most cherished values: self-determination. But there are side effects.

The proliferation of formal borders can easily frustrate the flow of goods, capital, people and ideas, depending on the policies each country imposes at its door. Far more troubling are the radical forms of violence that sometimes accompany the quest for a separate identity, which can include terrorism, civil war, and ethnic or religious cleansing. Some of humanity's ugliest and most intractable conflicts of the past quarter-century have been about asserting nationalist or religious identities: Northern Ireland, Somalia, Rwanda, the former Yugoslavia and Chechnya in the 1990s; Darfur, Sudan, Ukraine, Iraq and Syria in the twenty-first century; and through it all, the struggle between Israel and Palestine, or between India and Pakistan over Kashmir. And many others. The identity conflicts gaining momentum today in the United States and Europe are far less violent, but do terrible violence to the popular civility upon which democratic governance depends.

Competing

Finally, 'connected' suggests a reaching out to one another in a spirit of cooperation. We have done that, more and more, on cross-border issues: health, security, the economy and the environment. For example, the global energy trade, which keeps the world's lights on, betrays an interdependence that transcends many deep geopolitical divides. See Figure 3.4. And the 2015

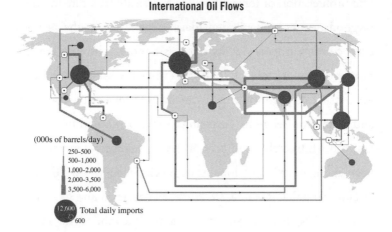

FIGURE 3.4 *The global oil trade defies many deep geopolitical differences.*
Source: BP (2015). Statistical Review of World Energy (64th edition). *London: BP.*

Paris Climate Accord saw 195 nations come to a science-driven consensus that alternative fuels must power most of our twenty-first century.

But contest, too, motivates our reach. We may see the whole world with new eyes, but we have not lost our appetite to control our piece of it , nor our suspicion of those others with whom we share it.

Of course, all European territorial 'discoveries' of the first Renaissance were contests against local peoples who had long before laid their own claims. Each new land grab also provoked contests within Europe. The sighting of the New World was followed shortly after by a legal battle between Spain and Portugal over who owned it. Columbus had made his voyage for Spain, but in a prior 1479 treaty – when the main axis of exploration was still north–south, along Africa's coast – Spain had ceded any lands 'south of the Canaries' (including, as it happened, Columbus' discovery) to Portugal. Ultimately, the two empires agreed a new Treaty of Tordesillas in 1494, which redivided the world in east–west terms along a meridian '370 leagues west of the Cape Verde islands'. Spain claimed all discoveries west of that line; Portugal, all discoveries east. (The eastern point of South America, discovered in 1500, was found to extend east of the line, which is why Brazilians today speak Portuguese and not Spanish like their neighbours.) Of course, if two imaginary ships set off from that line in opposite directions, 180° later they'll meet again. A large part of what drove cartographers to remake their world maps, spurred Magellan to set off on his bold circumnavigation, and sparked Europe's elite to see the world as a genuine globe was the contest to draw the dividing line between Spanish and Portuguese authority on the *other* side of the world (and figure out into whose hemisphere the commercially important Spice Islands fell). The Renaissance not only discovered, but divided, the world.

Today, contest and suspicion remain at the heart of much of our global ambitions. The spread of democracy and market economics, while helping to connect countries and raise human welfare, also locked the east into a post-Cold War order that disproportionately advanced US and European interests. The growing diaspora of Russian speakers in Eastern Europe may help those parts of the world relate to one another, but it also gives the Kremlin a pretext for interfering in the local politics of its neighbours. The international collaboration between the United States, Canada, Russia and Denmark to map the Arctic sea floor – some of the remotest and harshest territory on the planet – aims ultimately to divide among them sovereignty over its untapped oil and mineral riches.

* * *

In political, economic and social terms, the new world is unrecognizable from the old. It has become a global tangle of choices and burdens, enablers and obstacles, interdependencies and conflicts that ensnare us all. The next chapter shows how living in it makes this the best moment, ever, to be alive.

4

Vitruvian Man

How human health, wealth and education have reached new heights

We have seen more progress in this century ... than our ancestors did over the past fourteen.

PETER RAMUS (1515–1572)[1]

One of the big ideas to seize the first Renaissance was something that eventually came to be called *progress*. Amidst so much tangible change, a broad philosophical shift began, from seeing ourselves as occupying an important but fixed midpoint (between God and the Devil) in the Great Chain of Being, to seeing ourselves breaking that chain and determining our own destiny. In the history of ideas, this was a major step, and part of what divided early modern Europe from its medieval past.[†]

[†]Recent scholarship by Craig Truglia suggests that the Muslim philosopher al-Ghazali reached the same breakthrough conclusion around 1106.

Humanity's new sense of its own progressive possibilities was expressed in the *Oration on the Dignity of Man*, a 1486 work by Giovanni Pico della Mirandola (1463–1494):

> The nature of all other creatures is defined and restricted within laws which [God] has laid down; you, by contrast … may … as the free and proud shaper of your own being, fashion yourself in the form you may prefer. It will be in your power to descend to the lower, brutish forms of life [or] … to rise again to the superior orders whose life is divine.[2]

The full essay is often called the 'manifesto for the Renaissance'. First, because of its origins: it was the scholarly embodiment of the newly connected age in which it was written. The author studied church law (in Latin) in Bologna and Greek philosophy (in Greek) in Padua, and picked up Hebrew, Aramaic and Arabic in Florence and Paris. His aim was to discover a fundamental philosophy of human nature that united Christian, Greek, Jewish and other branches of thought. Second, for its distinctly modern theme: we can achieve a higher state of being, if we but strive for it.[3]

The *Oration* shares a symbolic kinship with the iconic image of the Renaissance, Leonardo da Vinci's 1490 *Vitruvian Man*. See Figure 4.1. The circle is Heaven, harmonious and perfect. The square – four corners, four elements, four seasons – is Earth.[4] By placing man in the centre of both, Leonardo signals

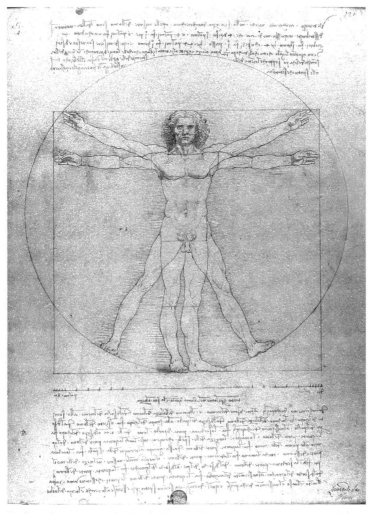

FIGURE 4.1 *A form full of possibilities.*

Leonardo da Vinci (c. 1490). Vitruvian Man. *Courtesy of the Gallerie dell'Accademia, Venice, Italy.*

our capacity to occupy either, and he urges us to realize the divine potential latent in our natural form. We look, and we see what we might be.

From misery to middle class

Leonardo's artistic vision had a real-life counterpart. In material welfare terms – health and wealth – the Renaissance saw Europeans attain new heights. This was especially true in contrast to the century prior.

The worst of times

In 1346, a Mongol army from Asia laid siege to the port city of Kaffa (in present-day Crimea). The Mongols had brought with them a terrible, deadly plague, and, it is widely believed, 'ordered corpses to be placed in catapults and lobbed into the city in the hope that the intolerable stench would kill everyone inside ... Soon the rotting corpses tainted the air and poisoned the water supply, and the stench was so overwhelming that hardly one in several thousand was in a position to flee the remains of the [Mongol] army'.[5] Those who did get away may have carried the plague with them all along the Mediterranean coast, and possibly caused one of history's deadliest pandemics. Between 1347 and 1353, the Black Death, as it became known, killed at least one-third and as much as one-half of Europe's population – seventy-five million people or more.[6] In far-away England, 30–50 per cent of the population died.[7] The Mediterranean was hit even harder. Florence saw its population fall by two-thirds, from some 120,000 citizens before the plague to perhaps 40,000 after.[8]

The depopulation and disruption caused by plague plus warfare (notably the Hundred Years' War between France and England (1337–1453) and Ottoman conquests from 1352 onward) depressed economic activity across the whole continent. Food output dropped for lack of peasants to work the fields; many who had survived the plague starved. Even money was in short supply. Europe's own mines were nearing exhaustion, and war with the Ottomans had interrupted the usual bullion trade with West Africa's Gold Coast. Royal courts groaned under the weight of their international debts.

It was a dangerous and often miserable time to be alive.

The best of times

By around 1450, Europe began to turn the corner. At about the same time (1453), France and England temporarily set aside their centuries-old territorial disputes, and the Italian powers (Milan, Venice, Florence, Naples and the papacy) signed a mutual non-aggression pact (the Peace of Lodi) so that they could enjoy the economic benefits of peace. As natural immunities developed, the worst bouts of plague subsided and bequeathed to Renaissance Europe a younger, hardier and smaller population, ready and able to participate in the continent's peacetime recovery.

Living standards lifted for plague survivors, from the bottom of society up. Among peasants, the sharp demographic shift forced major structural changes. Once-productive fields grew wild for lack of labour to cultivate them. To lure back scarce peasant labour, landlords were forced to cut rents and improve living conditions. In some places, like France, the crown went one better and offered peasants small plots of land that they could own outright, both to bring abandoned fields back under cultivation and to plough new ground to expand total agricultural output. (For the crown, it was a win-win. The fields got planted, the peasants got fed and the crown treasury gained a broad new tax base – one far more pliable and submissive before the king's taxman than the noble families at court.[9]) Throughout most of Western Europe, feudal serfdom, under which peasants worked land owned by their lord, gradually gave way to this new system. More and more, peasants rented or owned land for themselves and could sell their surplus produce and free time to the market.

New industry and trade connections also spurred improvements in peasant welfare. For most rural peasants, it was the first time they had ever owned their labour, and urban industries in the midst of recovery outsourced work to this new pool of (cheap) rural talent. When not busy with the planting or the harvest, rural peasants could earn income from merchants in nearby towns, spinning yarn or churning out craft pieces. Meanwhile, diet slowly began to improve as more nutritious and higher-calorie New World foods – such as sweet potatoes, peanuts, various beans, cane sugar and maize (after 1540) – made their way into European (also Chinese, Indian and African) stomachs.[10] Over the next 200 years, this agricultural exchange would profoundly improve European health (tobacco – introduced after 1560 – less so). The continent's population rebounded, and by about 1570 had recovered its pre-plague levels.[11]

Trade along the old routes also rebounded, and new intercontinental trade was emerging. These factors sustained a steady increase in demand for agricultural and manufactured goods. As trade networks between the town and countryside improved, and as improvements in farming techniques spread more widely, peasants in some regions began to shift some or all of their lands from subsistence crops, such as wheat, to higher value cash crops, like grapes for wine-making.

Those who were able to take advantage of these new circumstances earned a reasonably secure living and lifestyle. Some did very well, and a sort of peasant aristocracy emerged, many of them building homes that still dot the landscape of Western Europe (and are often far outside the purchasing power of the twenty-first century's middle class). See Figure 4.2.

FIGURE 4.2 *A wealthy peasant's home in Warwickshire, UK, built about 1480.*
Photo credit: Nat Alcock and Dan Miles (2012). The Medieval Peasant House in Midland England. *Oxford: Oxbow Books.*

Life in the towns also changed for the better. Italy's Mediterranean cities led the way. They were resource poor, but opportunity rich. Their physical infrastructure and social systems for trade, commerce and banking were far ahead of the rest of Europe, so cities like Venice and Florence benefited fastest from the turnaround in the continent's fortunes. Venice dominated European spice importing and was also the main port of entry for Asian and Levant porcelain, gems, perfumes, silks and other luxuries. It was also a major producer of wool and silk, glass and silverware, soap and sailing ships, and by 1500 was the chief global centre of book publishing. Florence, home of the Medici for centuries, was one of Europe's great financial centres. By the year 1500, Italy boasted the highest GDP per capita on earth. Its people were some 30 per cent richer than the Western European average, and two-and-a-half times wealthier per capita than those who dwelt in the great Ottoman, Egyptian or Japanese empires.[12]

During the Renaissance, these riches spread beyond the Mediterranean to other parts of Europe. The voyages of discovery generated a burst of new wealth for Spain and Portugal. Much of it flowed into the hands of princes, merchants and bankers, but a large swathe of Atlantic Europe was made better off by the sudden boost in economic activity. Europe's Atlantic port cities became new centres of commerce enlivened by enterprising merchants, sailors and craftsmen flocking in from the countryside in search of New World silver. Urban growth stimulated new demand for manufactured goods and new employment opportunities: in craft guilds and professional colleges; as peddlers, shopkeepers and servants; and doing the officious tasks of maintaining order, collecting taxes and keeping records.[†]

The last category hints at one of the greatest boons for townspeople: the growth of the state. The tax base was growing bigger and wider, which called for more tax collectors and accountants. Trade ventures, sea voyages and empire-building

---

[†] The illicit economy – thievery, prostitution – also did well.

called for more ambassadors, captains and clerks. New health protocols to manage disease (through quarantine) needed doctors and officials to enforce them. The introduction, then spread, of gunpowder – beginning with the cannons that had toppled Constantinople's walls in 1453 and progressing to the hand-held arquebuses with which the Spanish defeated the French at Cerignola in 1503 – prompted an arms race to finance and deploy new weapons and new fortifications against them. That called for bigger, better-trained armies, more engineers, more military experts and more bureaucrats to manage them. All this state-building in response to a changing world meant more, better-paying jobs for townspeople. Between 1480 and 1520, the French court in Paris doubled in size. Other courts swelled similarly. This increased the chances for exceptional individuals to rise above their birth, as many monarchs preferred to train competent commoners rather than give more power to the old feudal families. In Spain, several members of the royal councils rose from peasant stock. One of the most celebrated education reformers of the age, Peter Ramus (1515–1572), started life as the son of a charcoal maker and ended it as Regius Professor of Rhetoric in Paris.

A larger middle class emerged in the towns, comprising merchants, manufacturers and their employees, skilled artisans, artists and apprentices, and state bureaucrats. (They would play a large role in the flourishing that Part II describes.) But for those who remained poor, things also improved, thanks to the rapid spread of new ideas about poverty. Popular awareness of the problem was growing. In fiction, themes shifted from medieval knights and errant shepherdesses to modern misery set against desolate urban landscapes. The English humanist Thomas More (1478–1535) coined the word 'utopia' in a 1516 book by the same name to draw attention to realities that fell short of his vision.

The revisionist mood of the moment led thinkers like More to preach that poverty should not be the permanent blight on human society that everyone had always taken it to be. Radical solutions spread, in part thanks to another rapidly spreading idea – the Protestant Reformation, about which Chapter 8 says more. For Catholics, giving alms to the poor was an act of Christian virtue and therefore ought to be voluntary. Protestants focused more on the growing social problem of begging and vagrancy, which they sought to eliminate through public programmes. Almost simultaneously in the 1520s, some sixty Western European towns in what came to be Protestant areas invented centralized systems of poor relief. The particulars of these policy experiments varied, but typically included a prohibition on begging, a mandatory poor tax assessed against better-off townspeople, low-interest loan programmes to tide the needy over during temporary cash crunches, and education programmes to upskill beggars to become sailors, servants or other useful members of society.[13]

Measured in health and wealth, the preceding century had been one of the worst times in many European generations to be alive. Suddenly, from the peasantry to the palace, it was one of the best.

A new golden age

We can say the same today. Despite the many miseries that still plague our world, by macro measures of health and wealth, now really is the best time to be alive – even for the world's least advantaged. The chances of escaping poverty and living a long, healthy life are greater now than for any preceding generation.

And this time, the gains are almost global.

Top to bottom, human health has leapt to its highest levels ever

One of the most important measures of human health is life expectancy at birth. 'How long can we expect to live?' might be the single question that summarizes best the impact of nutrition, disease, drugs, medical science, disaster, war and lifestyle habits upon our health.

By this measure, the present age is unprecedented. Since 1960, global average life expectancy has risen by almost two full decades – from about fifty-two to seventy-one years.[14] It took 1,000 years to achieve the previous twenty-year improvement (although most of those gains happened after 1850); this time, it took only fifty. In 1990, only one-third of those who died had passed their seventieth birthday. By 2010, it was closer to one-half, and almost one-quarter of all who died had passed their eightieth. In just two decades, eighty has become the new seventy.[15]

These gains have been genuinely global. A baby born today in almost any country can expect to live longer than at any other time in that country's history. Since 1990, life expectancy at birth has risen by seven years in South Asia, by six years in East Asia, the Middle East, North Africa and Latin America, and by four years in Central Asia and developing parts of Europe. Even in sub-Saharan Africa, where economic conditions are poorest and HIV/AIDS hits hardest, infants born today can expect to live six years longer now than in 1990. A few countries have made once-unfathomable leaps. Life expectancy in Ethiopia and Bhutan has risen by fifteen years (from forty-seven to sixty-two and from fifty-two to sixty-seven, respectively); in the Maldives and Cambodia, by sixteen years (from sixty-one to seventy-seven and from fifty-five to seventy-one, respectively). A few countries, such as South Africa and Lesotho (where HIV/AIDS has cut average life expectancy by twenty years) and Syria (down twenty years since civil war broke out), have stumbled backwards, but these are exceptions in an otherwise extraordinary age of global progress in health.

Top to bottom, wealth has leapt to its highest levels ever

In the big picture, the most important wealth gains happen not among the rich but among the poor, for whom increased income and assets yield a dramatically different quality of life and powers of choice.

Today's poor share a special kinship with the Renaissance: life at the bottom of the pyramid has changed surprisingly little in the past 500 years. Then, poverty meant subsisting on a diet of bread, vegetables and gruel, with meat a rare luxury. Some sold their manual labour, and some ran a micro-business like making charcoal or hauling refuse. Most scraped by through some combination of both, plus heroic perseverance. They spent 60–80 per cent of whatever they earned on food, and most of the rest on clothing and shelter. They lived in crowded conditions and owned at best a few old clothes, a straw-filled sack to sleep on, a stool and maybe a table. What necessities they couldn't afford to buy, they begged for, shared or did without.

The extremely poor in our own time – defined by the World Bank as people living on less than $1.90 per day – similarly survive mainly on grain. The better-off among them sell their labour or run simple businesses – making street meals, stitching clothes or selling talk-time on their mobile phones. They spend some 55–80 per cent of their income on food and the rest on other necessities. They live in households of six to twelve people. A survey of the extremely poor in western India found that most homes have a bed or cot, but only 10 per cent own a stool and 5 per cent a table. They are undernourished and deficient in red blood cells (anaemic).[16] They are weak, frequently ill, and have a fair chance of developing serious vision problems or other disabilities. Particulars vary from place to place, but the overall picture remains consistently bleak.[17]

Fortunately, extreme poverty is a far less common picture than it was even twenty-five years ago. This is a moment of truly global economic growth. Between 1990 and 2014, real per capita incomes rose in 146 of the 166 countries and territories for which data is available.[18] Global real GDP per capita in 2014 crossed $8,000, almost 40 per cent higher than 1990 levels.[19] Even despite recent crises, the raw economic resources exist to transform the lifetime opportunities and powers of choice for the vast majority of humanity.

This transformation is well underway. Global poverty has plummeted during the past few decades. When the Berlin Wall fell, nearly two billion people (43 per cent of the world) still lived below the World Bank's international poverty line.

By 2015, and despite humanity growing by two billion people in the meantime, the absolute number of the extremely poor had been cut by more than half, to about 900 million people (12 per cent of humanity) – still too many, but a dramatic improvement.[20] It is also the first time in history that the ranks of the poor have thinned even as the human population has swelled.[21] Fifty years ago, development experts took for granted that extreme poverty was a permanent blight; today they debate whether forty, thirty or twenty years is the timeframe in which we might eradicate it.

In China, whose 1.4 billion people make up one-fifth of humanity, thirty-plus years of over 8 per cent year-on-year economic growth raised average incomes twenty-fold and lifted some 500 million people out of poverty.[22] There is much to criticize about China, including how it is handling its present economic slowdown, but much to admire in how it has broken from its impoverished past. It is the most successful development story in world history. India is close behind. Since 1990, its economy has also grown by nearly 8 per cent year over year, and the share of its population living in extreme poverty has nearly halved, from over 50 per cent to about 30 per cent.[23]

While the greatest strides against poverty have been made in these Asian giants, Africa, despite a late start, is catching up. In economic terms, the 1990s were a lost decade for Africa. In the sub-Saharan region, per capita growth was actually negative, at −1.1 per cent; *The Economist* declared Africa 'hopeless'.[24] But beginning in the 2000s, the continent's economy turned around. GDP has subsequently risen by about 5 per cent per year; six of the world's top ten fastest-growing economies this millennium have been African.[25] While sub-Saharan Africa's forty-plus individual economies still face major problems, the region's collective GDP ($1.7 trillion in 2014)[26] today stands roughly equal to Russia's and is anticipated to continue growing at about 4–7 per cent per year for the next decade.[27] The share of sub-Saharan citizens who are extremely poor has fallen from nearly 60 per cent in 1993 to less than half now, and is trending steadily downward.

Overall, the world today is far richer, and offers the poor far more opportunity and choice, than just a quarter-century ago.

Top to bottom, education has leapt to its highest levels ever

One of the first things people do when their powers of choice expand is spend more time in school. Education is both a consequence of development – something people who can choose, do choose – and a catalyst for further health and income gains.

Education for many

The first Renaissance saw schooling transformed from a relative luxury to a more and more precious commodity, of practical and spiritual necessity to many.

In 1450, fewer than fifty universities dotted the continent. By 1550, there were nearly three times as many.[28] See Figure 4.3. German enrolment in higher education, largely stagnant through most of the medieval period, doubled over the century.[29]

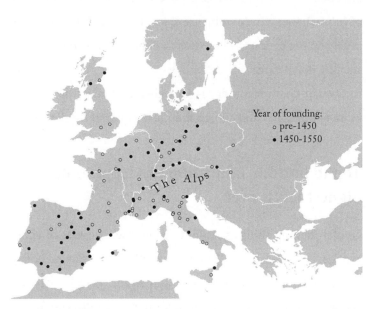

FIGURE 4.3 *Universities proliferated across Europe during the Renaissance.*
Source: Hilda de Ridder-Symoens (1996). A History of the University in Europe. Cambridge, UK: Cambridge University Press.

Partly, numbers grew because the overall population was rising. But it was also because the student body broadened beyond clergy and nobility to include townspeople. Increasingly complex financial, commercial and trade ventures demanded a talent pool with better literacy and numeracy; booming state bureaucracies needed more people with legal training. Good work was available for those who got some of either, so many more did. Meanwhile, new technology (the printed book) dramatically improved access to education by making it possible to supplement traditional (high-priced) oral instruction with lower cost self-study.

Partly, numbers grew because of the spread of new ideas about what getting an education meant, by movements such as humanism (which fostered renewed interest in ancient writers), and by religious rethinking stirred by the Protestant Reformation. The core curriculum of higher learning throughout medieval times – theology, law and medicine – was useful only to specialists. Many people saw no need for even elementary learning. But most Protestants, who, beginning in the 1520s, took half the continent by storm, did. One of the big ideas that eventually set Protestants apart from Catholics was that people didn't need a mediator (e.g. a priest) to worship God; everything they needed to know was in the Good Book – including in its translated versions. Suddenly, reading became a new pathway to salvation, and everyone who believed this had a reason to learn what squiggles on paper meant. As part of their vision to bring people back to a purer Christian message, many Protestants also advocated taking formal schooling away from the monasteries and putting it into the hands of the state. The idea was seized upon by ambitious monarchs eager to beef up their own authority, and a flurry of new state-run universities opened up.

Humanism had its origins in the previous century, having been catalysed in no small part by a man named Petrarch (1304–1374). Obsessed with ancient Greece and Rome, Petrarch travelled to their famous sites, collected their coins and even wrote letters to their dead luminaries. He was also a politician, and he found kindred spirits among Florence's elites. He gave to their city's governance a powerful layer of myth: they were the old Roman Republic reborn, guardians of its civic virtues against that modern expression of corrupting Empire, the papacy. Petrarch brought the political debates of the classical world back to life in his contemporary Italy.

When, in the next century, a wealth of classical works were recovered and reprinted via Gutenberg's marvel, Petrarch's dream of restoring classical greatness suddenly took on a new reality and infused education with new prestige and purpose. With the passage of time, the emphasis shifted from the core medieval curriculum towards the 'humanities': grammar, rhetoric, history, poetry and moral philosophy – branches of learning aimed not at filling specialist roles but at cultivating capable and virtuous citizens. This curriculum, geared as it was towards a broader audience, inspired a number of new schools. Some were radical in their ideas about improving access. Vittorino da Feltre's secular boarding school, 'The House of Joy', admitted girls as well as boys so that they, too, could partake of a classically inspired curriculum that included drawing, music and physical education among its subjects.[30]

In the span of a century, education's place in popular society broadened from a curiosity meant for the few to a means of unlocking the potential of the many.

Education for all

In our own century, we have bundled humanism's aspiration for a more capable, active citizenship into the legal language of human rights. Article 26 of the 1948 Universal Declaration of Human Rights, the core document in this language, affirms that 'Everyone has the right to education' and 'Education shall be directed to the full development of the human personality.'

We are well on our way to realizing this vision, beginning with the foundation of all education: literacy. In 1980, almost half the global population (44 per cent) was illiterate. Today, despite rapid population growth, that share has fallen to just one sixth. In just over a generation, humanity has added *three billion* literate brains to its ranks. The internet, like print before it, has given everyone a new, powerful reason to learn how to read and write. Among youth, illiteracy is just 10 per cent and dropping – which means that almost the entire incoming cohort of adults will possess the basic skills to take part in humanity's new knowledge networks.[31]

The next step up the ladder, formal schooling, has also been climbed worldwide. Since 1990, primary school enrolment in sub-Saharan Africa has more than doubled, and as of 2015, 91 per cent of primary school-age kids across the developing world were in school (versus 96 per cent in the rich world).[32] Globally, eighteen out of twenty will complete it and go on to secondary school (up from fifteen out of twenty in 1990).[33] Progress has been uneven across regions, but few countries have slipped backwards.

Importantly, the gender gap between schooling of girls and boys is rapidly closing. This matters, both because the idea that gender should limit one's life chances is repugnant and because educating girls make society far better off. Women who are more educated have fewer kids and are therefore less likely to die in childbirth and more likely to participate in the workforce. They also raise their kids' chances. Children born to more educated women are more likely to be born healthy, survive infancy and get immunized. They also spend more hours per week at study, score better on tests and are more likely to adopt good nutritional and other habits, while frowning upon bad ones (like smoking).[34]

For all these reasons, the developing world has recently put a lot of effort into educating girls, with some tremendous results.

Since 1990, female enrolment in primary school has risen from 73 per cent to over 87 per cent, and in secondary school from less than 40 per cent to over 61 per cent.[35] Again, progress varies by region – faster in the Arab states and South Asia, slower in sub-Saharan Africa – but the direction of change is universal. In one-half of developing countries, there are now at least as many girls in school as boys; in one-third, there are more. In some countries, the pace of change has outstripped all predictions. In just a decade, Morocco has achieved improvements in female enrolment that took the United States nearly half a century.[36]

It is on the highest rung, namely post-secondary education, that the most rapid and dramatic gains have been made, largely due to the expansion of higher learning in the development giants, China and India. Globally, the share of secondary school graduates enrolled in higher education has more than doubled since 1990, from under 14 per cent to over 33 per cent by 2014.[37] By our own estimates, the number of people alive today with a higher education degree is greater than the total number of degrees awarded prior to 1980. Every year, a further twenty-five to fifty million degree holders are being added to the total. Massive open online courses (MOOCs), like Khan Academy and Coursera, are helping to raise that figure even more rapidly.

Although higher education enrolment rates are highest in the developed world (at 74 per cent of secondary school graduates, versus 23 per cent in the developing world), in terms of absolute numbers the developing world is coming on strong.[38] Already at least 40 per cent of the world's science and engineering doctoral students and 37 per cent of degree-holding science researchers are in the developing world.[39] Women are rapidly advancing, too. Since 1970, post-secondary enrolment has risen four-fold for men but more than seven-fold for women, so that worldwide today – again, for the first time in history – there are more women enrolled in university than men.[40]

* * *

Humanity is healthier, wealthier and better educated than at any time in our history. The development gains we've made in the past few decades are not simply incremental improvements along long-term trends. Instead, we've crossed thresholds that will never be repeated and that mark this moment as our own golden age: the addition of nearly a full generation to global life expectancy since 1960; an absolute decline in poverty amidst a global population boom; near-universal literacy among the incoming generation of adults; a numerical superiority of women in education. Individual experiences vary. And massive challenges remain. Once-comfortable middle-class households in the developed world are now struggling. Nearly one billion people still live on under $2 per day. But for more people in more places than ever before, now *is* the best time to be alive – again.

Why now?

We are winning the battle against disease

As with the first Renaissance, the answer in the second begins with the decline of disease. Two major threats to human well-being are infectious diseases (caused and spread by specific bacteria, viruses and other parasites) and chronic diseases (long-term conditions like heart disease, cancer and diabetes, whose causes are complex and include lifestyle, diet, genetics and other factors). Both have proven highly vulnerable to our connective and developmental powers in this age. Against infections, such powers have enabled: improved technologies and practices for hygiene, public sanitation, clean water and pest control; vaccines, antibiotics and other drugs; improved crops and staple grains fortified with minerals and nutrients; growing public budgets and private incomes to invest in all these things; and the education to absorb them and apply them wisely.

In 1990, thirteen million children under the age of five died from four main categories of infectious disease: respiratory infections (pneumonia); diarrhoea; tuberculosis; and other childhood diseases like measles, polio, whooping cough, diphtheria and tetanus.[41] Most of these deaths were in the developing world. Almost no children in rich countries die from these causes.

In 2015, 5.9 million children died from such infections. An immeasurable tragedy has been halved, thanks to vaccination, safer drinking water, education and behavioural change.[42] Widening contraceptive use, improved access to pre- and post-natal care, and growing numbers of skilled personnel to attend births have also halved the share of mothers who die giving birth.[43] And the share of their children who are underweight has halved, too, from 29 per cent in 1990 to about 15 per cent today, thanks primarily to rising incomes and imported farming improvements. The effect of all the above is that 19,000 more children's lives are saved *every day* than in 1990, a remarkable achievement that's being surpassed each year.

At the other end of the human lifespan, we are also rolling back the scourge of chronic diseases, like heart disease and cancer. Across the developed world, the likelihood of dying from some form of cardiovascular illness today is less than half what it was in the 1960s.[44] Researchers are keeping us healthy through the spread of new technologies, like drugs that lower cholesterol and stents that can open up arteries without open heart surgery. But of equal impact has been the wide spread of preventive wisdom, to which we've all contributed. Smoking, once a ubiquitous behaviour, is now socially awkward. Alcoholics Anonymous has gone global. People consume less fat and do more exercise (or, at least, know they should). The importance of these spreading lifestyle habits shows starkly in global mortality statistics, which reveal two facts: first, the tide began to turn in the battle against chronic disease even *before* helpful drugs and surgical procedures became available; and second, places that cut themselves off from preventive wisdom continued to lose the war, even with new technologies on their side.[45] In Russia, where both the state and people (especially men) have resisted evidence telling them to drink and smoke less, average life expectancy today (sixty-six years) is some three years lower than it was back in the 1960s, and some thirteen years lower than it is today in North America and the rest of Europe.[46]

Humanity's remarkable drop in child mortality, plus progress in preventing and managing chronic disease, are together the reason why, between 1950 and 2005, the human population recorded the fastest doubling there ever has been – and, if demographic forecasts are correct, ever will be – in the history of our species.

This last-ever population burst has already paid big dividends in East Asia (mainly China) and South Asia (mainly India), and is just starting to pay dividends in Africa. Not so long ago, development economists were largely convinced that rapid population growth was a bad thing. In 1972, the Club of Rome, a non-profit think tank, published *The Limits to Growth*, a now-famous report that foresaw ecosystems devastated by pollution, natural resources mined to exhaustion and, ultimately, social collapse. But by 1990, we had come around to appreciate what the first Renaissance had already discovered: a burst of population growth can be a good thing. 'People are the real wealth of the nation', began the World Bank's 1990 Human Development Report. True, the bigger our population, the more it costs to support and feed us all. And true, the planet has limits. But each additional mouth comes with two hands and a brain. So long as there's enough food to go around (a caveat that the Renaissance met by bringing more land under cultivation, and that we've met by doubling world farm output through improved irrigation, fertilizer and seed development), the benefits – more hand power and brainpower – can outweigh the costs.[47] This logic holds especially in an open, connected economic environment where labour abundance can translate into a trade advantage and broad welfare gains.

We are reaping the benefits of connecting economies

The link between stronger economic connections and increased well-being is not automatic. Many cases have shown how this link works, while others have shown how interfering factors (such as inequalities of opportunity, poor governance or shock events) can break it.

Those caveats matter – and, as many households now realize, often cause gains made at the top to outpace everyone else's – but they don't negate the many ways that connecting global trade and finance have helped cut poverty, create wealth, and fund better health and education.

First, expanding trade creates jobs and raises incomes for workers by increasing the size and stability of the market for their products beyond limited and cyclical local demand. This benefit holds true for small-scale labour-intensive goods – for which an army of idle hands is a competitive strength – more so than for large-scale capital-intensive industries that employ just a few highly skilled people.[48]

In the Renaissance, the incomes of idle rural farmers improved when they started spinning fabrics for distant markets in the off-season. This is not so different from what happened in the late 1980s and early 1990s when Vietnam set itself up as rice grower to the world. In the span of a single year, 1987–1988, Vietnam transformed itself from a rice importer to the world's second largest rice exporter, and has expanded exports ever since (from 1.5 million tons in 1990 to about seven million tons by 2014). Along the way, the country improved rural nutrition, created 7.2 million new rural jobs and generated new annual revenues for small-scale farmers (in 2013, worth $3 billion).[49] A more recent example is Bangladesh, which has built a $23 billion clothing export sector that by 2015 accounted for over 80 per cent of the country's total exports and employed over four million people.[50] Yes, wages and working conditions in the sector are appalling, but they are improving (in 2013, the government raised the minimum wage for garment industry workers by 77 per cent).[51] Forced to choose between extreme poverty and poverty, many Bangladeshis choose the latter.[52]

Second, new economic connections promote competition. Depending on what conditions existed before (especially if there has been a monopoly), competition can increase the variety of goods and services people can buy, improve quality and lower prices. This means tight household budgets can stretch further, and small businesses can more easily afford to operate. In the Renaissance, cheaper grain shipped into Europe from the Baltics helped moderate the price of bread. Today, the global trade in wheat, rice and other cereals helps control the cost of dietary staples worldwide.

New linkages can also raise productivity. In one hour, someone sitting at a sewing machine will stitch more shirts than someone armed only with a needle and thread. 'Productivity' is the term economists use to capture that difference. It matters for human welfare, because the more we can do in an hour, the more valuable that hour is to someone else, and the higher the wage (and hence income) we can expect in exchange.

Connecting up the global economy increases our productivity through a variety of channels. The simplest is specialization. As trade links improved in the Renaissance, some farmers began to specialize in growing grapes instead of grain. They traded away the grapes (for more than the grain they could have grown), spent some of the proceeds on what grain they needed for themselves and pocketed the rest.

Specialization is still part of how we raise productivity through trade today (as the Vietnam example illustrates), but only a part. Another major way is through technological upgrading. New machines embed new technologies that demand the development of new skills in their users. Taiwan, a small, resource-poor island, has since the 1980s grown a $180 billion manufacturing sector – seeded by foreign technologies.[53] South Korea, whose manufacturing sector today is twice the size of Taiwan's, has done likewise. Technology borrowing from the United States and Japan in the mid-1980s helped South Korea get its start in advanced semiconductors.[54] In 2013, South Korea's chip-making industry overtook Japan's as the world's second biggest.[55]

Finally, stronger economic connections can change the very nature of work and the structure of the labour force in important, positive ways. In the Renaissance, the emerging rural craft and textile industry was a boon not only to idle farmers, but to rural women, children and the elderly, who had a new chance to join the labour force and improve their material conditions. Similarly, economic opening today has helped women to move out of agriculture and into manufacturing and service sectors, with positive consequences for their education, health, income and skill development.[56]

We are reaping the benefits of connecting people

Connecting people has also been a boon to human well-being.

For people not lucky enough to be born into a high-growth economy, migration can offer a way to participate in the welfare gains being made elsewhere. By moving from low-growth to high-growth economies, or from less developed to more developed places, people at all levels of skill and education can earn better incomes for equivalent work.

Migrants don't just pocket this difference; many send part of it home. Migration is a two-way street. People carry in themselves, their labour and their skills, and they often remit cash in the other direction. This informal financial support has expanded almost twenty-fold since 1990. In 2016, total remittances back to developing countries topped half a trillion dollars.[57] That is three-and-a-half times the amount of all official development assistance (i.e. foreign aid) those countries receive from other governments each year. And while it is not as much as foreign investment inflows, it typically goes to communities that foreign investment does not reach, and has proven to be far more reliable. See Figure 4.4. Speculative investors pull money out of one country and pour it into another according to whichever opportunity looks best that year, or that hour. Remittances are rooted in family. When crisis hits a country, remittances tend to increase, even as foreign investment flees.

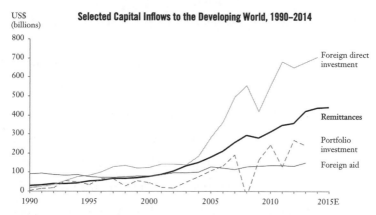

FIGURE 4.4 *Remittance flows are larger than foreign aid and more stable than foreign investment.*

Source: World Bank Databank (2015). World Development Indicators. *Retrieved from data.worldbank.org; Remittance estimates taken from World Bank (13 April 2015).* Migration and Development Brief 24.

Skilled migrant flows are often criticized as 'brain drain', especially in medicine. Some 95 per cent of Haiti's nurses and 60 per cent of its doctors leave to work in higher-income countries – an extreme case, but not the only one.[58] Clearly, a large-scale exodus of doctors or other professionals imposes costs back home, and working out how to encourage more to stay is a subject of active policy experimentation from Thailand to Tanzania. Even so, the weight of evidence suggests that migration's benefits to sending countries outweigh its costs in the long term. The Philippines, for example, is one of the world's largest exporters of nurses *and* maintains one of the best nurse-to-patient ratios among developing countries within its domestic healthcare system. Local incentives and training programmes generate sufficient supply to serve both markets.

Migration yields a net gain for human welfare in receiving countries as well. Fears that immigrants steal jobs and clog social services are exaggerated. Courage, ambition and ability are common traits among those who successfully overcome all the obstacles they face trying to reach the big city or a new country. As a group, those who do arrive pay more taxes than the cost of services they consume. They often take jobs that the host labour market is unable (nurses) or unwilling (domestic cleaners) to fill. And they help establish stronger ties between their host and home regions, which can be a resource for businesses. Take the Taiwanese and Israeli diasporas, who have helped build thriving high-tech industries on both sides of their respective migrations. These ties can also foster a more cosmopolitan brand of politics and give vital support in times of need. When, in 2014, Russia broke international law to annex Crimea, Canada was one of its most outspoken critics – in part because 1.3 million Canadians claim Ukrainian roots.[59]

We are reaping the benefits of connecting ideas

The final link between the new world we live in and the new heights of human development we've reached is the spread of ideas. One form these ideas take is practical knowledge, the transfer of which is a thread that runs through all of the connective forces outlined above. Its impact on development is so large because once knowledge has been created (often at great expense), the cost of sharing it is effectively zero. And, unlike other goods, the more people who consume knowledge, the easier it becomes for other people to consume it, too. Best of all, however knowledge is packaged – as a device, a pill or injection, or as a set of policy steps – by adopting it, less developed societies can leapfrog the years or decades that led to its development and reap its benefits immediately.[60]

These benefits are clear in the development statistics. See Figure 4.5, which graphs life expectancy at birth against GDP per capita. Named the Preston curve after the economist who first drew it in 1975, the graph shows that as people's incomes improve, their life expectancy moves up along a curve: faster gains at lower income levels, more modest gains after that. But over time the *entire curve* shifts upwards, so that at *every* level of income, life expectancy is higher today than in 1960. Why were we born onto a different curve than our parents? Answer: the knowledge environment has changed.

Some ideas that spread are positive, not because they enable us to do practical stuff, but in a more general way: they encourage us to think differently about what constitutes a good life. We call such ideas *values*. Democracy, whose dramatic expansion

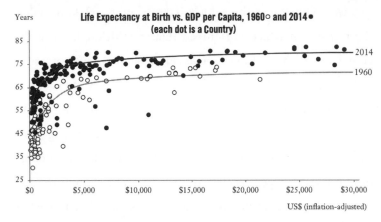

FIGURE 4.5 *The spread of new ideas and technology means that at every level of income, children born today are living longer.*
Source: *World Bank Databank (2015).* World Development Indicators. *Retrieved from data.worldbank.org; Adapted, with the authors' gratitude for his generous engagement on this topic, from Angus Deaton (2013).* The Great Escape: Health, Wealth, and the Origins of Inequality. *Princeton: Princeton University Press.*

in the past quarter-century was charted in Chapter 2, is the most important example here. Going back to Aristotle, one of civilization's big ideas has been that political participation is a unique human capacity, and that a good society is one that gives everyone a chance to develop and express their own political voice. Development economists, notably Amartya Sen, have added practical weight to this philosophical view by pointing out that, as a matter of empirical fact, democracies tend to make fewer disastrous-for-their-own-people policy decisions than other forms of government.

The spread of democracy also matters for global human welfare because it may help spread stability. As was the case 500 years ago, war is bad for development. Violence pushes people out of their homes, deprives families of income-earners and children of parents, and causes widespread physical and mental disability. Today, 70 per cent of infant deaths and almost 80 per cent of out-of-school children are concentrated in conflict-affected states.[61] Countries lose decades of progress when war breaks out.

Democracies rarely go to war with one another. While the validity of this statement depends entirely on how one defines 'democracy' and 'war', it remains true that as the share of the world's population living under formal democracy has grown, the total magnitude of large state-to-state conflicts has fallen – by some 60 per cent from its peak at the end of the Cold War.[62] Democracy's spread also shows a better way to solve domestic disputes. Military coups have almost disappeared from Latin America (which endured thirty such events between 1970 and 1989, but only three since then) and have become far less common in Africa (which saw fifteen in the 1990s but only five since 2000), as the perceived legitimacy of such acts declines globally.[63] And until the outbreak of the Syrian civil war in 2011, the number of deaths from civil war in the twenty-first century (some 40,000 per year) was trending at only one-quarter of the toll that prevailed during the 1980s (over 160,000 per year).[64] Although the media often skews our perception of the fact, worldwide violence has declined. The spread of ideas like democracy (also human rights, international justice and other related norms) is part of the reason why.

Tarnish on a golden age

The inventor of linear perspective Filippo Brunelleschi (1377–1446) taught that what we see depends on how we look at it. So it is with the gains of both the first and the second Renaissance. The view from the front is positive; from the middle or rear less so. Progress is polarizing. Some people take leaps forwards; those who don't, fall behind simply by not moving. The faster things improve, the more we need to turn our heads to see the whole picture.

Falling behind

In the Renaissance, the polarizing effects of progress were clear to see. While average welfare improved through much of the period, the margins of society, rich and poor, grew further and further apart. It was, in the words of the English historian W. G. Hoskins, 'a golden age for the Shearers … [that] left the Shorn with just enough on their backs to keep alive, and not always that'.[65]

Peasants who were able to take advantage of their new circumstances made major gains. Those who weren't fared less well. In the countryside, their landholdings tended to shrink over time. Plots that were once sufficiently large to support a peasant family were nibbled away by inheritance, which divided the parents' assets among multiple heirs; by legal actions (often crooked) brought by nobles bent on consolidating territory; and by bad luck – poor health, a failed harvest, burglary, disease or war – that forced a family into debt. For peasants, the road from debt to dispossession was short and well travelled. It didn't help that new competition from cheaper, imported grain – shipped by sea from the Baltics – depressed crop values.

In the towns, circumstances similarly grew tougher at the bottom of the economic heap. Data from the period is patchy, but every available example indicates that from about 1450 onward, as trade and new forms of manufacturing expanded, the gulf between rich and poor widened. By 1550, in nearly every sizeable Western European town, the top 5–10 per cent of residents owned 40–50 per cent of total wealth, while the bottom 50 per cent owned little more than their own labour. In the county of Suffolk, England (at the time one of the most 'industrialized' parts of Europe), just 1.5 per cent of the population commanded 50 per cent of the region's wealth, while the bottom half held just 4 per cent and four-fifths lived at or beneath the poverty line.[66]

A major cause was falling real wages at the bottom of the income scale. A constant influx of impoverished country dwellers kept town wages down, especially among the unskilled. Rural outsourcing by town manufacturers neatly sidestepped the regulations and collective bargaining power of the townspeople's guilds. Circumstances grew especially hard for women. Between 1480 and 1562, a nanny saw no increase in her pay; over the same period, the price of her daily necessities rose by 150 per cent.[67]

Stumbling backwards

The widening gap between rich and poor was driven by more than relative rates of forward progress. Sometimes, the poor were sent backwards. Shock events hit the poor much harder than the rich. Recurring harvest failures across Europe in the 1520s meant debt, and ultimately dispossession, for many farmers. Meanwhile, local fluctuations in market demand or consumer tastes could be life-threatening. Peasants who grew grain always had something to eat, at least. Peasants who opted to grow lucrative cash crops like grapes could find themselves starving if trade suddenly dried up – which often happened when disease or conflict erupted in the neighbourhood.[68] And conflict was coming (see Chapter 8).

All the while, the population continued to grow. For decades, population recovery was a positive for poor people, as the growing supply of labour boosted food output and raised demand for manufactured goods. But eventually, the numbers began to work against them. In 1450, across Western Europe, few able-bodied males lacked work. By 1550, youth unemployment was common – which again helped keep town wages low – while increased demand for housing made it possible for rural landlords to jack up the rent for tenant farmers.[69]

The widening gap between rich and poor betrayed the limits of the period's high-minded idealism. Humanists exalted 'Man', but many seemed to ignore the squalid condition of ordinary men. Relief programmes for the poor were often sustained less by a desire to help the poor and more by a desire to gentrify the streets by removing their unsightly presence. In many cities, the main thrust of poor relief became to manage the supply of low-cost labour. In Venice after 1529, beggars were put to work on merchant ships at half wages. Beginning in 1536, under England's Poor Laws, children of welfare recipients had to work without pay for other farmers or craftsmen. A law passed in Leuven in 1541 required the unemployed to gather twice a day at the town hall, tools in hand, or be struck from the welfare rolls. Those who made the rules argued that hard labour was good for poor people's souls, but for employers it had the convenient side effect of depressing wages for unskilled labour.

Geographies diverged

The Renaissance was a European phenomenon, and a Western one at that. Within Western Europe, the north (with its better trade links) began gradually to pull ahead of the south, and the Atlantic began to pull ahead of the Mediterranean (same reason).[70] Eastern Europe remained largely agricultural, and peasants there felt the weight of feudal oppression grow heavier, not easier. In gross economic terms, Asia largely stood still through the period.

Other continents were shoved backwards. In Africa, some 150,000 people were enslaved between 1450 and 1500, followed by another quarter million in the next century,[71] while in North and South America, Europe's Age of Discovery marked the collapse of pre-existing civilizations. It's true that exchange with Europe brought certain benefits to Native Americans. Europeans introduced new crops: wheat from Europe, rice and sugar cane from Asia, olives from the Levant, coffee from Africa. They brought new animals: domesticated cattle, sheep, pigs, hens, goats and draft animals. And they unveiled new technology: sailing ships, metal tools and weapons, and ploughs. They even reinvented the wheel – which a native Mesoamerican civilization had arrived at independently around 1500 BC, but knew only as a toy because it lacked domesticated beasts big enough to make a cart conceivable.

But the negatives – disease, plunder and subjugation – certainly overshadowed the positives, which shockingly few Native Americans lived to enjoy. Millennia of exchange among

Europe, Africa and Asia had integrated what disease experts call the 'viral reservoirs' of these continents. Such biological mixings produced history's great killers – like the Black Death – as well as resistance to them. The Americas had survived these waves of death untouched, in blissful quarantine, but the arrival of European explorers and conquerors injected indigenous populations with thousands of years' worth of nature's terrors. Smallpox, measles, influenza and typhus carried over by Europeans (plus yellow fever and malaria carried by African slaves) exterminated all but a few hundred of Haiti's few million natives, and killed off 90–95 per cent of Aztec (Mexico) and Incan (Peru) populations (which fell from at least twenty million to at most one million, and from nine million to 600,000, respectively).[72] With most of America's native population killed by disease, and the remainder killed or subjugated by guns, European empires claimed its wealth of gold, silver and arable land for themselves. From 1500 onward, for at least three centuries, the Americas supplied 85 per cent of the world's silver and produced 70 per cent of its gold.[73]

Fresh stains

When it comes to recent gains, Brunelleschi's notion of perspective still holds: what you see depends on the angle from which you look.

Step back and view humanity as a whole, and the story is broadly positive. The emerging global middle class – the middle third of humanity, by income – have seen their real income rise some 60–70 per cent since 1988. The bottom third have seen theirs rise over 40 per cent.[74] But compare the fortunes of the global top versus the global bottom, and a very different picture emerges. While *average* global welfare has improved, the *extremes* have spread further apart, so that today the top and bottom live in ever sharper contrast to each other. In 2010, the 388 richest billionaires in the world controlled more wealth than the bottom half of all humanity. In 2017, it took just eight people to make the same claim.[75] The bottom half of the world's population – 3.6 billion people – live, on average, on just a few dollars per day. They include 2.5 billion people who live without basic sanitation, 1.3 billion people who live without electricity and 800 million people who live without enough food.[76] The bottom half suffer 99 per cent of all child deaths, four-fifths of all deaths from chronic disease and three-quarters of all deaths from infection.[77]

Take one step closer and break humanity down into component *countries*, and the picture changes once again. Comparing countries, the first thing we see is a positive phenomenon economists call 'convergence'.[78] In aggregate, over the past quarter-century, the average income in poorer, developing countries has been catching up to the average income in richer, advanced economies – and quickly. Since 2000, fifty countries have enjoyed per capita growth rates greater than 3.5 per cent for a decade or more, and the number of countries classified as 'low income' by the World Bank has halved, from more than sixty-five to thirty-three.[79] This empirical evidence backs up an intuitive notion: less developed countries, which are just beginning to ignite the big engines of growth such as basic infrastructure, education and health, ought to grow faster than mature economies that already have all those things.

Some major caveats cloud this cross-country impression. As with people, so with states: the relative fortunes of the global top and bottom diverge widely. Since 1990, the average income in the world's twenty poorest countries has risen some 30 per cent in real terms, from about $270 to $350 – an increase of $80. Income in the twenty richest countries has also risen about 30 per cent, from $36,000 to $44,000 – an increase of $8,000.[80]

The country you were born in still largely determines the life you'll have. If you're European, you'll grow some 8–9 inches taller (a good summary measure of multigenerational health) than if you're Central American or South Asian.[81] If you were born in Niger, you can expect to live twenty-six fewer years and spend nine fewer years in school than if you were born in Denmark.[82] You're also much more likely to live through a military coup, civil war or other violent conflict, in which you may be killed, disabled, raped, orphaned and/or made a refugee as a result.

Finally, take one more step closer to peer *within* countries, and divergence once again dominates the picture. Within almost all countries, from the least developed to the most, the gap between rich and poor has widened over the past few decades.[83] Nigeria, now Africa's biggest economy, has also become one of the world's most unequal. In the last two decades, the total income generated by Nigeria's economy has almost doubled, in real per person terms. Shockingly, so has the share of Nigerians living in poverty (from over 30 per cent to over 60 per cent).[84] In the United States, the top fifth have seen their real incomes rise over 25 per cent since 1990; the bottom fifth have seen theirs *fall* 5 per cent.[85] The bottom fifth were earning *more* money back when the US economy had 40 per cent *less* income per person to spread around. Even European countries long known for income equality, such as Denmark, Germany and Sweden, have seen the rich pulling further away from the pack.[86] This separation is not only statistical; it is spatial. Just as your country of birth can predict your quality of life, so can your neighbourhood. Residents born in upmarket parts of Oxford, England, can expect to live fifteen years longer than those born in the city's poorer areas – and are far more likely to get their children into the city's eponymous university.

Falling behind fellow countries

'Falling behind' and 'stumbling backwards' are again the two main reasons why countries' fortunes diverge.

The first factor reigns over many differences, especially those impacted by technology, trade and investment. In theory, it costs nothing to share a new idea, but in practice, it can cost quite a lot to adopt it. Some of these costs are direct, such as buying or licensing new technologies, but the big costs are often indirect – such as teaching citizens how to use them. Globally, governments spend on average over $4,600 per pupil on public education; sub-Saharan Africa spends only $185 – and that figure is up 15 per cent from 1990.[87] The shortfall makes it harder to roll out everything from the science against smoking, to savings accounts, to semiconductors, to the conviction that women and men are equal. Countries that have good education systems, do a lot of their own research and industry, and have the budgets to build supporting infrastructure can put new technologies and ideas to use much faster than countries that don't.[†]

The digital divide is a current case in point, with big social consequences. The internet and mobile technologies help leapfrog barriers to information, education and communication. More than any other technology today, telecom infrastructure *is* progress.

[†]Education alone does not determine the pace of adoption of new ideas and technologies. How the education system explains the world and shapes social attitudes also matters. Saudi Arabia has reasonably high educational standards but still prevents women from driving. Germany is one of the world's best-educated countries, but bans both genetically modified crops and new nuclear power at the same time as the United States and China are embracing both these technologies.

But it's not equally available. The International Telecommunications Union (ITU) maintains a ranking of over 150 countries by their level of telecom infrastructure, including telephone and mobile penetration, household computer and internet access, and wired and wireless broadband subscriptions. The top twenty countries – all in Europe, North America and high-income parts of Southeast Asia – boast abundant internet bandwidth, high broadband penetration and more wireless subscriptions than people. On the other side of the digital divide, the bottom twenty countries – all African – still have limited (mostly dial-up) internet access, few users, weak wireless broadband penetration and poor links to international data trunks. In all, the ITU identifies thirty-nine 'least connected countries', home to 2.4 billion people, that fit this description.[88] (Innovative solutions, like Facebook's solar-powered drones and Google's high-altitude balloons, may soon help Africa patch some of these gaps.)

How countries fall behind in trade and investment is more controversial, but follows logically from the above. Although classic economic theory teaches that all sides benefit from more open trade (each is able to focus on what it does best and trade for the rest), the reality has proven far messier.[89] When regulatory roadblocks to the flow of capital, people, ideas and goods are taken down, the remaining disadvantages one country may have versus another become more glaring. Trade's benefits don't just 'trickle down', like snowmelt from a mountaintop, to deliver everyone their due. Rather, they *pool* – in those countries and cities that boast advantages along whatever dimensions of difference remain.

Some of these dimensions are natural. Singapore, for example, is blessed with a central location and deep harbours that make it the ideal Asian trading hub. Others are human made. Jamaica, another island nation, has more natural advantages than Singapore: more plentiful and lucrative natural resources, closer proximity to a big open market, and much better beaches. In 1960, these two islands had comparable per capita GDP. Since then, Singaporean GDP per capita has shot above that of the United States, whereas Jamaican real GDP has been flat for over fifty years. Infant mortality today is eight times higher in Jamaica than in Singapore. The island suffers from some of the highest homicide and rape rates in the world, whereas Singapore enjoys the lowest. One difference: Singapore took policy steps to attract investment and highly talented people, and build world-class education, transport, energy and IT infrastructure. Jamaica did not.

Location, resources, labour supply and skill levels, infrastructure, public policy choices, the quality of legal and financial institutions, prejudicial notions about race or gender – all are far harder to revise than tariff schedules. That's why, despite the dramatic reduction in global trade barriers over the past two decades, today just ten countries account for 60 per cent of all global trade by value; sixty countries account for 92 per cent. Certain countries in Africa have actually *reverted* to simpler economic stages (less manufacturing, more mining) as money and industry have relocated to other (more business-ready) African and Asian countries.[90] The International Monetary Fund once made its financial assistance to poorer countries contingent upon their opening wide their industries to foreign investment and competition. These days, it has grudgingly come to accept that doing so is folly unless the country has the necessary institutions and policies in place to compete along other dimensions as well.[†]

Falling behind fellow citizens

Economic transformation during the Renaissance – rural development, the shift from feudal to wage labour in agriculture, expanding competition from international trade in grains and goods – boosted the well-equipped and challenged the disadvantaged to keep up. So it is for individuals today.

[†]The tariff schedules themselves remain tilted against many developing countries. Lower income countries are still heavily disadvantaged by trade agreements that invite foreign investment and competition in, but have not opened reciprocal access for their domestic industries to reach out – particularly for their core industry, agriculture. Farmers in poor countries have to surmount trade barriers for their produce that are twice as high as those that their developed-world peers face.

Falling trade and investment barriers have made it possible to relocate labour-intensive production to lower-wage places. Technological advances, especially in computing and robotics, have made it possible to replace more workers with machines. (By apt coincidence, 'robot', from the Slav word for 'work', came from Eastern Europe in the fourteenth and fifteenth centuries, and originally referred to that portion of a peasant's week – usually two to four days – when he worked for his landlord without pay.[91])

Both these trends have increased profits to owners and investors, and lifted wages for those with the managerial and technical skills to manage these new dynamics. But they have depressed incomes for those wage-earners whose jobs have been lost offshore or to new machines. In short, economic opening has increased the premium paid to skill, and magnified the pay gap between the less- and the better-educated.[92]

Stumbling backwards

Good governance can help laggards catch up quickly (as China, Ghana, Singapore and many other countries have demonstrated). But sudden, unintended steps backwards – social, economic, environmental, biological and conflict shocks – can wipe out the hard-fought gains of even the most competent development programmes. Such shocks are coming more frequently. Rank the world's ten deadliest natural disasters since 1980; eight hit after 2002.[93] Now, as 500 years ago, these shocks hit the poor hardest. Poor people and poor countries are the most susceptible to traditional catastrophes, to war (developing countries are host to all of the ten largest war zones and 86 per cent of the world's twenty million refugees),[94] and to the emerging risks to be discussed in Chapter 7. They lack the funds to take preventive steps – like researching new technologies, storing food and fuel, building seawalls, or training public officials in disaster preparedness – that could reduce their vulnerability. They lack the funds to rebuild roads, schools and hospitals in the aftermath of a disaster. And they lack the funds to build up their population's resilience through unemployment insurance, health care, pensions and private savings. In the developed world, HIV/AIDS is a chronic but manageable condition. Across most of sub-Saharan Africa, it has been an economic and social catastrophe. Shocks can push people already struggling with subsistence out of school, out of work and into abject poverty, as well as into crime, abuse, ethnic violence, suicide and starvation.

Other steps backwards can be blamed on bad or failed governance. North Korea's regime has done nothing for its people since the 1990 collapse of Soviet support, preferring to let them revert to the 1950s than to admit that its economic ideology is wrong. Somalia fought a bloody civil war from

1991 to 2012 that not only forced its population to sit out two full decades of Renaissance progress, but also made it one of the worst places on earth to be born. Today, one in ten children die in their first year, formal education has largely disappeared, the incoming generation of women is 75 per cent illiterate, and per capita income (at $284 per year) is barely one-fifth the average in a region that is already the world's poorest (sub-Saharan Africa).[95] Syria boasted one of the best healthcare systems in the Middle East prior to the 2011 outbreak of civil war. By 2014, 60 per cent of its hospitals were destroyed, half the country's doctors had disappeared, and broken vaccination programmes had led to the re-emergence of polio and measles.[96]

Finally, some stumbles are the fault of bad business. Renaissance Europe's plunder of the Americas has been repeated, on a smaller scale, in places that are likewise on the margins of public attention. Foreign business has played a role in some of the worst scandals of recent decades, including the 1984 Bhopal Union Carbide disaster, the destruction of Indonesian and other rainforests, and, in a long list of developing countries, suppression of workers' rights and support for dictators. Civil society organizations like Transparency International, Greenpeace, The Extractive Industries Transparency Initiative and others are helping to raise our awareness and hold these businesses to account, but opportunities to cheat remain bountiful.

Glimpsing greatness

The polarization of people's well-being introduces huge stresses into our societies. A Renaissance is a stormy moment. The same wind that pushes us fast and far also kicks up big waves. Growing sentiments of exclusion and neglect are causing people to opt out, even mutiny, just when we need all hands on deck. Still, the divergence of fortunes at the top and bottom doesn't change the broad truth: the world is a dramatically healthier, wealthier, more educated place than before this second Renaissance began. This is especially true for people born poor, who stand a better chance now of escaping poverty and living a longer, healthier life than at any other moment in history.

The positive achievements dominate, for two reasons. The first is *scale*. The blunt fact is that the worst cases of failing states and backward stumbles are relatively small, while the best achievements of the past couple of decades are very big. The combined populations of the six least developed countries in the world do not quite equal the population of a single average-sized Chinese or Indian province.

Some argue that this fact exposes humanity's recent achievements as hollow. Take China out of the equation, and the broad picture flips from progress to stagnation. Yes, the total number of extremely poor people has halved since 1990, but

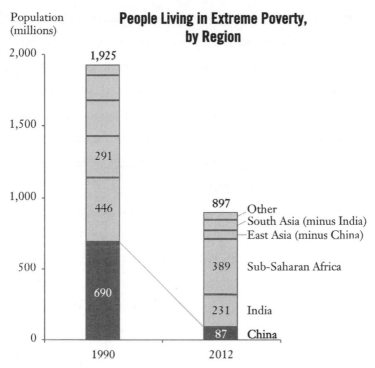

FIGURE 4.6 *The fall in extreme poverty has taken place mainly in China.*

Source: World Bank PovcalNet (2015). 'Regional aggregation using 2011 PPP and $1.90/day poverty line'. Retrieved from iresearch.worldbank.org/PovcalNet/index. htm?1.

in the world outside China it has fallen less dramatically. See Figure 4.6.

This argument is flawed. We ought to cherish equally each new breakout from the prison of poverty, wherever it takes place. Also, while China may have led the way, India and now

Africa are on track to follow its big development achievements over the next few decades. In economic terms, India's twenty-first century looks much rosier than China's. Its population is a similar size, but much younger. In the years to 2025, India will add 170 million more workers to its own labour force, while China's is already contracting (even with the recent revision of its 'one-child' policy up to two).[97] Major gains in health, wealth and education for India should follow.

Africa's future is less certain, but could be equally bright. To the rest of the global economy, the continent has only just been discovered. Several, but certainly not all, of its countries enjoy resource wealth (40 per cent of the world's gold and 90 per cent of its platinum are in Africa), which, in the hands of good governments, could be invested in public infrastructure and skills. And good government is better understood: citizens know their rights much better and are holding those in power accountable with ever-rising frequency.[98] Africa is also blessed with a looming demographic dividend. Its working-age population will balloon from 500 million people now to over 1.1 billion by 2040.[99] If local governments can learn how to foster neighbourhoods instead of slums, and if national governments can better integrate their too small economies and build better institutions, Africans might banish extreme poverty from their midst before mid- century.

The second reason why the health, wealth and education achievements of this second Renaissance outweigh the shortcomings is their *breadth*. Divergence over the past two decades is strongest along economic dimensions. But while GDP is a good place to start measuring human progress, it's a bad place to stop. Consider: China's GDP has grown a full 5 per cent faster than Tunisia's for over thirty years, yet over the same time frame, female life expectancy in Tunisia has risen by fourteen years (from sixty-three to seventy-seven), versus only seven years in China (from sixty-nine to seventy-six).[100] Tunisia caught up with, and has now overtaken, China on one of health's most fundamental metrics. The spread of so many low-cost ideas to improve health and education means that wider human progress today depends more on how well countries exploit these ideas than on how fast incomes grow. If, instead of concentrating only on income, we look at life expectancy, years of schooling and income together – a combined statistic that its Pakistani creator, the late economist Mahbub ul Haq, dubbed the Human Development Index (HDI) – then by this measure virtually *all* countries for which data exists are better off since 1990, and poor countries are clearly converging upon the rich.[†]

[†]The exceptions are a handful of states – such as Zimbabwe, Iraq, Syria and Somalia – that have been knocked backwards by civil war or HIV/AIDS.

At present rates of progress, by 2050, more than three-quarters of humanity will attain the same score on the development index that the UK enjoys today.[101] The biggest leaps are happening in countries we don't talk nearly enough about – like Rwanda, which since 2008 has risen faster up the HDI – seventeen places – than any other country.[102]

* * *

We see humanity's potential more clearly now, because we suddenly stand so much closer to it. In the first Renaissance, this glimpse of our own greatness inspired the consequences for which the age is famous: genius.

PART II

FLOURISHING GENIUS

How the present age generates
genius and raises the scale of collective
achievements

5

Copernican Revolutions

Why big shifts are happening now

Paradigm shifts

In 1504, Nicolaus Copernicus (1473–1543) – by day, church administrator; by night, avid astronomer – set himself up to observe something special: a once-in-twenty-years Great Conjunction of Jupiter and Saturn.[1] For Copernicus, stargazing was a form of devotion: what better way to worship God than to study the heavens? And so, during the seven years he had lived in Italy studying medicine and church law, he seized every chance to feed his private passion: taking electives in geometry, assisting astronomy professors with their nightly observations, and consuming the theories and star charts of other astronomers, both ancient (Ptolemy) and contemporary (Peurbach, Regiomontanus), as fast as they came into print. Now, one year after returning to his native Poland, he set out with his astrolabe and his trusty almanac (the 1492 edition of the *Alfonsine Tables*) to chart the planets' march towards each other.

What Copernicus saw troubled him, in two ways. First, his almanac proved not so trusty, after all. The *Alfonsine Tables* had been compiled in the thirteenth century: they computed the position of the sun, moon and the known planets from 1252 onward, and were a staple of medieval astronomy. But they were inexact. The 1504 Conjunction occurred, as predicted, but the timing was off by one to two weeks and its location in the sky was off by one to two degrees.

His second worry was philosophical. The *Tables* had been based on Ptolemy's model of the heavens, which Copernicus deemed too messy, too inelegant, to reflect the mind of God. Ptolemy had held the earth to be the fixed centre of the universe – an obvious fact, confirmed daily by the rising and setting sun. But the planets were more troublesome wanderers. Seen from earth, they performed a weird dance, scurrying first this way, then that, dimming and brightening at odd intervals. To explain it all, Ptolemy had conceived an elaborate array of cycles, epicycles and equants – strange and complex rules of solar, lunar and planetary motion that had stood for 1,400 years simply because they worked. They reliably predicted when and where all the heavenly bodies would be – within one to two weeks and one to two degrees.

These worries preoccupied Copernicus for the rest of the decade, and around 1510, he had an *Aha!* moment.[2] It was an insight so pure in its simplicity that it felt divine, yet so startling that he waited over thirty years to publish his thinking in full – and then, only at the persistent prodding of a pupil who had been smitten with the tentative draft Copernicus had circulated to a small group of scholar-friends around 1514. Let the sun, not the earth, be the centre of the universe; let day and night be the result, not of the sun's motion, but of the earth spinning on its own axis; and let the earth be a planet that circles the sun like any other.

It was an absurd set of claims. If the earth really were spinning eastward on its own axis to produce night and day, its speed would have to be enormous. How could anything – towers, trees, people – stay standing upright? How come birds and clouds weren't being flung through the sky by the air's momentum? Copernicus didn't know. Moreover, if the earth were spinning around the sun, then why did the stars appear fixed? Just as objects in our vision shift from side to side when we wink one eye and then the other (an effect called parallax), so, too, should the star field shift each year if we do, in fact, travel from one side of the sun to the other. Convinced his theory was right, Copernicus could only surmise that the stars *do* shift, but must be so far away – a thousand times farther than Ptolemy had dared imagine – that our eyes and instruments cannot see the difference. Early nineteenth-century telescopes would prove the Pole correct, but in the sixteenth century, contemporaries scoffed at the untestable notion. Tycho Brahe spent his life compiling the most meticulous record of the heavens ever in an effort to prove Copernicus wrong. Ironically, his data helped demonstrate the superiority of the Copernican model over Ptolemy's, and hastened the former's acceptance.

Copernicus challenged the deep assumptions upon which all astronomy was based – and overturned them. The twentieth-century philosopher Thomas Kuhn coined the phrase 'paradigm shift' to distinguish this special class of achievement. Because our working assumptions are deeply embedded in our thinking, such shifts are extremely difficult to make. (Copernicus' 1543 book, *On the Revolutions of the Heavenly Spheres*, was banned by the church for over 200 years.) They're also extremely important, since every paradigm has limits and eventually those limits must be confronted. Otherwise, progress stalls. Copernicus' heliocentric theory had its own flaws – the sun is no more the centre of the universe than the earth is – but it took astronomy past Ptolemy and raised many new avenues of productive inquiry. How might we prove that the planets orbit the sun and not the earth? In 1610, this question prompted Galileo Galilei (1564–1642) to point a recent Dutch invention (the telescope) skyward and gather fresh evidence from the phases of Venus and the moons of Jupiter. How best to describe a planet's orbit? As an ellipse, Johannes Kepler (1571–1630) discovered. He derived three laws of planetary motion that made new almanacs accurate to within two-tenths of a degree.[†] And why, if the earth really were spinning through space, could no one feel it? Inertia, answered Sir Isaac Newton (1642–1727) – and the answer became the first of his Three Laws of Motion. The impact of Copernicus' work extended far beyond the time horizon of the Renaissance and far beyond astronomy. He laid a fresh foundation atop which all modern physics was built.

When genius became general

We label this rare class of achievement 'genius', and during the Renaissance it became startlingly common. Philosophy, science, technology and art all made radical breaks from the principles that had governed their craft. Put together, these society-wide paradigm shifts constituted what historians now recognize as the transition from the medieval to the early modern world. Their common core was the philosophical move, noted at the start of Chapter 4, from honouring humanity's God-given place in the

---

[†]The remaining inaccuracies were due to forces Kepler did not know about – the gravitational tug of the planets upon one another (specified by Newton) and general relativity (specified by Einstein).

Great Chain of Being, to striving to rise above it. This radical rethink of the meaning of life was accompanied by a gradual shift in the locus of truth, from Revelation to observation. This new thinking transformed our picture of the earth (see Chapter 2) and, through Copernicus, transformed our picture of the heavens.

In medicine, this new way of thinking began to shift our model of the human body from spiritual to anatomical. Human dissection became commonplace in medical schools, and accurate diagrams of our skeleton, muscles, veins and arteries, organs, nervous system and brain were printed widely. The heart, found Michael Servetus (1511–1554), was not the residence of the soul, but a pump. Chemistry began to shift from alchemy to experimentation. The practice of trying to transmute lead into gold according to ancient recipes gradually gave way to gathering fresh data about what reactions *do* occur, to develop better methods to distil alcohols, acids and other substances, and to see what effect these potions had on sick people.

Fresh fields of study were born. Today, Niccolò Machiavelli is deemed 'Machiavellian' because his famous treatise *The Prince* seems to advocate violence and deceit as good leadership traits. But 500 years ago, the real shock was that in addition to composing the usual flattering lies about the virtues of the ruling class, he published observations of their actual behaviour. Political scientists have been doing the latter ever since.

Hand in hand with these new ways of looking at the world came new tools and technologies. Seaworthy ships were made bigger, tougher, with more versatile sails and rudders – and became *ocean*-worthy. Compasses and other navigating devices became more accurate and made it possible for pilots to sail on headings they'd never dared before. Agriculture began to adopt new practices (like stall-fed cattle and crop rotation) that raised farm output for the next three centuries. Mining, having exhausted Europe's shallow ore bodies, plumbed new depths and began to confront (and overcome) the technical challenges of doing so: draining water, venting air, hauling ore vertically, and preventing floods and explosions. Metallurgical engineers built the first blast furnaces (which produced more and better iron) and developed new alloys. Hydraulic engineers recovered the ancient Romans' fascination for waterworks and took it forwards, developing dams, pumps and conduits to do work in mines, in mills and at ports. Architects designed new hoisting machines that enabled them to raise giant domes of a scale not seen since the days of Caesar. Early violins, guitars and other instruments arrived, and led musicians to compose new forms of music.

The shifts we remember best today occurred in the visual arts. Medieval art could be elegantly simple and mystical – but also flat and formulaic. Its main purpose was religious – to tell a sacred story. Plagiarism was common practice; innovation was irreverent. Slowly, those norms were replaced with the notion that the artist's job was to capture a fragment of the world as he saw it, and it produced works that were increasingly lifelike, original and secular. See Figure 5.1.

The shift began with artists like Brunelleschi, who pioneered linear perspective (showing depth on a flat canvas by drawing far-away objects smaller), and Jan van Eyck (c. 1390–1441), who, rather than paint idealized nudes, instead stood naked people in front of him and captured the details that marked each individual. By the height of the Renaissance, Leonardo da Vinci

FIGURE 5.1 *The Renaissance transformed the visual arts.*

(a) Madonna and Child, fourteenth century (?).

Provenance unknown, probably Crete (c. 1400?). Our Lady of Perpetual Help. Courtesy of the Church of Sant'Alfonso di Liguori, Rome, Italy.

(b) Madonna and Child, fifteenth century.

Sandro Botticelli (c. 1480). Madonna of the Book. Courtesy of the Museo Poldi Pezzoli, Milan, Italy.

and Michelangelo had mastered art's new ideals. See Figure 5.2. Today, their works are admired for their great beauty, but back then, they were also admired for their originality. No one had ever painted a portrait quite so lifelike as Leonardo's *Mona Lisa*. His secret, born of years studying how the eyes actually see, was to leave the corners of her mouth and the contours of her body indistinct and let the viewer's brain, not the painter's brush, fill in the details. Likewise, Michelangelo's careful study of human anatomy gave us marble sculptures that were somehow both

FIGURE 5.2 *Leonardo and Michelangelo married real-world observation with individual inspiration.*

Leonardo da Vinci (1503–1517?). Mona Lisa. *Courtesy of the Musée du Louvre, Paris, France.*

Michelangelo Buonarroti (1513–1516). Dying Slave – detail. *Courtesy of the Musée du Louvre, Paris, France.*

contorted and graceful, with every muscle and sinew polished in its proper place.

None of these revolutions were immediate. Copernicus stubbornly insisted that the planets' orbits must be circular, since God thinks in circles;[3] the chronicle of Renaissance medicine is likely to make modern readers wince; Leonardo dabbled in alchemy along with everyone else. A Scientific Revolution had barely begun, and would take centuries. But enough early successes were achieved under these new paradigms to validate and accelerate them. In 1450, Western Europe lagged far behind China and the Arab world on many measures of progress, such as science, exploration, navigation, iron- and steel-making, weaponry, agriculture, textiles and timekeeping. But by 1550, as the Harvard historian Niall Ferguson showed in this 2011 book, *Civilization: The West and the Rest*, Europe was leapfrogging them along all these dimensions, and boasted more organizational and energy resources than any previous civilization on earth.[4]

It was arguably the greatest, fastest flourishing of genius in human history.

New shifts

Until today.

Our own Copernicus-scale shifts have already begun. Those described in Part I – from closed to open political and economic systems, and from the analog to the digital medium – are the broadest, but in narrower domains the same phenomenon is underway. In diplomacy, the absolute sovereignty of states over their own affairs – the bedrock of international relations going back to at least 1555[†] – is being challenged by humanitarian notions of a 'responsibility to protect' other countries' citizens, an international criminal court with jurisdiction to try 'crimes against humanity', and the growing realization that no state can achieve domestic prosperity without links to the international community (as the case of North Korea epitomizes). In business, the very concept of 'the firm' is being reinvented. The old idea – that entrepreneurs assemble firms because it's more economical than obtaining every good and service they need from the market – is being challenged by digital platforms that drive transaction costs down and make a new range of fractional services possible. New thinking sees the chief value of the firm in the unique set of values and practices it harbours. The nature of work is likewise transforming, from full-time employment to temporary contracts. Since 1995, more than half of all jobs created across advanced (OECD) economies have been part-time, self-employed or freelance.[5] Digital freelance platforms

---

[†] In 1555, the Peace of Augsburg established the principle of *cuius region, eius religio* (Whose realm, his religion) within the Holy Roman Empire. It gave princes within the Empire the power to determine the religion (Catholic or Lutheran) of their own state.

like Upwork, Task Rabbit and Thumbtack are booming from Minneapolis to Mumbai.[6] In art, the basic division between artist and audience is being broken, and participation in the act of creation is becoming commonplace.

But the clearest proof is in the sciences. The genius of the first Renaissance is obvious with 500 years of hindsight, because we can contrast how Europe changed with how other regions of the world, under different local conditions, did not. Today, of course, we don't have that luxury. We cannot step 500 years into our own future, and we cannot easily contrast places: the connective and developmental forces shaping our own age are global. So it's difficult to judge, for example, whether social media is simply a more convenient way of getting in touch with one another, or a fundamental shift from a physical to a virtual form of society.

In science, particularly the natural sciences, important leaps are more clear-cut. As Copernicus discovered, it's very hard to rewrite the basic principles that underlie science. Theory and practice are backed up by decades, sometimes centuries, of hard data, and changing them means confronting that body of evidence head-on with something objectively better. On the other hand, if that argument can be won, then science makes a more rapid and decisive transition to the new paradigm than any other field. (No one wants to do further research down a path that's been proven wrong.) This means we can spot big shifts, even in the short term, and trust that they'll endure.

The natural sciences are a vast, complex ecosystem of human brainwork, comprising many fields and subfields, but in oversimplified terms, there are two basic branches: life sciences (the study of living things) and physical sciences (the study of non-living things). The first branch proceeds from physics (what matter is) to chemistry (how matter behaves) to biology (living arrangements of matter). It ends at medicine – how we apply the life sciences to prolong life. The second branch likewise has its foundation in physics and chemistry, but then explores materials (non-living arrangements of matter) and ends at engineering – how we apply our understanding of materials to make useful things.

In both branches, the shifts underway right now are very big indeed – and, if we take the time to understand them, as beautiful as any leap in art. Taken together, they are the best evidence yet that our lives are about to transform. One branch determines the quality and duration of life for each one of us. The other makes all the stuff we fill life with.

Life science: from medical treatments to genetic transformations

For most of medicine's 5,000-year history, we've taken the human body as a given. We've been 'tiny pawns in a play which we did not write', in the words of James Watson, who co-discovered DNA with Francis Crick in 1953. The role of medicine in this drama has been treatment: to explain how the human body works and why sometimes it doesn't, so that we can better prevent illness or fix the body when prevention fails. Medical explanations have evolved over the past few millennia – from gods and spirits, to 'humours', to germs and bad choices – but medicine's role has remained constant: namely, to combat these enemies.

Treatment, which can be crudely summarized as drugs plus surgery plus education, has served us very well up until now. Medicine developed vaccines to shield us from some of history's deadliest killers, including smallpox (1790s) and polio (1950s). Researchers isolated insulin (in 1921), a natural protein produced in the pancreas to control blood sugar levels, and supplied it en masse to the quarter-billion diabetics whose own insulin supply isn't up to the task. They discovered penicillin (1928), and from there a whole class of antibiotics and antimicrobials to defend us against infection. As understanding of the body's chemistry grew, scientists developed new drugs to tweak it for our purposes. They invented the contraceptive pill to regulate fertility, antidepressants like Prozac to regulate our state of mind, statins like Lipitor to lower our cholesterol and Viagra to prolong erections.

Medicine's list of surgical achievements is equally impressive. Take transplants, for example. Transplants rank among medicine's highest triumphs, because they demand deep knowledge of an organ's mechanics *plus* mastery over the body's chemical factory – which otherwise would reject the transplanted cells. In the 1950s, surgeons accomplished it with kidneys. In the 1960s, they followed that up with the pancreas, liver and heart. A decade later, they managed the lungs. Fast forward to today, and medicine can replace your ovaries, your penis, your legs, your arms, your hands and – since 2010 – your entire face, with parts donated by someone else. The first human head transplant is scheduled for 2017. So total is our command of the human body now that we can even turn it off and back on again. In the 1970s, a cold, lifeless, breathless body would have been declared dead immediately. Today, surgeons can suspend us in that condition for half an hour, and we re-emerge as if from nothing more than a deep sleep (after the first half-hour, brain damage becomes progressively more likely).[7]

The success of preventive education, while less headline-grabbing, is equally profound. Simply schooling us all to quit smoking has done more to thwart lung cancer than all drugs and surgeries combined.[8] And getting nearly everyone to wash their hands has likewise been our greatest victory against the spread of infection, from restaurants in Tokyo to favelas in Rio de Janeiro.

Limits

For all its successes, the treatment model has limits. Chief among them is aging. Even the best-treated body grows old, breaks down and dies. The second limit is genetics. Despite all our efforts, our own nature can work against us to impair our body's functions or make us more vulnerable. And the third is chronic illnesses, which have defied treatment in large part because their cause is very often rooted in some combination of the first two. Take cancer. We know that if there is a history of cancer in our family, we are more likely to develop cancer ourselves. That's genetics. But it's also age-related. The DNA we're born with is not exactly the same as the DNA we die with. During our lifetime, as the cells in our body divide, die and replace themselves, over and over again, they accumulate little mutations. The older we get, the more mutations our cells collect. Collect the wrong ones, and they can start to multiply uncontrollably – which is what cancer is. Other chronic illnesses – diabetes, Alzheimer's, multiple sclerosis – have likewise frustrated medical research.

To surpass these limits, we need to surpass the treatment model. And that is what medical science is beginning to do. Instead of striving to maximize our quality of life within the limits that nature has handed to us, scientists now understand our nature deeply enough (they think) to set a far bolder ambition: to transform our bodies so that fewer and fewer of these limits apply.

The book of life

The study of genes dates back to the 1860s, when an Augustinian friar, Gregor Johann Mendel, patiently bred some 30,000 pea plants and deduced from his monkish observations that the nature of a 'child' plant must be due to a combination of dominant and recessive traits inherited from both parents. By around 1900, scientists had figured out that those inherited or 'hereditary' traits are carried by chromosomes inside the nucleus of the cell. And by the 1950s, they had located within chromosomes the ultimate vault for our genetic inheritance: a clever, two-strand or 'double helix' molecule dubbed DNA.

DNA is nature's language for storing and copying genetic information. It's *digital*. But instead of 0s and 1s, each strand comprises a long sequence of A, C, G and T – adenine, cytosine, guanine and thymine, which are four simple molecules present in all cells. These four molecules have a special property: A will only bond with T, and C will only bond with G. If one spot of the first strand reads C-G-A, the same spot on the opposite strand must be G-C-T.

The genetic data of all life on earth is secured by this one fact. Nature exploits this simple chemistry (A = T, C = G) to copy genetic information accurately each time a cell divides.

But DNA is more than a vault for storing genetic information until the moment comes to produce offspring. Other molecules, called RNA, are constantly streaming in and out of that vault, scribbling down a short snippet of the DNA code (a gene), then carrying that information out to one of the cell's factory floors: a ribosome. Snippet in hand, the ribosome follows the same digital decoder to assemble a corresponding string of amino acids. Once assembled, these 2D strings fold themselves into complex 3D shapes. We call these diverse 3D shapes 'proteins'. The ones that build muscle and bone are only a small, familiar subset. Proteins are involved in everything: from converting food into fuel, to producing and eliminating chemicals, to fighting off infections and transporting oxygen. Researchers think the human body contains some 100,000 different proteins in all; collectively, they make up perhaps 75 per cent of our body's dry weight. DNA is the language in which each and every one of them is encoded.

DNA holds a big part of the answer to what makes me *me* and you *you*, but also to how the human body works, from the molecular level up. Consequently, since the discovery of this genetic code, we've tried very hard to understand it. Unfortunately, it's (a) very long and (b) written in a language we don't read. Picture an ordinary sheet of office paper filled edge to edge, top to bottom, with a string of As, Cs, Gs and Ts in 12-point font, something like:

gtgaacaagaaatgatgctttgtctggtatgcatggtaaataatgccccttgc
tctctgcttcatgatcacatgtgatacttctaacatagatagcacatgtaaatccagtgg
ccttgactgcaactcaagagagcattttggccaagtacaaacccactagtcatga
aaaaaaaaaaaaaaccaaatcaaagtaaattgatggtattgacatttgtctatgaaa
aacaa

The human genome would fill one million such sheets (about the area of ten football fields). And it's unbroken by any spaces or punctuation whatsoever that might help us make sense of it.

Since we cannot read it directly, scientists' only tool for making sense of DNA is comparison. They compare the DNA of a person who suffers from, say, cystic fibrosis, with that of a person who doesn't, and identify the significant differences. Then they look at the DNA of other people who suffer from cystic fibrosis to see which of those differences they all share in common. In 1989, cystic fibrosis became the first genetic disorder whose DNA root was isolated in this way. (The snippet above is just 230 of the over 230,000 letters that spell it out.) Comparison proved a powerful tool for translating DNA into meaningful text. But it was a slow process. By 1990, all global 'libraries' of decoded DNA fragments put together amounted to much less than 1 per cent of our total code.[9] Many biologists believed the job of isolating all our genes to be beyond human capability.

Genius

No one believes that anymore. The field and its prospects look totally different today.

In 1990, the world's geneticists were scattered across fewer than 100 labs, mostly housed inside universities. For the most part, they researched independently and kept their collaborations within national boundaries. Today, they populate thousands of public- and private-sector labs and testing agencies, and the number and complexity of their research linkages – across both economic sectors and national borders – have knitted the whole field into a genuinely transnational scientific endeavour. The Human Genome Project, launched in the early 1990s to map the full genome, was an American-led affair. The Human Proteome Project, its follow-up act launched in 2010 to map all humanity's proteins, is a global endeavour comprising twenty-five research groups housed in nineteen different countries.

This thicker, denser community has been further transformed by the arrival of new, better instruments and techniques to perform their work. One of the big bottlenecks to the comparison method had been DNA sequencing. Once the hard work had been done to locate the gene responsible for cystic fibrosis (on our seventh chromosome), the real hard work began: namely, to write out the actual string of A, C, G and T at that location. It was a labour-intensive and technically demanding laboratory process involving long hours hunched over test tubes, centrifuges and electron microscopes. An expert researcher doing nothing else could sequence perhaps 100,000 letters in a year. At that rate, it would take 30,000 to 50,000 person-years to sequence the whole human genome. So no one tried. Because there would never be enough time or money to sequence it all, scientists didn't sequence *anything* until they had a really good idea about why that particular snippet might matter. Sequencing had to be rigorously hypothesis-driven. Otherwise, it could be a black hole that swallowed up researchers' whole careers without giving anything back.

But beginning in the 1980s, innovators committed to breaking this bottleneck served up a number of technical innovations. Sequencing machines arrived to automate many of the lab technicians' decoding tasks. DNA copy machines were invented that could take a single DNA snippet of interest and make millions of copies overnight, which, in turn, enabled a new generation of faster sequencers designed to apply brute force to now inexhaustible source material. Mathematicians developed new statistical models to puzzle out how to stitch any number of snippets back together into their correct order, and the 'shotgun sequencing' technique (basically, blasting the entire genome into tens of thousands of very short segments) was born to take advantage of this new 'sequence now, line up later' capability. Finally, computer scientists supplied bigger and better hardware and software to crunch, compare and store the swelling volumes of data being generated by these new techniques.

The abrupt amplification of brain and computing power flipped the genetics research model on its head. The old model said: we can't boil the ocean, so let's make a good guess about which cupful matters and boil that instead. The new model says: we *can* boil the ocean, so let's do that and see what we find. In the end, it did not take 30,000 years to sequence the full human genome; it took fifteen. And sequencing time and costs are still falling – faster even than Moore's Law. See Figure 5.3. It took fifteen years and cost $3 billion to sequence the first genome; today, it takes less than six hours and costs only $1,000 to sequence another.[10]

By 2003, geneticists had written out all ten football fields of the human blueprint. While that was an important popular milestone, its scientific significance was limited because they had no other human genomes against which to compare it. Today, they do. Science has already sequenced over 250,000 full genomes and millions of partial ones.[11] With this data, plus

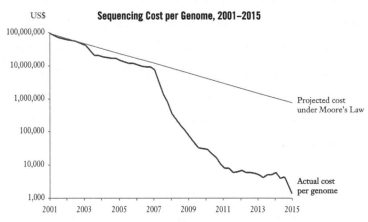

FIGURE 5.3 *Genome sequencing costs are falling faster than Moore's Law.*

Source: Kris Wetterstrand (2015). 'DNA Sequencing Costs: Data from the NHGRI Genome Sequencing Program (GSP)'. National Human Genome Research Institute. Retrieved from www.genome.gov/sequencingcosts.

the computing power to scour through it, researchers have identified the roughly 20,000 genes that code proteins, and, for the majority of those genes, have already figured out which proteins they print.[12]

There is no book

Now that life scientists deal in whole genomes, they've begun to discover many things they didn't even know they didn't know. The role DNA plays in biology is vastly more complicated than was thought just ten years ago. Science has learned that only 1–2 per cent of our total DNA actually codes for any proteins. Researchers' first thought was that the other 98 per cent was just junk – evolutionary leftovers that natural selection hadn't weeded out yet. Now, they're not so sure. At least some of that 'junk', it's now known, store different instructions: not to make proteins, but to more finely regulate the proteins already being printed. What makes humans so much more complex than fruit flies is only partly that our DNA prints more proteins, but mostly that our bodies manipulate those proteins with far more sophistication. Research has also discovered that some inherited traits aren't coded in our DNA at all. 'Epigenetics' is the name of this field of study, so new that scientists only agreed upon the word in 2008.

Most profoundly, science is now asking us to give up the idea that DNA is a blueprint at all. It is, rather, a warehouse – full of useful ideas that nature has been accumulating since life began. Yes, out of DNA come proteins, which in turn make cells, which in turn make tissues, which in turn make organs and from there, an organism. But DNA does not *determine* the organism, any more than a warehouse of parts determines the car that is built from it. That car is built by the machines on the warehouse floor that ferry parts from their shelves to the assembly line; by the assembly line staff and robots that request the parts and weld them together; by designers and engineers who decide how the car should perform; by executives who decide to build a car and not a truck. Every level in the system can communicate with every other; every level can cause a new chain of events that shapes every other. So it is with life. Since about the year 2000, *systems biology* has begun overturning reductionist, deterministic notions of DNA with this new realization.[13]

Nature, transformed

There is no going back. Recent breakthroughs in biology have changed humanity's relationship with nature for good. The most immediate power they confer is self-knowledge. Our own strengths, weaknesses and tendencies – whether pacific or pathological – are being given physical foundations. So are our futures. Soon, medicine will be able to simulate our own aging with software. But beyond simply projecting what we will look like in twenty-five years, our virtual doubles will serve as risk-free labs in which to test how our bodies uniquely respond to new drugs, surgeries and lifestyle choices. Drug discovery will leap forwards, as the emerging capability to quickly and cheaply simulate mass clinical trials will render today's methods obsolete.

With heightened self-knowledge, we will personalize medical treatment. Due to our recent population growth and low child mortality rates, today the human species boasts much more genetic variety than ever before. Of late, natural selection has had neither time nor opportunity to prune new mutations from the human gene tree. This matters to health, because it turns out that the oldest parts of the human genome – those lines of our DNA code that have been battle-tested over eons of evolution and are the same in almost all of us – are also the most bullet-proof. Most of the genetic weak spots in our armour lie amidst so-called 'rare variations' – more recent lines of code that occur in fewer than 1 per cent of people. In other words, human beings are the same, but different. Mass-produced medicine glosses over the latter point; personalized medicine will embrace it. In 2015, the US Food and Drug Administration (FDA) approved the first 3D-printed drugs, which can be custom-made to match each patient's ideal dosage requirements and absorption capabilities. And parents can already purchase genetic tests to screen their children for hundreds of known mutations and disorders. The day of a sequencing machine in every doctor's surgery is beckoning.

We can also hack DNA. We can open up nature's warehouse to fix bugs or, theoretically, add new features. Nature does this all the time – with viruses. A virus is just a snippet of DNA with some protective layers added, which enters a cell nucleus and writes itself into the host DNA to change the cell's function. 'Gene therapy' is the label science has given to this new capability, and researchers have been reasonably successful at it so far. They've engineered viruses that can reprogram our own cells to make the missing protein whose absence causes cystic fibrosis, to override an inherited blood disorder so that our blood cells produce sufficient amounts of haemoglobin, and to direct our body's own antibodies to seek and destroy cancer cells or HIV, to name but a few recent laboratory achievements. In late 2013, the world's first approved gene therapy drug, Glybera, made it to market. It's a virus that, when injected into a pancreatitis patient's bloodstream, infects cells and reprograms them to correctly produce a missing protein needed to break down fatty acids. Gene therapy still faces many limitations – chiefly, that it cannot rewrite our whole body's DNA, only the DNA of the cells it infects – but it proves that DNA debugging is doable.

Gene therapies are a modest application of humanity's new genetic powers. We are already capable of far stranger things. Scientists have cross-bred species in a petri dish that nature has never mated, giving birth to live, healthy beefalo (buffalo-cows), geep (goat-sheep), ligers (lion-tigers) and zorses (zebra-horses).

They've inserted the jellyfish genes that cause fluorescence into cats, so that the latter glow in the dark. They've inserted genes from the wormwood plant into a species of yeast, so that instead of secreting alcohol, the yeast secretes a scarce anti-malarial drug. We don't yet know the full extent to which DNA codes are compatible across species, but scientists are experimenting in labs across the planet to find out. Eventually, every plant, animal or bacterium with which we cohabit the earth may contribute blocks of ready-made code that genetic programmers can combine to produce chimera organisms that serve human needs and fantasies.

The next milestone for this field, called 'synthetic biology', will be to design a totally new organism from scratch. Why limit ourselves to nature's code bases? Search online for 'custom DNA synthesis', and you'll find dozens of private labs that will synthesize almost any DNA sequence you give them for under $0.20 a letter.[†] They'll mail you back the test tube in two to four weeks. With this power, we could one day accelerate evolution: start with horse DNA, simulate a thousand years of its evolution on a computer, synthesize the result and impregnate a living mare. Would the colt thus born be a thousand years more advanced than its mother? Or perhaps we will create a bacterium that chews atmospheric CO_2 and secretes petroleum.

[†]Risky sequences are blacklisted.

Part of this is already possible: scientists can sequence the full genome of a bacterium, tweak it on a computer, synthesize a physical version, implant that version into the vacated nucleus of another bacterium and watch that cell *become* their artificial organism.[14] But they're still using an existing life form's DNA as the starting point. Researchers don't understand enough about how all the different levels of a biological system relate to design their own organism from the ground up – yet.

Of course, the most profound power is to alter the human organism. In a modest, tightly controlled fashion, science has already begun to do so. These controls are self-imposed; they are political and ethical limits only. The technology to tinker more aggressively already exists. For example, in 2015, Chinese scientists edited (with mixed success) the genomes of eighty-six human embryos to modify the gene responsible for a fatal blood disorder.[15] If we choose to expand this line of research, we may one day soon give birth to the post-human, a more evolved form of us: healthy and active long beyond a lifespan that we now consider normal, possessing physical and cognitive powers that far outstrip our own. As our confidence in our new genetic and chemical powers grows, will we continue to deny ourselves these powers? Under what circumstances might we eventually decide to wield them? Julian Savulescu at the Oxford Martin School is one philosopher who has suggested that those circumstances may already be upon us: for the sake of our own survival, he asks, should we not try to reprogram human behaviour at the genetic level to make ourselves more peaceful and less self-interested?[16] Hasn't history shown – many times over – that we are poorly adapted to coexist with one another?

Perhaps that's right. Or perhaps that's wrong, and human enhancement will divide us more profoundly than war ever could. Who will decide? Will it be the private sector? Scientists? Governments? What if some governments permit human enhancement and others don't?

In these first decades of the second Renaissance, the life sciences have suddenly, irrevocably put nature's power to create and modify life into human hands. It's a crude power now, but it is growing far faster than our wisdom and institutions for handling it. It is exhilarating – and dangerous. It will present us with the most profound choices we have ever faced as a species.

Physical science: from scaling down to building up

The same, but smaller

If Albrecht Dürer (1471–1528) were to walk inside one of Intel's semiconductor plants, he would find much of what was going on remarkably familiar. A leading German artist and intellectual, Dürer was an early adopter of ironplate etching. He would take a flat iron plate, coat it with varnish, and then draw on it by scratching through the varnish with a sharp stylus. Afterwards, he'd bathe the plate in acid, which ate at the iron wherever he had scraped the varnish away and thereby transferred his drawing into the metal. That, in a nutshell, is how we make transistors on a microchip today. We've replaced the iron with silicon and the artist's stylus with ultraviolet rays, but the concept is the same.

The main difference is scale. Dürer etched fine lines less than a millimetre apart; we etch features into silicon that are a million times finer. See Figure 5.4. We do this because one of the cardinal rules of engineering is that if we can accomplish the same thing, smaller, that's better. Smaller means cheaper, because less raw material is needed. Smaller means more energy-efficient, because there's less inertia and friction to overcome. And smaller means faster, because the moving parts have less distance to travel. It's simple physics.

Moore's Law, and its associated seventy-year free fall in computing costs, is physical science's best testament to the benefits of scaling down. A computer computes via a collection of switches, each of which can be either on or off, 1 or 0. The more we can pack into the same space, the more calculations it can do per second. The first switches, vacuum tubes, were each about the size of a thumb; in 1946, 20,000 of them were packed into a room two-thirds the size of a tennis court. In the 1950s, engineers replaced tubes with individual transistors about the size of a fingernail, and put 10,000 into a cabinet the size of a refrigerator. In the 1960s, they figured out how to

FIGURE 5.4 *The same concept, a million times smaller.*

(a) Iron plate etching.

Albrecht Dürer (1518). Landscape with a Cannon. *Courtesy of The British Museum.*

(b) Etched silicon wafer.

Photo credit: Eric Gorski (2010).

etch transistors directly into silicon. By 1970, one fingernail could hold over 2,000 transistors; by the mid-1980s, twenty million. Today's transistors are fifty times smaller again, with features just 10–30 nanometres (billionths of a metre) across. You could easily fit one billion of them onto a fingernail, and five million of them onto the dot at the end of this sentence, right here.[17] Each and every one is a working switch. Pump electrons through it, and it's a 1; switch the electrons off, and it's a 0.

In 1965, Moore expected his empirical Law to hold true for another decade; it has done so for another half-century. For fifty years, every time we've wanted more power out of our electronic devices, engineers have taken the sixteenth-century art of etching and found a way to shrink the technique further. But our computers still struggle to tackle a wide range of complex questions in a useful timeframe. Some questions are old (What will the weather be in two weeks?); many are new (Will the protein I just synthesized fold into a useful molecule?). And scaling down will not satisfy our need for speed indefinitely. The smallest atoms are about 0.05 nanometres in size; that's the fundamental limit to how small our building blocks can go. But long before we get there, at about 10 nanometres, familiar physics starts to fall apart and a different set of rules – quantum mechanics – takes over.

Physical limits

In scale terms, the difference between a metre and a nanometre is the difference between the planet earth and a marble. Quantum mechanics is the branch of physics that attempts to explain how very tiny building blocks of matter and energy – atoms, photons, electrons and the like – behave. The earliest theoretical work on quantum properties goes back to at least 1877, and many of the most famous names in twentieth-century physics – Bohr, Planck, Heisenberg, Schrödinger and others – made the foundational discoveries that forced scientists to think of the world in a new, quantum way. But it is only recently that we've gained the power to (1) actually see the quantum properties these physicists predicted and (2) manipulate matter at the atomic scale. The first has been an unqualified success. In little over thirty years, quantum mechanics has become the most successfully tested theory in the history of science: what it predicts is what we find, at the deepest level of reality we can penetrate.

The second has been rougher going. The basic problem, in quantum-mechanical terms, is that all matter has both particle and wave properties. At large scales, we can disregard the latter, but the smaller we go, the harder that is to do. Imagine a sea of small ripples. If you are on a cruise ship, you can ignore them; if you are in a kayak, they may capsize you.

The ripple that threatens to capsize chip-makers is the probabilistic nature of very small particles, like the electrons they send streaming through transistors. In classical physics, something is either there or it isn't. But in the subatomic realm of electrons, quarks and gluons, nature isn't like that at all. An electron doesn't occupy a single place. Rather, it occupies *all* possible places simultaneously – until we look at it, at which moment it *does* settle in a single place. Where we find it in that moment isn't set by Isaac Newton's laws of cause and effect, but, rather, by laws of probability. Most of the time it's where Newton would expect, but sometimes it's not.

This weird indeterminacy is completely contrary to our experience and intuition. 'God does not play dice', Albert Einstein, a sceptic of quantum mechanics, famously declared (to which Niels Bohr, a believer, replied, 'Einstein, stop telling God what to do.'). Nevertheless, everything acts this way at the subatomic level. Ordinarily, we don't notice anything strange, because at any one moment only a tiny share of the subatomic stuff that makes up, say, this book is doing something really improbable (like passing through your hand). But sometimes we can see this weirdness on a macro scale. The best example is the sun. According to familiar physics, it should not be burning. Its core temperature, about fifteen million degrees Celsius, isn't nearly hot enough to start a fusion reaction; the sun's hydrogen atoms don't have the energy to overcome the repulsive force that separates them. But quantum mechanics says: it is merely *extremely improbable* that hydrogen atoms will fuse at that temperature. True, they can't push through the repulsive barriers separating them, but a rare few will pop up on the other side anyway. The sun contains so many hydrogen atoms that even the extremely improbable happens fairly often – often enough to sustain the fusion reaction that lights up our sky. And so, even though the sun shouldn't burn, it does.

For the same reason, there's a limit to how small a reliable on/off switch that uses electrons can be – perhaps 7 nanometres. Any smaller and we won't be sure if the switch is on because we told it to be on, or because some naughty electrons defied classical physics and leaked across from a neighbouring transistor. It's improbable, but there are so many transistors on a chip that even the improbable would happen often enough to garble its function.

At present rates of progress, scientists may reach the scale limit of a reliable silicon switch within a decade – although they might buy us another decade by swapping silicon for some other material that forces electrons to behave better (the present best candidate is graphene). Such processors will power the next generation of consumer tech and search engines, but even the fastest new chips will still not be fast enough to solve many important problems – not in a time frame that's useful to us. That's because they're built to test each possible value of each variable one by one, and the more we learn about our world, the more values and variables we introduce. It can take a long time to test them all. Say you have 100 coins from 100 different countries, and you want to see what every combination of 'heads' and 'tails' looks like. That's 2^{100} possible combinations – an astronomically large number. Even if you had a laptop 1,000 times faster than today's fastest, it would still take billions of years to run through them all.

Computing genius

The end of silicon scaling is nigh – but it was only ever going to take us so far. Its imminent demise means we must reinvent how we store and process information.

Instead of shrinking down the familiar features that work at the micro scale, can we scale up the uncanny phenomena that define the nano? Our present computers are inherently limited because they're built atop a simplification – that a particle is either there or it isn't. In fact, it's both, and in theory, that makes it a far richer carrier of information than its current use indicates. If, instead, we could somehow exploit an electron's ability to be in two different states simultaneously – called *superposition* – then it could do two calculations at once. Two electrons could do four. Three could do eight; four could do sixteen; and so on. Processing power would grow exponentially. Just 100 electrons working together could test 2^{100} combinations *instantly* – that is to say, billions of years faster than any laptop. And if we could somehow *store* information into an electron's different states, then just 300 electrons working together could hold more information than could *ever* be stored the old way – even if we rearranged every single atom in the universe into a pattern of 0s and 1s.[18]

That's the theory. In the past two decades, we've begun to put it into practice. Some of the first applications have been prime number problems. Given a very large number (say, 250 digits long), which prime numbers divide evenly into it? Your laptop might crunch for decades and not find the answer – which is why most data encryption is based on prime number tests like that. In 2001, researchers built a quantum computer that successfully factored the number 15 into 3×5. In 2012, researchers factored 143 into 11×13, and in 2014, they pushed the quantum factoring record up to 56,153 (233×241).[19] It still sounds underwhelming, until you realize what a 'quantum computer' really is: a collection of atoms or electrons ('qubits'), upon whose quantum states we have mapped mathematical meaning, so that when they weirdly occupy all quantum states simultaneously they are, in effect, testing all solutions to our maths problem. Then we look at these particles, which causes them all to collapse into the one state they most prefer, which, when we map back into mathematical language, happens to equal the right answer.

Scientists have proved the quantum concept; the task ahead is to scale it up. In 2011, D-Wave Systems, a Canadian company, brought the first commercial quantum computer to market:

D-Wave One, with 128 qubits. In late 2012, researchers proved it's possible to make qubits out of silicon atoms – an important step, since everything we know about large-scale computer fabrication is still silicon-based. In 2013, Google announced the opening of its Quantum Artificial Intelligence Lab in partnership with NASA. The lab bought a D-Wave Two, which operates 512 qubits and can solve certain types of problems 3,000 times faster than today's fastest classical computer. In 2014, IBM announced a new five-year, $3 billion R&D investment to push chip fabrication into graphene and quantum processing. Intel announced its own foray into quantum computing in the autumn of 2015. Speculations vary, but a good guess is that by 2020, quantum computers will compete against, and replace, regular supercomputers for some specialized problems.

Meanwhile, physicists have begun to perform real-world applications. In the 1990s, they discovered quantum teleportation – roughly, how to pass a tiny piece of data from one place to another without its having to travel through the intervening space. Since then, they've been steadily boosting the reliability and distance of the quantum jump, with the idea of one day building a quantum internet. (As of today the distance record is greater than 150 km – a useful theoretical milestone, since that's also the minimum distance between the ground and orbiting satellites.) In the 2000s, quantum cryptography became real: it is now possible to generate a truly random passcode that is physically impossible to predict, to transmit it some 300 km, and for the recipient to know with absolute certainty whether it was intercepted en route.[20] Commercial versions of such systems have already secured bank transfers and the transmission of national election results. Government agencies are also on board. In 2014, leaked US government documents revealed that the National Security Agency was racing to build quantum devices for code-making and code-breaking applications. In the same year, the equivalent agency in the UK, the Government Communications Headquarters (GCHQ), mothballed one of its own prototype encryption projects because it was proven vulnerable to quantum attacks.[21]

Over the next few decades, quantum computers may help us answer big questions that are still well beyond our present understanding: how exactly the different levels of a biological system affect one another; how consciousness emerges; and what the ultimate fate of the universe will be. They may also transform our daily lives. Quantum sensors may have sufficient processing power to monitor from moment to moment all the chemicals present in our blood – the same as performing every available blood test, in real time, with instant results. Real-time status updates about our body would transform our habits, our basic notions of 'health' and 'disease', and our healthcare systems.

When popular technology changes, our intuitions change, too. We very quickly adopt new ideas about how objects should behave. Have you ever swiped your finger across a screen, only to discover that it's not touch-sensitive? In that moment of frustration, you've glimpsed the change that quantum technologies might work upon our thinking. Weird-seeming devices might begin to appear in our daily lives – new tools for sensing, communicating, computing and information-processing that behave very differently from the devices we're used to. They will be impenetrable black boxes, but spookily aware and instantaneous, and oblivious to distance and complexity. As these devices proliferate, quantum behaviours will begin to seem less strange and more natural. Our intuitions will align more closely to how, at a deep level, the universe actually works. And that will help us unravel more of its secrets, faster.

Manufacturing genius

Humanity's recent foray into the nanoscale realm has exposed the limits of how we compute information – and promises a new path that will one day lead us to nature's deepest mysteries. But it has also exposed the limits of how we build things – and granted us new powers to manipulate matter.

In the early 1980s, scientists in Zurich invented a new quantum-based device, the scanning tunnelling microscope (STM), and imaged individual atoms for the first time. By the mid-1980s, they even managed to pick them up and move them around, one by one. Excited futurists began to run with the possibilities: imagine little nanoscale robots building machines and materials from the bottom up, atom by atom, with absolute precision at the absolute minimum scale. Some fantasized that we'd produce fuel from air, extract pure water from sludge, and assemble spaceships out of sand and CO_2. 'Scarcity' would vanish from our lexicon.[22]

Unfortunately, just as some quantum ripples don't let us scale down silicon transistors forever, other nanoscale phenomena won't let us scale down our machines. The two pervasive problems are random motion and stickiness. Random motion is standard physics, and is what causes a single drop of food colouring to spread through a whole glass of clear water. The water may look calm, but at the nanoscale it's a roiling ocean of colliding H_2O molecules. Stickness is a quantum thing, and is what causes cling film to cling to a salad bowl, or two smooth pieces of glass to stick together. The physics is esoteric, but basically, most things adhere strongly to each other when their surfaces come into contact. At the macro scale, we don't notice it much because most smooth-looking surfaces are rough up close, and points of true contact are few. But at the nanoscale, stickiness is as ubiquitous and dominating as gravity is for macro things. Put together, these two phenomena, random motion and stickiness, make building anything in the nanorealm like trying to assemble a tower on a ship during a hurricane, with every worker, crane, bolt, girder and raindrop covered in fast-contact cement.

A new voyage of discovery

The forces that engineers are familiar with – tension, compression and the like – don't reign at nanoscale. And the materials they're used to building with don't have the same properties. Carbon is black, but if you make a sheet just one atom thick, it's more transparent than glass. The atomic realm was the great unknown all around us, and so in the 1980s, materials science set out (armed with its STMs and other new tech) to discover what's down there, what rules govern, and whether any weird properties native to that realm could be brought up for our use.

Progress has been explosive: we've seen new cities of gold and returned with the evidence. In 1990, a total of 230 academic papers on nanoscience had been published in the journal *Nature* and all its subsidiary journals. By 2015, the count had passed 11,000. (For comparison, it took seventy-one years for research into evolution to pass the 11,000-article mark.[23]) At the turn of the millennium, the first commercial applications of nanotechnology began to appear, and by 2015, thousands of such products had already swelled into a $1 trillion market.[24]

Silver nanoparticles kill bacteria. How exactly, we don't yet know, but socks, teddy bears, bandages, dental implants and public subways have already been laced with the stuff to prevent disease and speed healing. In 2015, scientists developed the 'Drinkable Book' (paper laced with silver nanoparticles) as a portable low-cost solution to filter sewage into drinking water.[25] Geckos, we've figured out, hang from walls and ceilings by exploiting quantum stickiness: their feet sport billions of nano-scale hairs that make many points of true contact with any surface. Entrepreneurs have made a synthetic version with processes borrowed from the semiconductor industry, and as they tweak it, 'gecko tape' will find uses in defence (all-terrain robots), manufacturing (replacing many screws, rivets and glues) and even athletics (fumble-free gloves for American football players). Other discoveries will have a wider impact. Scientists are working, for example, on artificial photosynthesis to make fuel from sunlight and CO_2, faster DNA sequencing (the idea is to pass a single DNA molecule through a tiny hole that can feel the electrical difference between A, C, G and T as each passes through it) and super-thin, unbreakable condoms spun from nanofibres.

One of the most versatile materials being brought back from the nanoscale realm is graphene, first captured in 2004. Graphene is simply a sheet of pure carbon, one atom thick. We are all familiar with carbon's other forms: diamond, which is the hardest stuff in existence, and graphite, so soft we use it in pencils to write. Graphene combines the best of both. It is transparent and diamond-tough, yet can be spun into flexible fibres (strong enough to reach outer space) and cut into any 2D shape we desire (say, a roll-up display screen or solar cell). It conducts heat ten times better than copper, and electricity 100 times better than silicon (which excites chip-makers). While still expensive, it is rapidly becoming a macro-reality. In the first year after its discovery, scientists struggled to produce graphene sheets wider than a human hair. Some ten years later, they can print flawless rolls up to 100 metres long.

A unifying breakthrough

What scientists cannot yet do is build useful objects one atom at a time, or build robots that can do it for us. Most of our nanoscale engineering to date involves bulk materials: chiselling features into a surface with UV lasers (gecko tape), pumping specially prepared vapours across a copper sheet to deposit a super-thin film (graphene), mixing chemicals in a test tube to produce a desired molecule one beaker-full at a time (silver nanoparticles) and so on. Three-dimensional printing, which can dramatically cut time and waste out of conventional macro-manufacturing, can so far only deposit grains at micrometre scales – small enough to print precision parts for the aerospace industry, but not tiny enough to tap the weird properties of matter that emerge at scales 1,000 times smaller. Likewise, our ability to build robots – making and assembling motors, gears, arms and other mechanical parts – is still stuck in the micrometre realm. Scientists have worked out some theories about how a nanoscale robot might navigate through hurricanes of random motion or keep itself unstuck, but testing such robots with a prototype could be decades away – or never.

To make true nanomachinery will likely demand a radically different design approach. As with making computers, instead of trying to shrink macro-mechanisms to nanosize, we'll need to exploit the distinct features of reality at that scale and engineer our machines in ways that are native to that environment.

One promising approach is to mimic biology. The broadest insight to emerge so far from the nanoscale realm is that the farther down we go, the blurrier the distinction between 'physical' and 'life' science becomes. Traditionally, engineering has not mimicked nature. Airplanes don't flap their wings. But the intersection of the two is where some of the most fruitful science is now being done. Engineering supplies the tools and platforms for investigating nanospace; nature supplies an endless catalogue of elegant solutions to the engineering problems one finds there.

Nature, it turns out, is the ultimate nanoscale engineer. Bacteria, some just 200 nanometres long, are in many ways the nanobots we wish we could build.[26] They have tiny power plants that can run on sugar. They have molecular assemblers, called ribosomes, just 20 nanometres in size. They're programmable, with a DNA logic board. They self-repair, self-replicate and navigate the random, sticky nanoscale environment via a clever twisting motion.

More instructive to human engineers is how *unlike* our wished-for nanobot they are. Bacteria aren't general-purpose machines. They're highly specialized: each species exploits particular properties of nanoscale matter to do one particular thing well. And they *self*-assemble, with the help of subtle forces already present at the nanoscale. The main self-assembly trick is protein folding. A protein starts out as units of amino acid, each just 1 nanometre long, stitched together into a long chain by a cell's ribosome. It turns out that each type of amino acid (life uses twenty-three altogether, and repeats them often) has a unique electrical charge. As the chain gets printed, every unit in it attracts or repels every other unit according to its charge, and the 2D chain contorts into a 3D structure in a complicated balancing-out of these forces. This folded tangle has just the right shape and all the right surfaces to build structures or interact usefully with other proteins.

Can we assemble our own nanostructures in the same way? Knowing the final shape or function we want to achieve, can we figure out the equivalent tangle and work back from that to the amino acid chain that folds into it?[†] Lab work to date points to yes. In 2010, scientists coaxed DNA to fold itself into a sort of

---

[†]Protein-folding is one domain where exponentially more powerful computers are needed. Given twenty-three amino acids, a chain 100 units long can be assembled in 23^{100} possible ways. If we made just one physical test molecule of each, together they would weigh more than the entire universe.

basket, with a lock on the lid, and placed a drug molecule inside it.[27] Only cancer cells have the right key. If the basket bumps into one, the lid springs open and the drug is released on site. A 'DNA nanobot' like this may one day replace chemotherapy and other current cancer treatments that kill plenty of healthy cells along with the bad.

* * *

Medicine is gaining nature's power to design life; engineering, the power to design matter. This is not ordinary progress, but the revolution that comes when we hit the outer limits of our present paradigms and adopt new ones.

If history is any guide, these breakthroughs will usher in an era of rapid human achievement. Some of it, we can already see coming in the form of emerging technologies. Some remains more speculative. Will we crack how the brain works, and create medicine to regenerate it as we have begun to regenerate other organs? Will artificial intelligence replicate or surpass human cognition? No one knows, but these achievements no longer seem so far beyond our capabilities.

We cannot step 500 years into the future, but we can be certain that when the history of the twenty-first century is written, a title theme will be how we developed our new powers of nature – and the wisdom or folly with which we exercised them.

The formula for flourishing genius

A flourishing of genius does not just 'happen'. It arises as a result of specific social and intellectual conditions that enable creativity to shine forth. Why did genius shine so spectacularly during the Renaissance? And why is it happening now?

Part of the credit goes to the rare individuals – the genius*es* – who are born into a given age. Individuality is a crucial component to every instance of genius. As Brian Arthur, today one of the world's foremost thinkers on the topic, observes, the *Aha!* moment, when a new principle overturns an old, 'wells always from an *individual* subconscious'.[28] Often, something strange or unique in a person's focus tips the odds of a breakthrough in their favour. Copernicus focused on finding purer-than-Ptolemy harmony in the heavens. Leonardo focused on the study of optics and engineering. Michelangelo focused on marble blocks, each of which he believed had a figure trapped inside, begging for release. And when such focus produces an *Aha!*, whatever follows will embody its author's uniqueness.

But the presence of great, focused minds is not itself sufficient for genius to erupt society-wide. If it were, Western European civilization could never have caught up to, then surpassed, China between 1450 and 1550. China had a technological head start and, assuming that big-brained individuals form a constant share of the population everywhere, twice as many smart people upon whom to draw.

Europe's leap forward during the Renaissance suggests that something else mattered: *collective* genius. Every person possesses a unique fragment of capability; collective genius happens when society nurtures and connects those diverse fragments. Diverse minds bent on a problem can spark original ideas and contributions that accelerate individual breakthroughs, or take those breakthroughs forward. The number of individual geniuses may be a constant share of the population everywhere, but collective genius varies widely with societal levels of learning and linking up.

'All the world is full of savants, learned teachers, large libraries; and I am of the opinion that neither in the time of Plato nor of Cicero nor of Papinian were there such facilities for study as one sees now', wrote the French author Francois Rabelais (1483–1553) in the 1530s.[29] The biographies of those who made the biggest breakthroughs of the first Renaissance show that their singular achievements all owed a deep debt to the tangled, rapidly developing age into which they were born, and to the collective genius that flourished under such conditions.

Leonardo is the most famous polymath from Tuscany that history remembers, but he was far from the only one. The early humanist Petrarch (1304–1374) was Tuscan, and long before Leonardo's birth, Tuscan engineers realized that they had much to gain from dialogue with Petrarch's students of ancient Greece and Rome. The classical world's temples, domes and roads were still in use, 1,500 years later. What was the secret? The ability to creatively combine past solutions with present technical problems, or to communicate those combinations in drawings, was already highly prized and spreading fast at the time and place of Leonardo's birth. Leonardo reached a new peak in these arts, in part because he had the good fortune to grow up in a moment when the supply of knowledge about the past, and the speed with which new combinations spread, shot up.

Mainz, Gutenberg's hometown, was a crossroads for two very different domains: wine-making and coin-minting.[30] The former contributed many styles of grape press and the engineering craft to tinker with them; the latter, metal-working skills for making moulds and experimenting to find the best alloy for casting individual letters – one that would melt easily, cast well in a mould, yet survive repeated pounding in a press. These critical crafts were deep and local, but once Gutenberg successfully combined them, the diffusion of his press was guaranteed by the more general forces we mapped in Part I (despite his own best efforts to keep the technology secret).

As for Copernicus, he did his groundbreaking work in the quiet Polish district of Varmia, a place he himself styled a very remote corner of the earth.[31] But he spent his formative years, from the age of eighteen to thirty, hopping from one great hub of European learning to another. In 1491, he entered the Jagiellonian University in Kraków, where for three years he studied logic, poetry, rhetoric and philosophy alongside other brainy youths from across continental Europe. There he read major scientific works of the past and present that were just becoming widely available in print: the ancient geometry of Euclid and the recent trigonometry of Regiomontanus; the classical astronomy of Ptolemy and the recent astronomical tables by Peurbach; and major Arabic scientific works in their Latin translations.[32] (The latter may have been pivotal. A sun-centred universe had first been proposed by the Greek Aristarchus in the third century BC. Europe had forgotten Aristarchus, but Arabic scholarship had not; it's possible Copernicus borrowed inspiration from their writings.[33]) In 1496, he moved to Italy, and spent the next seven years networking with the continent's leading scholars. It is thanks to this network that Copernicus changed how the world sees the heavens. His 1543 book *On the Revolutions* was banned. His intellectual heir, Galileo, was harassed by the Inquisition for holding heretic views. But when Copernicus posted his draft ideas to an increasingly connected circle of scholar-friends back in the 1510s, he set loose an idea that could not be contained.

Fast-flowing ideas, brains and incentives

Whole bookshelves have been written on the question of what environmental conditions make genius flourish in some times and places, and not others; the full discussion is beyond the scope of this book. But the above stories highlight three conditions in particular that made fifteenth- and sixteenth-century Europe ripe for a collective heyday (and which, today's scholars tell us, are still decisive).

The first condition was a jump in the velocity, variety and richness of the flow of ideas. It is an obvious, but essential, point: the more quickly ideas flow, the more rapidly new and fruitful combinations of ideas can emerge. Variety matters, too, because, as Gutenberg found (and contemporary research confirms), the big leaps tend to happen when seemingly unrelated domains collide.[34] And the richer the flow, the more complexity it can carry. 'Let no man who is not a mathematician read the elements of my work', Leonardo wrote, because he believed only a learned person could adequately appreciate the ideas he was testing.[35]

Part I showed the connective forces that caused this jump. New exchanges between civilizations, expanding trade and financial links, social mobility, urbanization and migration together created many more contact points between diverse people and their ways of life. Then and now, one of the best ways to push the limits of our present thinking is to meet people who think differently.

The most direct catalyst of this enhanced flow of ideas was the new medium of print. The printing press was what today we would classify as a 'general-purpose technology'.[36] Unlike, say, the violin, whose arrival transformed music but affected little beyond that sphere, the press affected virtually every domain of activity. It multiplied the available body of knowledge and broadened the network of practitioners in every field. Among scholars, the medieval practice of writing letters to friends and holding local debates evolved into publishing booklets for wide distribution and critique. Engaging greater numbers of people brought a wider set of knowledge, experience and ideas to every important problem.

Print helped distribute another general-purpose technology: mathematics. In 1494, Luca Pacioli printed his *Summa de Arithmetica, Geometria, Proportioni et Proportionalità* in Venice, and helped launch the mass adoption of arithmetic in Europe. Prior to print, it was mostly only learned elites who knew Hindu-Arabic numerals. Most maths was still calculated with Roman numerals and an abacus, and the need for the latter piece of hardware meant most people couldn't afford to do their own sums. The spread of arithmetic made maths something that everyone with a stick of charcoal could afford to do, and multiplied the population that could understand, express and develop complex ideas in numbers.[37]

The second condition that helped collective genius flourish was a booming stock of well-educated, well-fed brains to tap this idea flow. A vast amount of effort by unknown others precedes a breakthrough like Copernicus': teachers and masters passing on unwritten, tacit know-how to students and apprentices; failed attempts that discover dead ends so that others don't have to; technical tweaks to devices and instruments that make it possible to probe deeper into a mystery; countless debates, oral and written, with other people's viewpoints to firm up one's own grasp of a craft or surprise the mind into new directions. The more brains that understand a craft and grapple with its limits, the more likely it is that someone will surpass those limits.

The third condition that helped collective genius flourish more strongly in Renaissance Europe than in other places was strong private and social incentives to reward risk-taking. China was a monolithic bureaucracy. There was little marketplace for ideas beyond those the state approved, and promising ventures – like Zheng He's 1405–1433 naval expeditions to explore the Indian Ocean and East Africa – could be scuppered by imperial decree. Europe, by contrast, comprised many small, weak states. Competition and war between them (and with the encroaching Ottomans) urged each to invest in discoveries that might offer a military, economic or cultural edge. Demand for new weapons, warships and public defences was high, and purse strings were loosened for whomever could design them (Leonardo spent a fair chunk of his productive lifetime designing military contraptions).[38] Wealthy cities endowed new schools, universities and professorships to tackle commercially important problems (like calculating longitude at sea). Meanwhile, rich families pumped money into new art, sculpture and architecture: it helped the emerging class of wealthy merchants gain a veneer of gravitas, and it was one of the few socially acceptable forms of ostentation.[39]

On the supply side of this emerging marketplace for ideas, individuals who offered good ones were free to profit from them. Gutenberg's wunder-machine was copied so quickly and widely that he made no money from it, but the generation of inventors after him fared much better. In 1474, the city of Venice adopted the world's first formal patent legislation. As the law's preamble noted, if 'provisions were made for the works and devices discovered by men of great genius … more men would apply their genius … and build devices of great utility to our commonwealth'.[40] By the mid-sixteenth century, such provisions were common across Europe.

Ripe again

The same conditions are present now, only stronger and more widely felt.

Part I laid plain the core evidence. Developmental forces today have raised the global population of healthy, brainy people to its highest level ever. Connective forces – in politics, trade, finance, population migration – have tangled human society together. These same forces have also impacted the spread of *ideas*. The volume, variety and richness of their flows through this tangle have exploded.

New general-purpose technologies

New general-purpose technologies have once again made mass communication cheap and abundant. Increased computing power has made the flow of ideas more diverse and abundant, and advanced the complexity of what we can say to each other. Thanks to the compound growth in computing power identified by Moore's Law, the smartphone that fits in our pockets today is faster than the Cray-2 supercomputer – the world's most powerful machine in 1990, which weighed in at 5,500 pounds and had a price tag of $35 million.[41]

Moore's Law has brought the internet to all our fingertips, but it has also taken us to the edge of the universe. Over the past twenty years, as our computing power has swelled, we've pushed our conversations further and deeper into very complex systems of maths, astronomy, biology, engineering, geology, weather, war, economics and other subjects. Whole new industries have followed our conversations into these domains, so that today we work with ideas that two decades ago were beyond our comprehension. The fracking industry uses today's supercomputers to model what happens when we drill a bunch of holes into the ground and inject high-pressure liquids to release gases trapped inside rock formations. Medical science is working to simulate brain activity, so that we can understand how the brain works and how drugs or surgery may alter it. Public health officials simulate a pandemic's spread to get a sense of where the highest-risk areas are located, which nodes of our transport systems need to be shut down first, and how far a virus might spread before we find, mass-produce and distribute a vaccine. Engineers model the stresses on new ships twice as big as the biggest ever built before, and on skyscrapers twice as tall (Saudi Arabia's Kingdom Tower, due in 2018, will be a kilometre high). And filmmakers convincingly bring to life fluorescent planets, black holes, alien robots and mutant superheroes.

New contact points

The freer flow of ideas today is also evident in the idea-rich contact points that have multiplied between different peoples, products and lifestyles.

It's clear in academia. Globally, some three million students go abroad each year on short- and medium-term stays. In the OECD, two-thirds of foreign students are from the developing world, with the number of students coming from Asia rising the fastest. China sent virtually no students abroad thirty years ago. Today, it sends more than any other country.

Given the chance, many top foreign students choose to stay put after they graduate and give back to their host economy. A 2011 survey showed that among the top ten patent-producing universities in the United States, foreign-born inventors were named on three-quarters of all patents filed.[42] Other graduates compete in the global market for research talent. Over 40 per cent of Oxford University's academic staff are foreigners – from nearly 100 countries – and that ratio is rising.

These academic migrants spread and connect the world's brainpower. Cross-border research collaboration, which accounted for fewer than one-tenth of all published papers in 1995, now accounts for almost one-third.[43] The most heavily collaborated paper in academic history – a May 2015 physics paper based on research at the Large Hadron Collider in Geneva – counted 5,154 co-authors from all over the world.[44] Curing cancer is now a twenty-four-hour research effort by virtual teams from leading labs around the world. At the end of their day, researchers hand off their latest labours to the next time zone; the next morning, they pick up where their foreign colleagues left off. And all but two of the last fifteen Nobel Prizes in science have gone to international teams of researchers.[45]

The freer flow of ideas is clear in the trade of idea-rich goods, like pharmaceuticals, chemicals, machinery, computers and other electronics. Over the past twenty years, trade in high-tech manufactures has quadrupled in nominal terms, from $1.4 trillion in 1995 to $5 trillion today. But it has also spread. In 1995, the developed world sold three-quarters, and bought two-thirds, of all traded high-tech goods. Today, that trade is split nearly 50–50 with developing countries, on both the buy- and the sell-side. The knowledge needed to produce such goods has been shared around the world.[46]

Finally, the faster, richer flow of ideas is clear in social media. On Twitter, one-quarter of all 'followers' are from countries other than the original Tweeter. Facebook conversations link every region of the world. See Figure 5.5. The result is that popular culture spreads ever faster and farther. In 2003, one of the very first Internet memes, *Star Wars Kid*, swept the planet. Within three years, it had been viewed an estimated 900 million times.[47] In 2015, *PewDiePie*, a YouTube channel, racked up 900 million views every three *months*.[48] Run by a Swede, Felix Kjellberg, the channel – which broadcasts his video game-playing antics – became the first ever to cross the ten-billion-view mark, in late 2015. Earlier the same year, Islamic extremists stormed the Paris offices of *Charlie Hebdo*, a satirical newspaper, and killed twelve people in retaliation for its cartoon caricatures of the Prophet Muhammad. Within twenty-four hours, the Twitter

FIGURE 5.5 *International Facebook friendships stitch the world's conversations together.*
Image credit: Facebook.

hashtag '#JeSuisCharlie', meant as a way to reaffirm freedom of expression, was retweeted 3.4 million times, in every country of the world where Twitter wasn't blocked.[49]

* * *

The world suddenly contains more brains, healthier and better educated, exchanging an exploding volume and variety of ever more vivid ideas – globally, instantly and at near-zero cost. These conditions describe an ideal world for creative breakthroughs, both individual and collective. They are why big shifts are happening now, and why the genius of this second Renaissance has the potential to far surpass the first.

Will we live up to that potential? Or lose faith in it?

6

Cathedrals, Believers and Doubt

Why feats that were once beyond us are now common, and why we all should embrace the flourishing that's underway

(even though its consequences won't always be what we expect)

Collective efforts

Individual geniuses hog the headlines, today and in the history books; we celebrate and lionize those persons who break through long-standing limits. But they are only the tip of the iceberg – the visible sliver of something massive and profound beneath the surface. Underlying the genius of Copernicus and da Vinci, Elon Musk and Stephen Hawking is a larger story: the expansion of talents and capacities across a wide population of people.

The last chapter showed the role collective *genius* plays in our present flourishing. Each of our brains is unique, and when conditions permit us to nurture, connect and focus many minds – like right now, through mass literacy and digital linking up – together we can co-create breakthroughs that complement and accelerate individual achievements.

Collective *effort* is a second form of Renaissance co-creation, and while it flourishes under the same conditions, it contributes to society in a different way. Genius, in its individual and collective forms, injects *originality*. As the last chapter showed, genius can break us out of the prison of prevailing thought and help us see the world in new ways. It moves society forwards by infusing the present with the uniqueness of those now living.

The main contribution of collective effort is *scale*. It builds wonders and tackles problems that no individual, no matter how gifted, could manage alone. If they are to be done at all, they must be done together. Michelangelo designed the great dome atop St Peter's Basilica; collective effort raised it.

And we are raising many more.

Scaling new heights

St Peter's Basilica in Rome. The Cathedral of St Mary in Seville. The Cathedral of Our Lady in Antwerp. In 1550, they stood, in that order, as the three biggest churches in all Christendom

(St Peter's and St Mary's still stand first and third today, by area). All three had been begun or finished in the preceding century.

Most of Europe's cathedrals had been built during the Middle Ages, but the greatest in size were more recent additions to the skyline. The glory building began in Florence with the Basilica of Saint Mary of the Flower, or *Duomo*. Ground broke on the cathedral much earlier, in 1296, but it was its final, crowning dome, engineered by Brunelleschi and completed in 1436, that put the Duomo into a new class of collective achievement. Based on the ancient Pantheon in Rome, Brunelleschi's giant dome was a visible shout-out from the geographic heart of Florence, to all who saw it, that the values and aesthetics of the classical world had been resurrected here. It was also a technological triumph. One way to judge a society's engineering prowess is the distance that its buildings' roofs can span without internal supports. The ancient Romans had set the bar high: their Pantheon spanned 43 metres. Brunelleschi's dome (44 metres) was the first to eclipse that mark in 1,300 years.

Cathedrals were a measure of collective capability – of what could be done, together. Brunelleschi is the name history remembers, but he didn't raise his dome alone. It was the endeavour of a whole community. It took enormous wealth and generations of skilled manpower to realize such ambitious stonework. It's no coincidence that the old St Peter's, which had been built under the Roman Emperor Constantine I in 360 AD and had stood in near-ruin for centuries, was torn down and rebuilt (several times larger) during the Renaissance. Nor is it a coincidence that the cities of Seville and Antwerp would raise the two next-largest houses of God in the same century. The former was a smallish Spanish town until Columbus' 'discovery' transformed the place into the international trading hub for New World goods; the latter was a Dutch port town that during the sixteenth century grew into the premier financial and mercantile centre for all Europe. Developmental and connective forces – the step-changes in wealth, health and education, political and economic integration, and urbanization – breathed life into grand visions. 'Let us build a church so beautiful and so great that those who see it built will think we were mad', said Seville's residents, according to local oral tradition.[1] So they did. When they finished their mad labour, in the 1520s, their cathedral supplanted the Hagia Sophia in Istanbul as the world's largest – a title the latter had held for nearly 1,000 years, and which Seville's St Mary's held for less than 100.

Collective power in the Renaissance also raised new cathedrals of knowledge – libraries. It wasn't just that libraries got bigger – although that was part of it. In 1450, a well-stocked library contained 100 manuscripts; by 1550, it was common for individual scholars to own over 100 books themselves.[2] The continent's largest libraries ballooned from 2,000–3,000 volumes to 15,000–20,000.[3] This quantitative boom was thanks to Gutenberg's invention: somewhere between 100 and 150 million copies of some 100,000–150,000 titles were sold in the first century of print, and many of them found their way onto the shelves of court, monastic and university libraries.[4]

But more important than the size and number of these libraries was the breadth of their contents, and therein lay the collective feat. Famine, plague and war during the Middle Ages had fragmented the written inheritance of Western civilization across all the courts and monasteries of Europe. Much was lost; much that survived lay forgotten on dusty shelves. Then print arrived, and in its first century printers hungry for new material hunted down this scattered heritage – in particular, works from classical Greece and Rome, for which demand was insatiable.

Printers became scholarly tomb raiders. They operated networks of manuscript diggers stretching as far and wide as the age allowed – which, given the rising economic linkages between Europe's major population centres, was from the Atlantic coast to the Black Sea. Aldus Manutius (c. 1452–1515), one of Europe's most prolific publishers at the time and the inventor of *italics*, drew rare manuscripts out of Italy, France, Germany, England, Poland and Hungary, and sent search parties as far north as Scotland and as far east as modern-day Romania.[5] His Aldine Press published 120 titles (totalling at least 100,000 copies) in his lifetime, including the very first Greek-language editions of more than ninety classical writers – Aristotle, Plato, Herodotus and the like.[6] Aldus' editions were sold across Europe, accompanied sea captains wherever ships sailed, and formed the foundation of classical Greek study everywhere (including at the authors' Oxford, where many of his now priceless first editions still remain).[7] He produced a library which was not limited by place or time as the great libraries of the past had been, and which knew no boundaries except the boundaries of the world. This, at least, was the opinion of Desiderius Erasmus (c. 1466–1536), who spent time on Aldus' editorial team and whose own far-flung network probably helped uncover several manuscripts.[8]

Each press was its own business, competing to be first to market with the next great work by Plato or Ptolemy, but almost every new book was a massive collective effort. Behind each book was a team of scholars drawn from all across Europe, working hard to piece together which pages from which surviving manuscripts constituted the authoritative text that was 'fit to print'.[9] Sometimes, as with Aldus' 1496 *Theocritus*, the task proved to be beyond a single printer's resources. But 'something is better than nothing', Aldus explained in his preface to that work (a bit of collaborative wisdom that's still popular among start-ups today); he offered up his own team's attempt as a foundation upon which peers could – and did – improve.[10]

Competing together and building atop one another's successes, Europe's proliferating presses reassembled the greater part of Western civilization's surviving knowledge base. They also duplicated and distributed it everywhere demand existed, so that by 1550, what had once been scarce and fragmented was available, whole, to virtually everyone who could read – including those in the New World, where the first press opened in Mexico City in 1539.[11] Arguably, this collective feat was the most important intellectual achievement of the first Renaissance.

Contemporary cathedrals, latter-day libraries

Five hundred years later, a relatively small team of people, aided by cranes and heavy machinery, can raise buildings multiple times bigger than St Peter's, and decades faster. But in many other domains, scale still defeats us – or has done. Now, the lift in our collective capabilities is bringing our own mad visions within reach.

Most of us are already acutely conscious of these new powers: impossibilities just a decade ago are now commonplace occurrences. Contemporary cathedrals like Wikipedia and open-source software (Linux, Apache) have been built, click by click, by tens of thousands of individuals. These people are scattered worldwide but brought together on the internet by common interests, and their collective works have become the most widely used in their respective domains. Wikipedia has put most print encyclopedias out of business; Apache powers 60 per cent of all Internet servers.[12] Like the libraries of the first

Renaissance, Facebook and YouTube have been pulled together by multitudes of people and, in many ways, chronicle humanity. *Collaboration* has become a buzzword and part of our daily lives: a metric against which our job performance is measured, a criterion in our grant applications, a priority within corporate strategy and government planning, and a whole new software industry.

With the spread of mobile data connections, collaboration has now become part of our every moment. In the first Renaissance, people went to the town square to find each other; in the second, the town square is always with us, in the form of real-time, location-based data on our identities, choices and behaviours. We go to it anytime to fulfil an ever-widening range of needs – to shop, eat, exercise, travel and meet with one another. We can match partners for love or sex (Tinder, Grindr), match entrepreneurs with investors (kickstarter.com, indiegogo.com), drivers with riders (Uber, Lyft), spare rooms with travellers (Airbnb), public stewards with street-level concerns (SeeClickFix.com), people in need with good Samaritans (causes.com, fundly.com), problems with the talents to solve them (hackathons, InnoCentive.com) and victims with aid-givers and watchdogs (ushahidi.com), to name a few.

None of these feats or forums were possible even ten years ago. Now, they are an integral part of how we all talk, learn, create, share, do and help, and allow us to do all these things more quickly, more efficiently, at a bigger scale and (sometimes) privately.

But the most ambitious of our new collective efforts are less familiar. They aim not to assist us in our daily lives but to defeat long-standing scale limits that fetter human civilization and science – limits that even our constantly growing computing resources have failed to overcome.

The first is language, which divides human culture and knowledge into mutually unintelligible islands. English, today's *lingua franca*, is understood by only about 25 per cent of the world's population – to widely varying degrees.[13] You would need to speak more than fourteen languages to reach half of humanity with native clarity, and more than forty to reach three-quarters.[14] The internet, humanity's principal site for speech and its storehouse of knowledge, is likewise compartmentalized by language walls; what we see depends on the language we use. English speakers tap the richest reservoir. Half the world's Tweets and most academic research online are English-only.[15] The English-language edition of Wikipedia, with five million articles, is more than 2.5 times larger than the next-largest edition (German, at 1.9 million), and more than fifteen times larger than the median of the top fifty editions.[16] On the other hand, English users remain almost totally oblivious to massive phenomena unfolding in the non-English web, like Chinese social media (whose main messaging platforms – Weibo and Weixin – far outstrip Twitter in terms of user base and chat volume),[17] or Nollywood (Nigeria's Hollywood, which mobile video has helped to balloon into the world's second-largest filmmaking centre, behind only India's Bollywood). The aggregate result is that while cross-border data flows have leapt some twenty-fold since 2005, only about half of that international traffic escapes its region of origin.[18] That's far less than cross-border goods (68 per cent), which, even though they're physical, are less impeded by linguistic and cultural gaps.[19]

A fully multilingual web would be a gift of incalculable worth to civilization. Unfortunately, so far it has been beyond our capabilities. To translate just one sliver, the full English edition of Wikipedia, into just one other major language would cost at least $100 million and take over 10,000 person-years.[20] Even if someone were willing to pay for it, there may not be enough translators living to make the attempt, depending on the destination language. Computer-driven translation engines can automate the task somewhat; they can often give us the gist of what a foreign utterance means. But, as users of every engine from the 1990s' *AltaVista Babelfish* to today's *Google Translate* can attest, much meaning, most clarity and all style are still lost in translation. That's because, whereas human translators start by recognizing the whole meaning of the source and then try to express it faithfully in destination-language terms, computers start by recognizing individual words – or at best, phrases – and then stitch together foreign analogues with no conception of the overall result. It will take a few more years before they get really good at it.

Nevertheless, a multilingual web is already starting to look feasible. What hadn't been factored in before is how widespread the impulse to learn another language is – 1.2 billion people strong, by recent estimates.[21] And it turns out that translating bits of the web is useful practice that many language learners enjoy and are willing to do for free. The result is a colossal jump in our aggregate translation resources. It has already made its presence felt in entertainment and other popular content. In China, Hollywood blockbusters and hit HBO television series are available online within a day of their US release, complete with Mandarin subtitles (the latter having been added by avid fans practising their English). Khan Academy, an online education portal, has seen most of its 6,000 instructional videos subtitled into one or more of sixty-five languages by volunteers. TED, another online portal, has attracted more than 22,000 volunteers to translate over 80,000 'TED Talks' into more than 100 languages. Altogether today, we estimate that the global pool of volunteer translators totalled some two to four million people, who in a single year gave humanity twenty-five to fifty million hours of free translation service in areas such as entertainment, education, news and disaster relief (e.g. by translating victims' Tweets in real time for emergency responders).

Clever business models are figuring out how to scale up our collective translation power even further and apply it to public content that volunteers neglect (or to private content in exchange for a fee). Duolingo, founded by Carnegie Mellon computer science professor Dr Luis von Ahn, is one example. It's a web- and app-based study platform that gives language learners a real sentence from the web – say, from a Wikipedia article or a CNN news story – and challenges them to translate it. When several students translate the same sentence the same way, the system deems that translation to be reliable and then gives or sells it back to the owner of the original text. The study tool is free for users, game-oriented and effective, so language students are rushing in. Duolingo launched in June 2012 with 300,000 users. Three years later, it had twenty-five million (12.5 million active) studying thirteen different languages, with another eight languages in development.[22] If enough Duolingo users advance from beginner to upper levels of second-language proficiency, they will crunch right through many of the web's once insurmountable language walls in short order. With one million advanced users, Duolingo would be able to translate the complete English Wikipedia in about 100 hours.

The second scale limit that we are cracking collectively is scientific data analysis. 'In many parts of science, we're not constrained by what data we can get, we're constrained by what we can do with the data we have', says Chris Lintott, an astrophysicist.[23]

Data is plentiful; our capacity to sift through it is not. That's because our computer-driven devices keep getting better and better at collecting the data researchers want – in Lintott's case, images of distant galaxies – but they are still quite poor at recognizing the patterns we're looking for or at separating meaningful signals from meaningless noise. The result is a massive, ever-growing backlog of data-to-be-studied-someday. CERN's Large Hadron Collider in Switzerland produces nearly a gigabyte of new data every second about how fundamental particles behave.[24] The world's DNA sequencing machines together churn out 1–2 gigabytes per second about how our genes work.[25] At NASA, data floods from the sky: its various missions generate about 150 gigabytes per second of new observations about our universe.[26] (For comparison, today, Facebook's 2 billion-plus users together uploaded over 5 gigabytes per second. Can you keep up with the whole world's news feed? NASA's problem is thirty times bigger.) The same deluge swamps climatologists, geologists, sociologists, economists and most other data-driven researchers. Science has already gathered the answers to many big questions. We just don't know it yet.

But we will soon. Our other feats of collective genius have led scientists to recognize that while computers may find it difficult to recognize patterns and filter out noise, the human brain does it easily. The mistake was to exclude anyone who wasn't wearing a lab coat from doing scientific work. Now, by redesigning research methods to focus computers on what they do best and inviting volunteer masses to donate human brainpower where it's needed most, 'citizen science' is starting to break through the analytical bottlenecks that plague a wide range of disciplines.

In 2007, Chris Lintott and Kevin Schawinski co-founded Galaxy Zoo, inviting amateur stargazers to help them catalogue and classify some 900,000 galaxies that had been photographed from the year 2000 onward. The task would have taken one devout graduate student three to five years of $24 \times 7 \times 365$ labour to complete; twice as long if she double-checked her work. Instead, it took over 100,000 volunteers less than six months, and each galaxy was re-checked an average of thirty-eight times. By mid-2014, several hundred thousand Galaxy Zoo volunteers had crunched through seven giant-scale data sets, compiled a catalogue of galaxies ten times larger than any previous version, and produced forty-four scientific papers' worth of results.[27] Along the way, they spotted rare astronomical phenomena that had been conjectured for years but never detected, and found others, like *Hanny's Voorwerp*, that were entirely unexpected.[28] Hanny van Arkel, a Dutch schoolteacher, got an object in the sky named after her – an honour that even professional astronomers rarely achieve.

Galaxy Zoo expanded into Zooniverse (zooniverse.org) – today, the world's largest citizen science portal, with over a million registered volunteers. Together, they tackle oversized data sets in dozens of active projects, spanning astronomy, biology, ecology, climate science and the humanities.[29] A project called Planet Four enlists Martian lovers to help map the surface of the Red Planet. In Chimp & See, animal lovers help spot leopards, elephants and chimpanzees as the animals walk, charge or swing past hundreds of cameras strewn across Africa's forests. OldWeather asks the public's help to transcribe ships' logs going back to the mid-nineteenth century (old logs form the most complete set of long-term climate data in existence, but like ancient Greek texts in Aldus' day, they lie scattered, gathering dust, in maritime museums and archives the world over). Ancient Lives assembles archaeology buffs to help translate thousands of 2,000-year-old Egyptian papyri (no knowledge of hieroglyphics required). Higgs Hunters invites anyone to help sift through data from the Large Hadron Collider for more evidence of the Higgs boson and other exotic particles.

Zooniverse is only one citizen science platform. Others include Tomnod (tomnod.com), where volunteers scour satellite photos to help stop illegal fishing or search for missing aircraft, and EyeWire (eyewire.org), a game that helps to map the human brain. Around the world, millions more volunteers are taking part in thousands of ambitious projects that would not otherwise be feasible.[30] Citizen science has become a force multiplier in field after field of research. Output that once would have occupied a productive lab for a lifetime can now be coordinated by a handful of curators in just a few years.

Citizen science isn't a panacea. Substantial expert effort is still needed to put data into a crowd-accessible form and to curate each project carefully so that results can withstand tough peer reviews. Sometimes it cannot be done. Data sets full of pictures, sounds and unusual text lend themselves to public participation more readily than, say, the endless stream of numerical values being pumped out by the world's particle accelerators. And as the data generated by our research devices continues to swell, even research teams a hundred thousand strong will need to speed up their work if they want to keep pace. The Square Kilometer Array, a giant radio telescope due to go live in 2020, will on its own generate as much new data each day as 5,000 Facebooks.[31] The Zooniverse team is working on how to raise its game – for example, by sorting the more accurate volunteers from the rest, and rechecking their work less often – to help meet these challenges.

Citizen science platforms need to get smarter, and they will. The best work being done right now marries citizen scientists with machines that can learn from them, so that as humans spot new galaxies or distinguish a leopard from a cheetah, the machines learn how we do it and improve their own algorithms. That frees human resources to focus on the most complex cases. In the meantime, existing platforms have already delivered some answers whole decades sooner than science expected to find them, and helped us tackle questions we never imagined we could.

Collective doubt

So what?

Flourishing genius would catapult sixteenth-century Europe past the rest of the world on many measures of progress, but that was only clear in hindsight. In an age pregnant with immediate anxieties – Turks encroaching from the east; incessant warmongering among Europe's diverse princes; economic, social and religious upheavals brought about by rapid change – the public took little notice of artistic, scientific and technological leapfrogging. If the latter did not make their own lives better, why care about them?

By this test, Columbus' discovery of the New World was for several years deemed a non-event when weighed against the real prize: a swifter sea route to the fabulous riches of Asia.[32] The newly found lands, bereft of important commodities like spices, seemed scarcely profitable at first, and their inhabitants lacked religions or refinements of the sort that Europeans recognized. Seen from some perspectives that prevailed at the time, the great voyages westward across the Atlantic had found nothing at all.

Likewise, Copernicus' scientific work seemed almost wholly disconnected from life's priorities. Even among the educated few who understood what the Polish scholar had done, the revolutionary importance of his claim that the earth spun around the sun was far from obvious. He had no proof for his 'heresy', only a theory that better fitted the facts. And its value was mostly esoteric – to help astrologers divine better horoscopes. Society would need another century or two to accept the idea that the obscure symbolic language of geometry and maths could help them understand physical reality in a way that the Word of God could not. As the publisher's preface to many copies of Copernicus' *On the Revolutions* anxiously acknowledged, '[T]hese hypotheses need not be true nor even probable ... they are not put forward to convince anyone that they are true, but merely to provide a reliable basis for computation ... [L]et no one expect anything certain from astronomy, which cannot furnish it, lest he accept as the truth ideas conceived for another purpose, and depart from this study a greater fool than when he entered it.'[33]

Even Gutenberg's press, so obviously an improvement over handwriting, was met with many shrugs at first. For making just a few copies of any book, a scribe was faster, far cheaper and less risky. The upfront investment Gutenberg needed to cast and arrange thousands of metal letters was considerable. The economics only made sense in large-volume runs. But books were a luxury: useful to few, owned by even fewer. Could any title command orders by the hundreds? (The Bible did not immediately come to mind: it was a specialist text whose reading demanded expert guidance – wasn't it?)

Again, so what?

Similar doubts hover over our achievements today. A growing number of serious voices in academia and industry worry aloud that, far from flourishing, the breakthroughs and inventions that matter to us here and now are becoming fewer and smaller.

Statistical stagnation

Economic statistics are a dismal oversimplification of reality. They fail to measure many things that matter to us – like the beauty of Michelangelo's *Creation of Adam*, or the case with which we can now make and maintain global friendships. But they do measure some other things that matter quite a lot: namely, our incomes, and how fast we can expect our incomes to grow. The blunt question demanded by the numbers is the same that greeted Columbus once his 'failure' became known: If flourishing genius doesn't deliver us tangible gains that we can take home, is genius really flourishing?

The most damning number is output per hour of work, or 'labour productivity' in economics-speak. How much 'value' does one hour of work produce? Our incomes vary directly with the answer we can give. Economists figure that this is a good way to track the technological progress of a society. ('Technology' includes more than just machines. It also includes things like laws, regulations and business models.) Depending on whether I harvest my crop with a two-handed scythe or with a GPS-guided combine, the number – the value of one hour's work – will vary quite a lot.

Right now, this number is worrisome. Robert Gordon, a guru of US growth economics, pored over a century of US productivity data and concluded, in 2012, that all our recent technological achievements don't amount to much in real terms. For the first eighty years of his study, from 1891 to 1972, US labour productivity grew about 2.3 per cent per year. That's sizzling-fast in macroeconomic terms (at that rate, productivity doubles with each new generation), and its speed and duration are proof that the technological changes to which those generations bore witness totally transformed their lives for the better. Eventually, however, the United States completed that transformation: its citizens all had cars and electricity and clean, running water. After 1972, productivity grew much more slowly – only 1.4 per cent per year – while economists waited for the next big thing to come along and give productivity a new lift.[34]

Fortunately, it did. Computers and information technologies arrived to change the world of work again; by 1996, productivity growth was up to a brisk 2.5 per cent per year. Unfortunately, this time, the sizzle very quickly fizzled. Technology adoption was swift. By 2005, the United States had installed industrial robots, barcode scanners, cash machines, PCs and e-commerce more or less economy-wide, and productivity growth fell back to about 1.3 per cent again. It's been stuck there since. This is disappointing news for everyone: average US wages rose 350 per cent in the forty years between 1932 and 1972, but rose only 22 per cent over the next forty. In other words: for all its hype, the computer has had less impact on people's incomes than the flush toilet.[35]

Missed expectations

Even without numbers, our present-day stagnation is plain. Consider this argument from Garry Kasparov and Max Levchin. A person born in the United States in 1875 had three choices if she wanted to get from A to B: walk, ride a horse or take a boat. She hauled her daily water and sewage, burned wood, coal and oil for light and heat, and performed most of her labours with either human or animal power. Assuming she didn't die early (due to poor sanitation, life expectancy at the time was only forty years), she lived long enough to witness a world in which people drove cars, flew through the sky, made water appear at the turn of a faucet (and flush away just as easily), commanded lights with the flick of a switch, and employed machines to do everything from wash their clothes to calculate their payroll. In her lifetime, she witnessed the invention of: electricity and all its spin-offs; automobiles and highway systems; running water and indoor plumbing and heating; the radio and the telephone; flight; as well as the vacuum tube, penicillin, radar, rockets and atomic weapons. And anyone born in 1950 witnessed the dawn of the space age, transistors and computers before the age of thirty.

Together, the above inventions defined modernity. They also imbued people with the expectation that technology would deliver a utopian future.

Now fast forward to today: that expectation has been disappointed. See Figure 6.1. Except for a few more gadgets and a lot of brushed aluminium and digital displays, today's kitchens are much the same as those of our grandparents. Today's cars drive fractionally faster on the highway than theirs did – and far slower in the cities, due to congestion. Now that Concorde has been shut down, it takes us the same six hours to fly from New York to London that it took them. (We don't even fly to the moon anymore.) Despite the hundreds of billions of dollars we've ploughed into medical research in the last forty years, rich people only live some 8 per cent (five years) longer than their grandparents, and we suffer from the same chronic diseases: cancer, heart disease, stroke, Alzheimer's and organ failure.

As Peter Thiel, who co-founded PayPal, put it: 'We wanted flying cars – instead we got 140 characters.'[36]

FIGURE 6.1 *To date, many expectations of the future have been disappointed.*

Diminishing dreams

All the above has sown a deeper doubt: that humanity's glory days may be permanently past. Is it possible that there are only so many one-time transformations humanity can work upon itself – and that we've already made most of them? Before, we couldn't harness electricity; now we can. We couldn't maintain sanitary living conditions; now we can. We couldn't get from any A to any B; now we can. We couldn't talk to anyone anywhere anytime; now we can. Whatever's left – driverless cars, or even quantum teleportation – might be incremental in comparison.

And perhaps whatever truly fundamental transformations do remain to be made, if any, will be much harder to achieve. We've picked clean the low-hanging fruit. Looking back, doubling human life expectancy the first time was simple: roughly, we separated our animals (horses, cows, pigs, chickens) from our homes, separated potable water from sewage, and stumbled upon (then mass-produced) the stuff in mould that kills off bacteria (penicillin). Doubling our lifespan *again* will be hard. It will require us to understand aging at the genetic level (where it's coded) and the cellular level (where the code is executed), then figure out how to halt it.

Until recently, business executives in major drug companies saw proof of these diminishing returns each time they (glumly) reviewed their research and development spending. As a percentage of sales, the pharmaceuticals industry invests more into R&D – nearly 18 per cent – than any other industry, except aerospace.[37] Such spending has rocketed over the past eighty years as pharmaceuticals quest for the next big breakthrough. In 1990, the global industry spent about $25 billion on the task. By 2000, spending had doubled to $50 billion, and by 2010, it had more than doubled again, to $130 billion.[38] But despite some notable successes – such as statins, which lower cholesterol, antidepressants and AIDS medications – research output did not keep pace. The number of genuinely novel drugs that made it into the public's hands each year stayed stubbornly flat.

The result was the depressing decline shown in Figure 6.2 – an undeniable downward trend in new drugs per research dollar spent. There was no leap. No Michelangelo moment. Only a difficult grind along a difficult road – one that became harder with each next step.

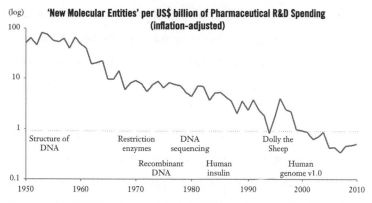

FIGURE 6.2 *Until recently, drug R&D productivity had been in long-term decline.*

Image credit: Bart Janssens, Simon Goodall, et al. (2011). Life Sciences R&D: Changing the Innovation Equation in India. *Boston: Boston Consulting Group.*

So hard, in fact, that some began to give up. In December 2011, Novartis shut the doors to its neuroscience facility in Basel, Switzerland, abandoning its drug-discovery work on brain disorders. In doing so, it joined the ranks of GlaxoSmithKline, AstraZeneca, Pfizer, Merck and Sanofi, all of which either shut down or scaled back their attempts to find new drugs for brain diseases because years of investment hadn't produced results they could sell.[39]

Four reasons to believe

We've laid plain the individual and collective genius that will write much of twenty-first-century history. Its flourishing seems self-evident when one considers the connective and developmental forces that make up our present. Yet the idea that genius is erupting now provokes a deep scepticism among many esteemed people – including some at the forefront of humanity's bold step-taking. So, who is right?

The good news is: we are. Not because the economists have their data wrong, not because the sceptics have their facts wrong, but because economic statistics and public expectations are poor yardsticks for measuring the impact that genius is already having on our lives.

1. Genius defies reduction to economic terms

Genius – including both exceptional individuals and exceptional collective achievements – brings into our world much more than economics can count.

Sceptics locked onto growth statistics make much of survey evidence showing that over two-thirds of adults in the developed world believe that the next generation will be worse off than themselves.[40] While that's a good insight into the general mood of the adult population, the more important question is: What does the *next* generation believe? Would they rather go back thirty to fifty years to live in the world of their parents and enjoy the same peaks of job security and income growth? Or would they rather march forward into a highly uncertain future?

Despite the recent comeback of vinyl records, we expect an overwhelming majority would choose the latter. Why? Because, while we value income security and wealth accumulation, we also value health. We value freedom, autonomy, participation, connection, influence. We value our new nearness to the deepest mysteries of life and the universe, to our sport idols and to our politicians. We have a hard time quantifying these things, but they are real and important. Would the next generation give up their extraordinary gains along all these dimensions in exchange for their parents' jobs?

If not, then the economists are missing something.

Not everything that matters can be measured. Economists understate the flourishing of genius now underway because they focus only on the stuff they can quantify: namely, economic activity. To economists, breakthrough ideas matter insofar as they can be exploited to produce *new* economic activity, in which case they are 'innovations' whose impact on our lives can be measured and analysed in economic terms.

But genius, as we've defined it, is a far more profound thing. Yes, genius can produce innovations (for example, when Gutenberg's printing press or Google's search engine launches whole industries), but its broader role is to *drive change*. The last chapter emphasized this role in the applied sciences, but without genius, social progress along *every* dimension of human striving – wealth creation, health, art, the pursuit of knowledge or justice – would eventually grind to a halt as we exhausted the possibilities of our present ways of thinking and doing. The job of genius is to break us out of these prisons before their bars become stifling.

When we do break free, new economic activity is just one possible consequence. Other consequences also matter. Astronomy, for example, may someday soon make the most significant yet least exploitable discovery in human history: life on other planets. Twenty years ago, the reigning assumption was that earth-like planets were rare things. Now – with better telescopes, cleverer computers and tens of thousands of amateur astronomers helping out via the internet – we know how wrong we were. The most conservative present guess is that the Milky Way alone is home to at least ten billion other planets of the right size, temperature and orbit to support life. Just add water. Mars, NASA discovered in late 2015, already has some. The chance that alien life exists somewhere in at least microbial form has been upgraded from remote to virtually certain. Soon we'll have rovers digging into Martian creeks, and telescopes able to probe deeper into the atmospheres of far-away worlds, to tell us for sure. Meanwhile, the search for *intelligent* alien life is gaining fresh momentum. In July 2015, Russian physicist-entrepreneur Yuri Milner announced Breakthrough Listen – a ten-year, $100 million pledge to boost the time spent scanning space for E.T. from dozens of hours per year to thousands on the world's best radio telescopes. As the physicist Stephen Hawking said at the launch event, 'In an infinite universe, there must be other life. There is no bigger question. It is time to commit to finding the answer.'[41] That answer will change how we see the stars – and ourselves – forever. But it will not raise productivity one bit.

2. The tangible impacts of genius defy simple measurement

Of course, economic conditions matter, too. The discovery of life in outer space will be cold comfort to people who cannot afford adequate food, let alone a telescope. Some statistics paint a grim picture, and rightly so. Counting people's incomes is fairly straightforward, and right now such measures show a rapidly widening wealth gap between winners and losers over the past quarter-century. That's a real problem, and it needs a real solution. (Public frustration with economic injustices spoiled much of the first Renaissance and could do the same in the second)

But looking beyond personal incomes to society's overall material well-being is less simple. A person born in 1970 has seen the total human population double and per-person welfare increase some 40 per cent in his lifetime.[42] There are twice as many of us, *and* we're all better off: for any civilization, that's a giant win. Why don't our statistics help us *feel* it?

The answer is that, for all the importance we place upon them, concepts like gross domestic product and productivity were never intended as proxies for aggregate well-being and are deeply flawed when we take them as such. They fail to capture not only the intangible gains that flourishing genius brings us, but many tangibles as well.

Short versus long term

In 1997, at an Intel shareholders' meeting, one participant challenged the then CEO Andy Grove to defend the company's recent splurge on internet ventures. What return on investment could they expect? Grove replied: 'This is Columbus in the New World. What was *his* return on investment?'[43]

The lag between feats of genius and their full social and economic impact can be very long – especially for new general-purpose technologies. In the developed world, it took some seventy-five years for the economic boosts brought about by public sanitation, electrification and the adoption of fossil fuel to thoroughly express themselves in productivity stats; in the developing world, they're still driving growth. In comparison, the mass adoption of computers has less than a forty-year history; the internet, twenty years. Mass adoption of genetic sequencing has just begun. Quantum and nanotechnologies are barely escaping the lab. It's far too early to quantify the material gains our latest tools will gift to humanity. We only know that they will be broad and deep.

How long we have to wait depends, in part, on the domain. In physics, for example, the average time between a big discovery and its Nobel Prize is twenty-five years. It simply takes that long to see what new avenues the discovery opened up. In other domains, even that is fast. Number theory – essentially, the study of the properties of numbers – has a history stretching back to ancient Greece and India. It enjoyed a resurgence during the Renaissance, when, amidst the general revival of classical knowledge, Greek mathematics texts were translated into Latin. But it remained an obscure discipline. Some 2,000 years after its study began, the twentieth-century number theorist Leonard Dickson (1874–1954) remarked: 'Thank God that number theory is unsullied by any application.'[44] We don't say that anymore. The application, it finally turned out, is computing. Without it, we wouldn't be able to understand – let alone solve – the basic problems that arise when we try to make machines do a quadrillion calculations per second.

The lag also depends on the kind of breakthrough. Does it add to, or destroy, what existed before? If we find a cure for AIDS, we know immediately what to do with it, and we'll be able to start counting up its impact the very same year. Discovered, developed and distributed within the present pharmaceutical paradigm, an AIDS vaccine would be a new drug in a well-established kit. Contrast that with gene therapy. It may enable us to add lots of new drugs to our kit, but it also teases us with the possibility that we might one day throw out our whole pharmaceutical bag altogether. Why deliver little chemical warriors into our bloodstream, with all their unruly side effects, when instead we can alter the body's behaviour at a cellular – maybe even molecular – level so it returns itself to health? This new medical model would have titanic economic consequences – it could add a full generation to the workforce through improved life expectancy – but it would take a lot longer to realize those benefits than it would to give every AIDS patient a vaccine.

Counted versus uncounted goods

Measuring the long-term impact of present-day breakthroughs is hard. But even if we narrow our focus to short-term payoffs in the here and now, our accounting of genius is going to fall far short. That's because economic statistics like GDP are designed to count things that are exchanged in some market at some price, and many of our immediate gains have no price in any market. They're free.

Economists call these unaccounted-for benefits 'positive spillovers'. Instead of being packaged up properly and paid for in a market, value just sloshes over from one domain into the next. Metalworkers in the town of Mainz contributed the craft that Gutenberg needed to develop new alloys for his invention, but their 'R&D' didn't net them any economic returns from the success of the printing press. In the present day, patents and licensing fees are one way we try to make these otherwise free benefits countable. We use the law to restrict access to an idea, which forces would-be users to declare – in dollar terms – just how much it's worth to them.

But patents can only cover some cases, and spillovers are pervasive. The most familiar gaps in our accounting, and the most glaring, are digital goods. If one million copies of the *Encyclopaedia Britannica* are sold for $1,000 each, those sales directly add $1 billion to GDP. If one million users access Wikipedia, and Wikipedia stays free, that adds zero. If the user base swells from a million people to a billion, it's still zero.[45] Collectively, we are far better off, in tangible terms of time and money saved, but GDP is unaffected (or falls, if fewer encyclopedias sell as a result). GDP is likewise oblivious to how much we value a Google search (research shows that we save an average of fifteen minutes per query, or $500 per year),[46] or all the free entertainment and education we consume from friends and strangers online. It doesn't count the millions of hours people volunteer on Zooniverse.org cataloguing galaxies and whale calls – or unpaid work of any other kind. In short, macroeconomic statistics miss some of the biggest happenings in our economy. As 3D printing evolves, many of the physical goods we buy today will transform into digital goods we create, share, download and print at home, and the already giant gap between the gains we count and those we cannot will widen still further.

3. Genius defies expectations

The third point is to recognize that our expectations are not a reliable standard against which to measure feats of genius. We're bad at guessing where present breakthroughs will take us:

> I predict the Internet ... will soon go spectacularly supernova and in 1996 catastrophically collapse ... The Internet's naïve flat-rate business model is incapable of financing the new capacity it would need to serve continued growth, if there were any, but there won't be, so no problem.

> Robert Metcalfe, co-inventor of
> Ethernet and founder of 3Com, in 1995[47]

We're even worse at guessing what future breakthroughs will be. 'Where are the flying cars?' is the perfect refrain to illustrate how our thinking gets trapped inside present paradigms. In the 1950s and 1960s, suddenly everyone drove cars and rode in airplanes. The most disruptive 'next big thing' we could imagine was for our cars to fly, too. By definition, genius breaks with these simple, linear extrapolations from the past. That we do not all fly cars today – and that most of us have forgotten this idea entirely – is not a failure of genius, but, rather, a testament to how it shifts our focus and resources into completely unexpected directions. Our cars don't fly, but our ideas do – at speeds so far beyond the imagination of the 1960s that the metric system in those days didn't even have the language to describe them. (Prefixes like 'peta' (10^{15}) and 'exa' (10^{18}) weren't adopted until 1975.)

Of course, most of the time when people ask 'Where are the flying cars?' they mean it rhetorically, not literally. Their real question is, 'Why hasn't genius solved all our problems?' And herein lies the second mistake our expectations make. Genius is not a panacea.

We expect continuous technical improvement (smaller, faster, cheaper and more responsive). We expect relentless progress and growth. We equate 'genius' with 'new technology' and expect the former to invent the latter so that we can push annual upgrades through whatever limits reality might throw up.

But that's not how genius works. Genius can never eliminate our problems; it can only replace them with new ones. That's because every new technological solution we ask of it introduces new needs, limits and unintended consequences. Consider energy. Fossil fuel-powered machines have helped us to do more work, grow our cities and jet between them, but have also exposed us to the previously unknown consequences of carbon emissions. Renewable energy solves that emissions problem, but reintroduces two others that fossil fuels had solved quite nicely: how to store energy (in batteries, which spawn a whole other set of problems) and how to concentrate energy so it can do explosive work (like propel a car or jet plane). Nuclear fission has given us near-limitless electricity, but also weapons of mass destruction and a waste disposal problem for the next 40,000 generations. If one day we discover nuclear fusion (making energy the same way the sun does, by fusing hydrogen atoms together), the new problem could be how to keep it out of the wrong hands. That's hard enough for fission, when the raw inputs (uranium and plutonium) are very rare and difficult to purify. But any schoolkid can make pure hydrogen by dropping a nine-volt battery into a glass of salt water.

This inconvenient bargain holds true across all domains and time periods.[48] Machiavelli observed: 'In all human things, he who examines well sees this, that one inconvenience can never be cancelled without another's cropping up.'[49] Engineers in the Renaissance built ocean-worthy ships, which made voyages of discovery possible, but spread European germs to America. Engineers today build container ships half a kilometre long. Such ships drive down the costs of global trade, but their ballast waters disrupt whole ecosystems by spreading invasive species. Some 500 years ago, battlefield medics figured out how to keep wounded soldiers alive by applying antiseptic to gunshot wounds and sutures to amputated blood vessels. But they had few answers for the pain and disability they thus prolonged. Modern medicine is rapidly extending the lifespan of our bodies, but has few answers for the mental degeneration (chiefly, Alzheimer's) that more and more people now live long enough to suffer. Fracking stresses local water supplies. Advanced electronics create a global dependency on rare earth metals. DNA synthesis machines raise the spectre of genetically engineered bio-pathogens.

Genius will never solve all our problems.

4. The biggest feats lie ahead

But genius will also never cease to transform humanity in response to the problems we face.

We can be confident that the sceptics will be proven wrong on their gloomiest forecast: namely, that in terms of social and economic impact, no future feats of genius will rival the big, one-time modernizations we've already worked upon ourselves, such as electrification, sanitation and mass transportation.

This assertion is wrong, for two reasons. First, as explained above, at *every* level of technological development we will *always* be met by equally advanced problems.[50] These problems will drive us to change in response, and the more powerful our technologies become, the *more* impactful these changes will be.

At our present level of development, one of our biggest problems is how to extend rich-country modernizations to the rest of the world – and into the future. China has sustained high growth over the past forty years precisely because it is catching up on the transformations pioneered by the developed world. Over the next fifty years, we can hope that Africa and the lagging parts of Asia, India, Latin America and the Middle East will do the same. If we step out of the developed-world bubble and think globally for a moment, that feat in itself would suffice to make the twenty-first century humanity's best ever.

Too bad it can't yet be done. The fossil fuel infrastructure that powers the developed world is not viable through the twenty-first century on a global scale – or even on its present scale. If the developed world is to bank permanently the gains it's already made, and if the developing world is to catch up, we'll first need to work one of our biggest feats of genius yet to wean ourselves off coal, oil and gas. On cue, energy researchers are concocting a wide range of would-be solutions, from near-term improvements in engine efficiency and renewable power, to nanoscale batteries, organic solar cells and microorganisms that eat CO_2 and excrete liquid fuel.

Second, the sceptics' gloomy assertion mistakenly applies the law of diminishing returns to human creativity. Genius, they suggest, is like pulling balls from an urn, each one representing a new idea or technology. In the beginning, the urn was full, but each time we've gone back to the urn, we've had to reach deeper than the last. One day, the urn will be empty. One day, we will have exhausted our potential to advance.[51]

It's a compelling metaphor, but backwards. Genius is more like mixing compounds in an alchemist's lab. Each compound is an *existing* idea or technology, and in the beginning we had just a few – maybe some salt, sugar and common liquids. But then we tried mixing them together, and some of them reacted with one another to form new compounds. Before long, our once-sparse workbench was crowded with acids, alcohols and powders. Now, each time we enter the lab to cook up something new, we are confronted by a wider range of compounds than the last. We need never fear running out of combinations to try. The fear, rather, is that new compounds and their possible combinations are multiplying so fast that we may fail to find the really useful reactions that lie buried among them.

This metaphor is far closer to our present experience. In the sciences, the pace of discovery is generally going up, not down – as intellectual connections within and across disciplines proliferate, as our computers and instruments evolve, and as we leverage new collective capacities to help researchers crunch through mountains of possibilities.

It's certainly true in the pharmaceuticals industry, where recent breakthroughs in drug development have confounded earlier predictions that the urn would soon be empty.[52] Medicine's deeper understanding of how disease happens, afforded by genome sequencing, is finally starting to bear fruit.[53]

Recent blockbuster drug discoveries include: new weapons against heart failure, which in an aging world is now the leading cause of death; immunotherapies, which help to defeat cancers by boosting the body's own immune response, in place of (or in combination with) chemotherapy; oral pills to fight hepatitis C infections that are safer, faster and twice as effective as previous injectable drugs; and improved HIV therapies, which keep patients healthy longer and have simplified their daily 'cocktail' of drugs down to a single pill per day.[54] Even Alzheimer's, of which the industry had begun to despair, is now looking treatable. The first drug capable of slowing the memory-wasting disease may arrive in a few years.[55] And after thirty years of toil, in 2015, GlaxoSmithKline announced that its children's vaccine against malaria had passed final-stage trials. Once approved, it could help save half a million children's lives each year.[56]

Every new drug discovery adds another compound to the alchemist's workbench. And drug researchers still have quadrillions more possibilities left to test. Only 10 per cent of the estimated nine million species of life on earth have even been catalogued.[57] On average, some 30 per cent of the foreign DNA you carry around *in your own nostrils* is unknown. But all that will change. In our own lifetimes, science will likely deploy legions of robots under the oceans, across the earth and into our bodies, to discover life, to sequence it and, with the help of computers and crowds, make sense of the natural wonders we find. Meanwhile, the total number of artificial drug molecules that could in theory be engineered is very large – as many as 10^{60}, or three times the number of stars in the universe.[58] Today's computers help drug developers crunch through thousands of these artificial molecules at a time in the hunt for useful compounds. Tomorrow's computer-simulated drug trials, which will accurately predict a drug's real-world effects by testing it on a computer-generated patient, will crunch through them by the millions.

Whether feats of genius translate into profits for any particular industry is an open question (whose answer depends heavily on factors beyond the feats themselves, such as the price the public deems acceptable for important new drugs). Whether feats translate into economic growth as measured by the day's dominant statistics is even harder to say. More certain is that no matter how far we think we've come, intellectually and technologically, much more discovery and transformation lie ahead of us than behind. We are standing near the base of a steep learning curve.

Reasons to fear

Genius breaks through the limits that bind us.

Perhaps not all our chains are meant to be broken. Some hold us back; others keep us safe. Unfortunately, genius doesn't always discriminate. If the sceptics are right on one count, it is to point out that alongside our gains, genius multiplies many dangers that threaten to undo them.

Guns for everyone

[T]he explosion of the powder mixed with saltpeter was so violent, the balls flew through the air with such stupendous speed and with such horrible thunder ... this kind of artillery [has] rendered ridiculous all former weapons of attack.

Francesco Guicciardini (1483–1540)[59]

In the bloody domain of doing violence to one another, gunpowder broke through millennia-old limits of human strength, skill and speed, and armed our conflicts with chemistry instead.

Invented by the Chinese in the ninth century, gunpowder's European arrival was heralded with cannons, most impressively the great Turkish bombards used at the siege of Constantinople in 1453. They were a 'diabolical rather than human weapon', and within fifty years their power had been shrunk down and put into the hands of individuals, in the form of the arquebus (an early musket).[60] In 1503, at the Battle of Cerignola, some 6,300 Spanish, with 1,000 arquebuses among them, defeated 9,000 French in the first battle in history to be decided by gunpowder-based small arms.[61] French casualties outnumbered the Spanish four to one, and one of those killed by an arquebus volley was the French general, the Duke of Nemours. Neither the strength and skill he possessed from perhaps two decades of swordsmanship nor his costly plate armour could protect him from whizzing bullets fired by leather-clad arquebusiers, who had become proficient with their weapon in days and could deliver the same devastating blows even if weak, fatigued or sick.

Five hundred years on, communities everywhere must deal with the danger of portable cannons falling into the wrong hands. Meanwhile, like our predecessors in the first Renaissance, we too are taking very powerful tools, once accessible only to a few, and putting them into the hands of the many.

The gravest new danger we face as a result is bioterrorism. For all its destructive power, a gun has limits. One shooter can carry only so much ammunition; each bullet can travel only so far; and when the shooter is neutralized, the threat is ended. A virus suffers none of these restraints. Even a nuclear weapon has a finite blast radius, but a biological one – say, smallpox – expands until all potential hosts are either immune or dead.[†]

Only states and well-financed sub-state groups have the money and men to cause large-scale destruction with guns. To date, only states have proven able to develop and deploy nuclear weapons. But the DNA equipment needed to synthesize smallpox (or Ebola, or pneumonic plague) is available today in every advanced country and costs the same as a top-end office

---

[†]To hedge against this threat, the US Center for Disease Control has stockpiled enough smallpox vaccine to inoculate every US citizen in the event of an outbreak.

copier did thirty years ago – well within the budget of any well-financed non-state organization. That's only one ingredient in a very difficult recipe, and the scientific community is divided on how feasible it might be to engineer a genuine bio-horror – especially in secret. The risk is not zero, and it is going up, not down. We might soon enter an era when, for the first time in history, a single individual could hold in his hand the power to kill hundreds of millions of people.

The history of the Cold War has shown that when states hold such power, they handle it with grave respect. And yet, even then, they flirted with Armageddon. The story of guns tells us that individuals are far less reliable. Our chief defence against self-appointed messiahs and scourges may be the ability to keep secret the source code to nature's deadliest bugs. Will we succeed? In 2002, scientists synthesized polio from scratch, using a polio genome published in *Nature* back in 1981.[62] In 2005, scientists resurrected the virus responsible for the 1918 Spanish flu, one of the worst pandemics on record.[63] How long will it be before someone designs an artificial virus that's even deadlier? In 2012, precisely these fears provoked a six-month global scientific debate over whether the journal *Science* should publish an article detailing mutations that would enable the lethal H5N1 bird flu to spread easily among humans. In the end, the magazine's editors did publish it. Science, they reasoned, makes discoveries that can be used for good and bad. Since the potentially devastating consequences of new knowledge will not lock it away in peoples' heads, the world is better off knowing about discoveries when they happen. That way, we can prepare against their abuse.

Even before new DNA lab technology emerged to raise this threat level, we've had a couple of close calls. Aum Shinrikyo, the Japanese cult that carried out a sarin gas attack in Tokyo's subways back in 1995, was in possession of anthrax; members had already attempted several aerosol anthrax releases from Tokyo rooftops by the time they were captured. Luckily, the strain they used was too weak, and the aerosol too diluted, to start an epidemic.[64] On 18 September 2001, letters containing anthrax spores were mailed to several US media companies and two US senators, killing five people and harming sixty to eighty more. The FBI eventually concluded that a single disaffected scientist in a government biodefence lab had produced and delivered the spores. Had that lone scientist chosen to produce and distribute a larger quantity, the corresponding death toll would have been much, much higher.[†] In 2014, files seized from a chemical engineer with ties to the Islamic State exposed preliminary efforts to weaponize bubonic plague.[65]

[†] In the meantime, to prevent repeats in the future, the US postal service has been irradiating all DC federal mail, at an annual cost to the US taxpayer of $10–12 million per year.

Collective bads

Our new *collective* powers also present dangers – less cataclysmic, but more probable and pervasive. Chapter 2 touched on how the same infrastructure, networks and investments that connect us also make it easier to coordinate crime and violence; disseminate hate; train up would-be hackers, fraudsters and bombers; and trade every illicit good from drugs to fake IDs to child slaves. e-Books on how to obtain Semtex (a plastic explosive), video tutorials on constructing a mobile phone detonator, recipes to cook crystal meth, nuisance viruses and 3D-printed plastic firearms are readily available on 'dark web' marketplaces.

More insidious is how harmful ideas, once marginal or declining, can now knit together supportive communities big enough to attack our chief public goods (freedom, security, tolerance) and resilient enough to defy every attempt to eradicate them. Non-state extremist organizations are a prime present-day example of collective genius gone bad. The 9/11 attacks in the United States in 2001, the March 2004 train bombing in Madrid and the 7/7 attacks in London in 2005 demonstrated vividly that a competent, moderately financed community of extremists – Al-Qaeda claimed responsibility for all three attacks – can overcome public security to cause large-scale death and destruction at strategically and symbolically important places. The war in Afghanistan against Al-Qaeda camps and commanders, and the assassination of its leader Osama bin Laden in 2011, eroded Al-Qaeda's resources and profile but also inspired affiliate groups to form across Southwest Asia, the Middle East and North Africa. Extremism in our own societies is another example. Whether it is Islamic extremists seizing power in Iraq and Syria, or Christian extremists plotting violence against Muslims in the United States, these movements are in part enabled by the same infrastructure and technologies that helped match Syrian refugees with willing European host families in 2015.

Tough questions

Some other outcomes of individual and collective genius are less obviously bad, but do pose difficult questions about the kind of world we want to live in.

A world without jobs

One of the big factors driving productivity growth, from Gutenberg's printing press to today, has been the replacement of many workers with a few machines. As machines muscle their way into agriculture and manufacturing, workers who lose their jobs move into the services sector – which is where most of us are now employed. Services have proven difficult to mechanize. Customers want freshness, variety, creativity, spontaneity and friendliness, and those are difficult values to deliver through automation. We can automate the assembly of an engine; so far, it's proven harder to automate the assembly of a good haircut, or a good book.

Thanks to recent advances in artificial intelligence and robotics, that's changing. In 2004, autonomous cars seemed unlikely: 'Executing a left turn against oncoming traffic involves so many factors that it is hard to imagine discovering the set of rules that can replicate a driver's behavior', stated a pair of prominent economists.[66] Six years later, Google announced that its labs had done so. Today, Tesla's autopilot is a better driver than most humans. Other cognitive tasks that were once deemed too complicated to automate, but which machines can now do, range from showing empathy to mental health patients, to writing routine news stories, performing surgery, making financial trades, conducting science experiments and winning Jeopardy (IBM's Watson system, which did so in 2011, now has a job diagnosing cancer patients and suggesting treatment plans).

One prediction is that nearly half of all current jobs in the United States could be automated away within two decades – a wrenching retooling that Klaus Schwab, founder of the World Economic Forum, has christened 'the fourth industrial revolution'.[67] Productivity will skyrocket. Will automation create a vast pool of chronically underemployed people with nowhere left to go? Or will we build whole new industries in which machines *augment*, rather than replace, humanity's talents? In the first decade of the twenty-first century, if anything, it was the former: in 2010, only 0.5 per cent of the US workforce had jobs in new industries that hadn't existed in 2000.[68] What about the profits of automation? Will they be shared with workers to help them adjust, or will the gap between rich and poor widen to the point of social breakdown? In the second decade of the twenty-first century, the latter has become an urgent possibility. Unfortunately, rather than confront that future directly, populist politicians in some advanced economies are redirecting workers' frustrations against foreign trade and immigration.

Strong states

In the Renaissance, gunpowder empowered individuals, but it also helped strengthen the state. Pre-gunpowder, 'states' had been loose concepts: hereditary princes surrounded by small courts, backed up by noble allies. Then military budgets ratcheted up: first, to build more secure fortresses to withstand cannon fire, then to build bigger cannons to blast through them, then to raise bigger armies to assault and defend these new bastions. By the same logic, many merchant ships became floating fortresses. As the economics of war-making began to outstrip smaller players, 'the state' began to monopolize the use of force and built ever larger bureaucracies – tax collectors, accountants, planners – to keep up with the spiralling costs and complexity of a 'modern' military.[69]

Today, too, technology makes both individuals and the state stronger. Communications technology enables each of us to broadcast our own message, and it supplies the state with new resources to monitor what, up until recently, we had assumed to be our private lives. Significant trade-offs have been made between public security and citizens' privacy, without popular consent – or even foreknowledge. In the United States, the National Security Administration has collected the metadata (the who, what and when) of every phone call made by every American for at least a decade.[70] Foreign-focused email, chat and text message databases are far larger, and more than twenty other US government agencies have the ability to sift through them.[71] What else the state now keeps under surveillance, we don't yet know.

Is this a worthwhile trade-off? Do we have a choice? Our flourishing genius forces us to face these questions.

* * *

An age of discovery doesn't offer guarantees; it offers possibilities, and it's up to all of us to realize them. The sceptics are right on one other point: there's a lot we could do better to kindle acts of creation and collaboration in our communities. 'Tardiness', Machiavelli schooled his peers, 'often robs us of opportunity'.[72] For a vigorous action plan, see Part IV.

In the meantime, other forces are at work. In the first Renaissance, flourishing genius coexisted with sudden catastrophes and new conflicts people did not know how to solve. That people persisted in the midst of such ugliness to build beauty and achieve breakthroughs that we still celebrate, 500 years later, is their defiant legacy to future generations.

We are rushing headlong into similar storms. What will *our* legacy be?

PART III

FLOURISHING RISK

How the present age generates
risk and strains society

7

The Pox Is Spreading, Venice Is Sinking

How the age we're in magnifies systemic dangers and makes it harder to see them coming

The downside of linking up

In 1494, Ludovico Sforza, who for thirteen years had controlled the Duchy of Milan from behind the throne as regent for his too young nephew, stepped forward and seized the mantle of duke for himself. Alfonso II, the king of Naples (who himself had a claim to Milan), challenged the move and threatened to unseat this usurper. But Sforza was not without allies. Charles VIII, the powerful king of France, had a claim to the throne of Naples, and Sforza convinced Charles that now was the moment to press it.

Charles raised an army of 25,000–30,000 men – including 8,000 mercenaries drawn from all over Europe – to wage his Italian war.[1] Passing unimpeded through Milan, his men slashed and burned their way down the rest of the Italian peninsula and captured Naples in February 1495.

But Charles had miscalculated. His show of brutality and overwhelming force, which brought swift victory, also accomplished what no lesser threat could: it united the states of Italy and their allies in fear against a foreign foe. The Pope convened a Holy League to drive the French from Italy, and Venice, Spain, England, the Holy Roman Empire (very roughly, present-day Germany) and even Milan signed up. (Sforza had begun to fear that Charles would betray him and swallow his own duchy, too.)

On 6 July 1495, the massed armies of the Holy League met Charles VIII on a rain-soaked field at the Battle of Fornovo to decide Italy's fate – for the moment. The League had numbers on their side; Charles had the terrain. In less than two hours of fighting, the French lost 1,000 men; the League lost twice that many. Both sides claimed victory; neither pressed the other to continue. Charles retreated back to France and his army scattered.[2]

But he left something behind.

Italian battlefield doctors noticed the disease first. It was unlike any affliction they had ever seen or that had ever been recorded, going back to the time of the Roman emperor Marcus Aurelius and the medical treatises of his physician, Galen.

Plague was well known – its symptoms terrible, its consequences mercifully swift. The victims spat blood, and in three days they were dead. But this was something new, something crueller. It debilitated its victims in horrid ways and left them to linger through months, even years, of flesh-eating filth and disgust. A medical chronicler of the time described sufferers' bodies 'covered with acorn-sized boils that emitted a foul, dark green pus'.[3] These boils often appeared first on the sex organs. Those who survived the disease's first stages developed 'tumors the size of bread rolls and ulcers that progressively, but simply dissolved skin'.[4]

It also spread quickly, thanks to the 'Noah's Ark nature' of both sides' armies.[5] Troops from both sides of Fornovo returned home, and mercenaries dispersed. By summer's end, the mysterious disease had terrorized towns throughout Italy, France, Germany and Switzerland. By the following year, it had hit Holland and Greece; the year after that, England and Scotland. Within four years of its first appearance, it had already touched the whole of Europe. Within another five years, except for some still-isolated exceptions, it was global.[6]

From its beginning, it was less fatal to Europe than the Black Death. To the rest of the world, it was certainly less devastating than some of the other diseases spread by European sailors, like the smallpox that decimated the Americas. As populations adapted to the new disease in their midst, its most repulsive symptoms subsided, and it eased into the lingering, chronic venereal disease we know today as syphilis.

Too complex to untangle, too concentrated to keep safe

We all need to develop a heightened concern for a particular kind of risk. It is not the direct danger that confronts us daily – things like getting hit by a car or being robbed. We're all well aware of such specific hazards already. Rather, it is the risks we don't see – the kind that creep slowly below our threshold of observation, and then shock all of us together. These 'butterfly defects' are widely felt but hard for anyone to see coming, because their causes are far removed from our day-to-day experiences and concerns. Such risks are not specific; they're *systemic*.[†]

Systemic risks flourish in the present age because the same connective and developmental trends that stoke genius also create the two conditions under which such risks breed: complexity and concentration.

[†]Ian Goldin and Mike Mariathasan explore the phenomenon and its consequences in their 2014 book, *The Butterfly Defect* from Princeton University Press.

Complexity demons

Most of us are well aware of the rising complexity of the present age: we see the evidence in our own lives. Flip back to the figures and graphs throughout Part I, and this heightened complexity is clear to see: in shifting patterns of global air travel; in the rising variety and number of cross-border financial investments; or in the growth of internet infrastructure. Meanwhile, developmental forces amplify this complexity by raising the volume of traffic that flows across these many, diverse connections, and by adding new nodes – be they new cities, universities, industrial zones, ports, power stations, labs, conferences or journals.

We've seen some of the benefits that complexity can bring. It increases the number and variety of good things that can touch us and that we can reach out to, and it's a major catalyst of creativity and idea generation.

From a risk perspective, too, complexity can be a good thing. The greater variety and volume of connections and flows create redundancy, of which the internet is contemporary life's best example. When one link goes down, its traffic reroutes almost instantaneously to alternatives, so that our end-user experience is not often interrupted. Complexity breeds benefits.

But it also presents a problem. The more complex our interactions become, the harder it is for us to see relationships of

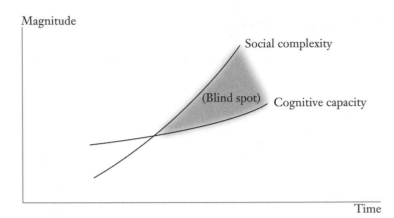

FIGURE 7.1 *We develop blind spots when complexity rises faster than our understanding.*

cause and effect. We develop cognitive 'blind spots' in our vision of the events around us. See Figure 7.1. How can we make good decisions, when we can't see their consequences?

Complexity was a big part of how syphilis struck the first Renaissance, and why it struck as hard as it did.

The spread of disease has always been among the first unintended consequences of population exchange; syphilis was just a terrifying case in point. According to the most widely accepted theory today on the origin of syphilis, its emergence in Europe just three years after Columbus discovered the New World was no coincidence.[†] Likely, his sailors carried it back to

---

[†] The theory of the American origin of syphilis is the most widely accepted, but has not been conclusively proven.

Europe with them.[7] Just as the new sea link between Europe and the Americas injected the latter population with a lethal cocktail of European bugs – smallpox, typhus, measles, influenza, bubonic plague, cholera, malaria, tuberculosis, mumps, yellow fever and others – so, too, it exposed Eurasia to a new plague against which local populations had no immunity. Likewise, the disease's swift propagation throughout Europe and Asia is best explained by the variety and volumes of new economic linkages in Europe and across the sea, over which goods, people and livestock flowed in ever-growing numbers.

The complexity of the disease's origin and spread also left people in the Renaissance at a loss as to how to respond. The state of medical knowledge at the time meant that the causes of most diseases were beyond their understanding, even though disease was a familiar danger and society had worked out some effective responses. During the previous century, the Black Death and its many aftershocks had taught them to recognize plague, quarantine its victims and avoid the settlements it struck until the disease disappeared. Later bouts of plague scarred Europe far less, because such protocols were in place. But syphilis, so suddenly, was in too many places to be avoided and at every level of society, from the peasantry to the papacy. And it didn't disappear. It lingered like its victims, a chronic blight that couldn't be avoided, and to which society had to, somehow, adapt.

The absence of any clear understanding of cause and effect left a cognitive gap that society stuffed full of stereotype, superstition and ideological agendas. The Italians called it the French disease, since obviously Charles VIII had brought it with his army. The French called it the Neapolitan (Naples) disease, since it had been unknown to France until her soldiers returned home from that Italian kingdom. The Holy Roman Emperor Maximilian I saw the disease as God's divine retribution against man for his sins. What else could explain the sudden universality of a completely novel affliction, one that let its victims linger in agony and shame to contemplate their misdeeds? The most popular explanation was that God was punishing people for sins of the flesh. 'God has raised up new diseases against debauchery', in the words of John Calvin (1509–1564).[8] People attached great significance to the fact that the disease often appeared first on the sex organs, and that soldiers and prostitutes (the two professions most associated with sexual licence and moral disorder) ranked among the first and most frequent victims. 'A night with Venus, a lifetime with Mercury' went the saying, referencing the mercury salves that became the common treatment.

Concentration dilemmas

Concentration is a less obvious consequence of human entanglement and development, but just as destabilizing. How developmental forces create concentrations is straightforward. Worldwide gains in health, wealth and education together yield a much bigger population that places far larger demands on existing social infrastructure, services, natural resources and the environment. Consider: humanity has been burning fossil fuels for millennia with seemingly little consequence. But now that a two-billion-member-strong global middle class has emerged, all wanting to drive cars, take flights, and run heaters and air conditioners, suddenly the collective weight of our energy consumption has to be reckoned with.

Concentrations also increase as the number and variety of our connections go up. At first glance, this seems counter-intuitive: if the variety of links across which goods, services, people and ideas flow suddenly increases, shouldn't that diffuse human activity?

Yes and no. While it's true that more connections open more choices for where goods, services, people and ideas *might* flow, these things do not flow randomly. Instead, they flow to wherever we deem most desirable. Governments concentrate public infrastructure, and businesses concentrate their operations, wherever is deemed to be most efficient. Immigrants and job seekers concentrate wherever work is perceived to be plentiful and the quality of life is seen to be good. Industries concentrate wherever the supply of supportive talent, ideas and capital is abundant.

Connectivity presents choice. When many people make similar choices, concentrations result. Concentrations are not only geographical, but also conceptual and behavioural – from the standardization of managerial preparation in the form of MBA programmes, to the homogenization of crops and farming practices in today's agribusinesses, to the global harmonization of regulations governing banking and trade.

Like complexity, concentrations carry positives and problems. Part II focused on the former. Concentrations bring wealth, ideas, genius and fragments of capability up to a critical mass that catalyses creative achievements.

We've already hinted at its problems. Concentrations put stress on the supply of infrastructure, on resources, even on the sociability and goodwill that help us live together in peace. The higher the stress, the greater the chance of failure. All else being equal, concentrations also mean that when something fails, the costs are likely to be higher and the consequences more severe for more people. Imagine two identical solar flares knocking out the internet planet-wide, one in 1990, the other today. The first would have frustrated some military researchers and the physics community. The latter would be a global catastrophe. (This is more than a thought experiment. In July 2012, a coronal mass ejection (CME) from the sun tore directly through the earth's orbital path, missing our planet by only one week. The US National Academy of Sciences estimated that, had the CME hit, the damages to planetary electrical systems might have exceeded $2 trillion – more than forty times the cost of the costliest hurricane in US history (Katrina).[9])

When syphilis struck the first Renaissance, one of the reasons it hit so fast and so hard was that people had begun to concentrate more in towns and cities. Urbanization compressed once self-sufficient families and villages into dense units of mutual interdependence. These crowded urban settings offered ideal conditions for the spread of disease. Rooms were overcrowded and public sanitation was stretched. Townspeople lived side by side with domesticated horses, pigs, chickens and their excrement. Itinerants were common; contact with new people and newly arrived travellers was frequent. Promiscuity was on the rise.[10] Poor environmental luck in the 1490s – flooding rivers, exceptionally cold winters – further weakened already vulnerable communities.[11]

Today, overcrowded and overstretched urban places are still a breeding ground for nature's killers.

New poxes

Disease has always been a fixture of human society. Flu epidemics affect an estimated 5–15 per cent of the global population annually, causing severe illness in three to five million people and death in one-quarter to one-half million people, every year.[12]

What is new is the emergence over the past few decades of fast-moving *pandemics* – viruses that spread easily among humans and can infect patients *worldwide* within a short time after their initial outbreak.[13] Already in the twenty-first century, humanity has confronted several such pandemic threats.

SARS

The first proof of these new fast-moving threats to global public health was Severe Acute Respiratory Syndrome (SARS). The first severe infectious disease to emerge in the twenty-first century, we've mostly forgotten about it by now, but in 2003 it suddenly seized the attention of the entire world, and 'pose[d] a serious threat to global health security, the livelihood of populations, the functioning of health systems, and the stability and growth of economies',[14] in the words of Carl Urbani, the World Health Organization (WHO) physician who first identified the disease (and died from it).

A viral infection with flu-like symptoms, SARS first appeared in November 2002, in Guangdong, China. Virologists now believe it transferred from bats to humans, either directly or via live animal markets in that crowded corner of Asia. By itself, the inter-species hop was unremarkable, and at any other point in human history might have prompted nothing more than a local epidemic. Such was the thinking in Guangdong, when Liu Jianlun, a 64-year-old doctor who had been fighting on the front lines of the outbreak, travelled to nearby Hong Kong and checked into a popular business hotel. Casual contact was enough to cause infection. The hotel's roster of international guests shared elevators, dining halls and other surfaces with Liu. When they flew home – to Canada, Singapore and Vietnam – they carried the SARS virus with them. Within just four months, SARS had spread to every continent except Antarctica. It was the fastest viral propagation in human history.

Luckily, it was far from the most dangerous. By July 2003, some nine months after its initial detection, 8,300 cases (including 775 deaths) had been reported in thirty countries. Once the pathogen had been identified, the same networks that had enabled its spread supported a swift, globally coordinated response under the auspices of the WHO. Aggressive quarantine measures halted the spread of SARS and contained what could otherwise have been a global catastrophe. Part of this success was thanks to planning. The Global Public Health Intelligence Network, an early warning system, alerted the WHO to the new viral threat when it was still in its pre-pandemic stages. Part of it was luck. The first epicentres of the pandemic – Hong Kong, Toronto, Singapore – all enjoyed advanced and robust public health systems able to mobilize and enforce mass quarantine protocols. Had SARS struck less developed centres earlier – say, Lagos or Kinshasa – its ease of transmission could have produced a far worse scenario. In hindsight, SARS was 'the pandemic that didn't occur'.[15]

Still, its costs were significant. While fewer lives were lost than in the average annual flu season, the mortality rate was far higher – almost 10 per cent – and many survivors developed long-term respiratory complications. The scare, plus quarantines, cost the global economy at least $40 billion in 2003. Tourism and travel industries were especially hard hit, but the epidemic also impacted several large manufacturing zones where workers became infected.[16] The disease has still not been completely eradicated, and as yet no vaccine exists that is safe for human use.[17]

Ebola

More recent proof of our rising vulnerability to disease is Ebola. If SARS is the pandemic that didn't occur, Ebola is the epidemic that did.

In December 2013, in a remote mountain village in Guinea, West Africa, near the border with Liberia and Sierra Leone, a two-year-old boy named Emile fell suddenly, terribly ill. It began as a severe fever, and within a few days progressed to severe diarrhoea and bloody vomiting. Within one to two weeks, he was dead from loss of blood and fluids. Following local traditions, his family washed his body and mourners journeyed from surrounding villages to embrace it. Shortly thereafter, several of them began to exhibit the same symptoms.[18]

SARS causes respiratory problems, and occasionally death – usually among older people with a prior condition. Ebola causes massive haemorrhaging throughout the body and historically kills 50 per cent to 90 per cent of the healthy people it infects. Laboratories that research it give it the highest risk classification, biosafety level 4, on a par with anthrax and smallpox. Worldwide, fewer than 100 facilities meet the protocols to handle it safely, which include multiple airlocks and showers, ultraviolet irradiation chambers, air and water decontamination systems, and biohazard suits with independent air supplies for personnel.

West Africa had never seen Ebola before.[19] Since its discovery in 1976, it was almost exclusively a blight on rural Central and East Africa, principally Gabon, Uganda, Sudan and the Democratic Republic of Congo – all some 3,000–5,000 km away. That fact, plus austerity-era budget cuts at the WHO totalling almost $1 billion in 2010–2011, helps explain why no one detected the outbreak until it had spread.[20] By the time the WHO first announced the Guinean outbreak in March 2014, Ebola had already enveloped neighbouring Liberia and Sierra Leone and killed sixty people. In June 2014, with over 750 cases and 467 deaths recorded, it became the worst Ebola outbreak ever.[21] By mid-2015, after 28,000 reported cases and over 11,300 deaths, the human toll had become twenty times higher than all previous outbreaks put together.[22] (The true toll, including unreported cases, may be two to three times higher again.) Meanwhile, the economic losses inflicted upon this already desperately poor region – losses that the World Bank put at up to $4 billion – could eventually kill more people than the virus did itself.[23]

If, like SARS, Ebola had struck places with robust public health systems, it could have been contained quickly. For all its deadliness, Ebola is not that easy to catch if one takes proper precautions. A person with measles infects on average eighteen other people; a person with Ebola infects on average fewer than two, in part because the disease kills its carriers quickly, but also because it doesn't spread well through the air. Body or fluid contact, which may include droplets transferred across a shared surface or handling an infected corpse, is needed. This means that, as long as a community has the capacity to identify and quarantine the sick, to trace and quarantine their recent contacts, and to properly equip front-line medical responders, any outbreak can be swiftly bottled. (The effective containment of Ebola in Nigeria illustrates that with the necessary will and resources it can be contained, even in a relatively poor country.)

Instead, it struck where public health systems are practically non-existent. The three hardest-hit countries – Sierra Leone, Guinea and Liberia – rank among the world's poorest, and all have been the site of recent military coups or civil wars. Sierra Leone's public institutions were just beginning to recover from a long civil war (1991–2002); wounds from Liberia's war (1989–2003) were even deeper and were still being patched over by foreign peacekeepers. Spain, which suffered one local case of Ebola when a nurse became infected after helping two patients from West Africa, spends nearly $3,000 per capita on its health system. Sierra Leone spends $96; Guinea spends $32.[24] The United States, which suffered a handful of cases among returning aid workers, has 245 doctors per 100,000 people.[25] Liberia had fifty doctors, total, in a country of 4.3 million people at the start of the crisis, and several died in the outbreak's early stages.[26] Low levels of education in the remote regions where the virus emerged made the task of these feeble public health systems even harder. Although attitudes eventually changed, at the beginning of the outbreak villagers distrusted officialdom; they mobbed (and, on at least one occasion, killed) health workers who attempted to isolate victims,[27] and persisted with a combination of traditional healing and funeral practices, which encouraged families to bring the sick and dying into churches to be touched by the congregation and faith healers. Sierra Leone's first reported case of Ebola was a traditional healer. The next several cases were the villagers who washed her body.

From the initial outbreak through its rapid spread and eventual containment, the West African Ebola epidemic was a distinctly new kind of public health emergency. How Ebola migrated some 3,000 km from any previous appearance is not yet known. It could be related to recent growth in intra-African trade, which between 1995 and 2012 grew over 10 per cent per year in nominal terms.[28] It could be related to massive refugee flows out of the Democratic Republic of Congo (although most of those flows have been to the Congo's near neighbours). It could be that climate change is altering the habitat of the fruit bats that are the virus's most likely natural reservoir. Population pressures are bringing villagers into closer contact with each other and with the animals that inhabit the forests and provide bush meat.

How the scale of the outbreak exploded *is* known: for the first time ever, Ebola escaped the countryside and reached cities – in large part thanks to the growing links between the two. That is also why the developed world belatedly stepped in with money, health workers and soldiers to help halt its advance.[29] Soldiers from the United States and the United Kingdom built makeshift hospitals. Mobile technologies were brought in to help trace victims' recent movements and contacts. Rapid DNA sequencing technology was deployed to map the virus genome in hundreds of patients and get a complete picture of the origin and variety of strains active in the outbreak. (Five of the scientists involved in the initial sequencing effort in Sierra Leone died from the disease.[30]) Major pharmaceutical corporations and government labs began to fast-track vaccines through human trials.

A rural epidemic in a faraway place is a tragedy. A lethal virus, normally locked up under the strictest safety protocols known, roaming free in large cities that are linked to the world by air and seaports, is a global security threat. 'Never before in recorded history has a biosafety level 4 pathogen infected so many people so quickly, over such a broad geographical area, for so long', the WHO stated in September 2014.[31] If the virus had spread to other regions with weak health systems, such as developing parts of Asia (with which West Africa has been aggressively boosting trade), a worldwide catastrophe could have followed.

Contagion?

Looking ahead, a worrying pandemic threat on the horizon is H5N1 (bird flu).

Like SARS, H5N1 originated in Southeast Asia, in or near Hong Kong, when the new virus crossed the species barrier from poultry to humans around 1997. H5N1 demonstrates that not only human but also animal populations are now one globally connected pathogen pool. We are all partly to blame. Although infected birds might migrate long distances, the overlap between when they migrate and when they're infectious to other birds is slight; without our help, H5N1 would have remained a local epidemic among Southeast Asian bird populations.[32] Instead, via commercial trade in live birds and animals, H5N1 is today endemic in avian populations worldwide. It has killed tens of millions of birds and forced the culling of hundreds of millions more.

Scientists and public health authorities are watching H5N1 very, very closely. Since 2003, some 600 human cases have been reported in fifteen countries (generally caused by close and prolonged contact with live infected birds).[33] Studies show that H5N1 is becoming progressively more pathogenic, can survive longer and is able to infect an expanding range of animals, including pigs, cats and dogs.[34] More than 60 per cent of human H5N1 patients have died, a rate that ranks H5N1 with Ebola and other lethal pathogens. Unlike Ebola, it spreads easily (among birds), like the common flu. Although it has not yet developed a reliable human-to-human transmission mechanism, lab researchers have already figured out the mutations that would give it that capability. Nothing but good luck prevents nature from duplicating this result.

The day we all hear of reliable human-to-human airborne transmission of H5N1, the world will come to a sharp stop. Would you get on a plane, knowing that a highly infectious virus with a 60 per cent kill rate might be on board with you? In reality, you won't face this choice: protocols already in place will shut borders and halt air traffic globally. Pandemic models show that a human H5N1 virus could easily surpass the Black Death of 1348–1350 as humanity's deadliest known extinction event. Depending on how early the pandemic is detected and how quickly a vaccine can be deployed, epidemiologists estimate that an H5N1 outbreak could infect up to one billion people and directly cause up to 150 million deaths.[†] Panic, riots, looting – in general, a fear-fuelled breakdown of social order – could push the death toll even higher. Survivors would suffer a global economic depression with losses in the trillions.

Other pandemic threats

The above three pandemic threats have so far grabbed the most headlines, but they are far from the only ones. In the past two decades, disease experts have identified more than thirty new or resurgent pathogens amidst human populations, including hepatitis C, Zika virus, cholera, malaria and the plague, and nature invents new ones each day.[35] In early 2013, a new bird flu, H7N9, was discovered in China; it causes severe respiratory problems and has been fatal in one-third of confirmed human cases. Unlike H5N1, birds infected with H7N9 can carry the virus without any signs of illness, making it much harder to detect.[36]

Another pandemic at least as terrible as any of the above is HIV/AIDS. To date, it has killed almost forty million

---

[†]In 2013, GlaxoSmithKline announced the first FDA-approved vaccine for a strain of H5N1. The first batch may arrive by 2017. Assuming it proves effective against a future pandemic strain, three months would elapse before mass quantities of the vaccine could be made available. Existing plans aim to produce one billion doses within the first year of the virus's initial identification.

people – more than the total population of Canada.[37] It was first identified by US public health authorities in 1981; at the time, perhaps 200,000 people worldwide lived with the disease. By the mid-1980s, that number had soared to three million; by 1990, to eight million; by 2000, to over forty million.[38] Still today, thirty-five million people are living with the disease; every year it kills over 1.5 million people and infects two million more.[39] But it does not threaten all humanity equally. More than two-thirds of those now living with HIV/AIDS are in Africa.[40] While persistent public health and education campaigns, plus antiretroviral therapies, have helped to contain the disease in the developed world, it continues to punish populations that are too poor to afford the necessary drugs or too slow to adapt their sexual practices to the reality of sexually transmitted diseases.

In its reach, persistence and consequences, HIV/AIDS is nothing less than a pandemic. That it no longer makes headlines in the developed world hints at another consequence of flourishing systemic risk: inequality. Renaissance moments magnify the differences in populations' capacities to prepare for, endure and recover from more frequent, more powerful shocks.

Future health demons and dilemmas

So far, humanity has demonstrated that we're up to these new global health challenges. The global system for dealing with disease is among the most developed and effective of all international coordination efforts. The WHO and the national health authorities of its member nations have, for the most part, contained pandemic threats since the Second World War. Newer, more focused agencies like UNAIDS are proving effective at mobilizing global responses to specific blights. Yes, diseases propagate faster and farther than ever before, but so do our detection and response efforts.

On the other hand, the challenges are getting tougher. The complexities are growing. Recent simulations have shown that a contagious airborne pathogen (like H5N1) carried into any major airport, on any continent, would be global within three days at most.[41] If the infected individual took just two plane journeys prior to a public health quarantine, more than five billion people (75 per cent of humanity) would need to be vaccinated to prevent a global pandemic. After three flights, global vaccination would be required.[42]

The concentration dilemmas are getting thornier. It is not a question of if, but when, a pandemic will strike a major political, financial or industrial centre and force its complete (albeit temporary) isolation from all physical flows in the global system – with hard-to-predict consequences for infrastructure services like energy and IT. But how can any large business avoid locating critical units in places like London, New York or China's Pearl River Delta?

The near-universal use of antibiotics and antimicrobials across the emerging global middle class, in everything from hospitals to cattle herds, is hastening nature's development of resistant superbugs. And our growing connectedness is spreading them worldwide. One superbug, MRSA, has already become a persistent nuisance (and occasionally, a serious threat) in hospitals and nursing homes everywhere. Another, a species of *Escherichia coli* discovered on pig farms in China in 2015, is resistant to colistin. Coliston is a powerful antibiotic that pig farmers mixed into feed to keep their herds healthy, but also humanity's 'weapon of last resort' for when all other known antibiotics fail. If this resistance spreads to other bacteria, once-simple infections could become untreatable.[43] For the health security of all, we must sharply reduce our antibiotic use (especially in animals) until replacements can be developed. But who can afford to leave themselves exposed?

In the developing world, cities are booming from a combination of migration and lower infant mortality. Cities offer better jobs, schooling, health and other services, and more opportunities than the countryside. They are also overcrowded and dirty. Human and animal populations are pressed side by side; the water supply is overstressed and easily contaminated. Such conditions were ground zero for SARS and H5N1, and will spawn many future pandemic threats. Those pathogens will threaten us all, and poor cities will be least equipped to confront them. But whether we are born among the rural poor, or born into an urban favela or slum, or born into an advanced economy that's questing for growth opportunities, how can we deny the lure of these emerging centres?

* * *

We have been tested many times, and for the most part, we have prevailed. But it is a biological certainty that pathogens will relentlessly assault our increasingly packed and interconnected populations and seek to turn our global shipping and transport infrastructure against us. Nature never gives up.

Merchants of destruction

Crisis then

Part I charted the transformation of Renaissance finance. New continental and intercontinental trade linkages, plus the lure of rapidly expanding coastal economies, shifted the centre of financial activity from the Mediterranean to the Atlantic. New financial instruments and markets were created to supply capital and insurance for increasingly complicated and costly mercantile activities. IOUs were deregulated so that they were no longer limited to the two parties who wrote them. Now, they could be freely bought and sold among third parties in secondary markets. That innovation gave rise to a continental money market, hundreds of times larger in value than the physical market it underwrote. The best-reputed merchant houses could write IOUs to the bourse on the strength of their name alone, with no goods to back them at all. In many ways, they could issue their own money.

Some sovereigns found this pot of easy money irresistible, and they approached merchant houses to raise vast sums on their behalf to finance their wars and ambitions. In one of the more famous episodes of the day, Charles I, king of Spain, borrowed some 850,000 gold florins from the Fuggers of Augsburg in 1519 to bribe the Electors of the Holy Roman Empire and get himself elected emperor.[44]

All of us today have some measure of wisdom about such situations. If we could, we might go back 500 years and warn Renaissance investors of what was likely to happen next. Unfortunately, they had to find out for themselves. The sixteenth-century Fuggers were so eager to lend out (at very high interest rates) to Europe's kings the large sums they could raise off the bourse, they discounted the possibility that even a sovereign might default. Charles I gained his sought-after office, but reneged on most of his debts. The Fuggers, and the myriad smaller investors across Europe who had bought Fugger bills, took heavy losses.

Crisis now

We, too, learned this lesson the hard way, during the 2007–2008 financial crisis and its prolonged aftermath. The hindsight-informed analysis has been repeated many times: American and European bankers played round after round of a highly lucrative game – lending cash to consumers and homebuyers, moving the debts and risk off their books through securitization and credit derivatives, then lending again – until households were drowning in borrowing costs and the balance sheets of big financial institutions were awash with hundreds of billions in bad debts that would never be paid off. The integration of emerging economies into global capital markets amplified the risk: China was generating lots of cash, saw few investment opportunities in Asia after the 1997 Asian financial crisis, and so ploughed it into the US economy by buying US government debt. The foreign cash infusion helped dampen domestic interest rates and kept the game going longer.

We did not clearly understand how fragile these activities made the global financial system, and we broke it. Households who took out big mortgages in the belief that housing prices would never go down turned out to be wrong. Quantitative analysts or 'quants' who thought they had packaged iffy debts cleverly enough to reduce their risk and maintain their return turned out to be wrong. The 'insurance' (credit derivatives) that firms purchased to hedge against default turned out to be inadequate. The consequences were stupendously bad. By 2009, the financial crisis had already tallied up losses of $4.1 trillion, across every market in the world.[45] Roughly fifty million people lost their jobs worldwide; among those who managed to stay employed, a quarter-billion fell into the ranks of the 'working poor'.[46] In Africa, it is estimated that 30,000–50,000 children died – from starvation – as a direct result of the global economic downturn that followed.[47]

By now, this story has been told so many times – in interviews, editorials, books, and Hollywood-produced documentaries and dramas – that the main lessons easily get blurred in the back-and-forth blame-casting. But viewed through the Renaissance lens, the take-aways come back into focus.[48]

Complexity limits our foresight

The first lesson is how rising complexity makes risks within the financial system harder to see. Colliding connective and developmental forces produced a global financial system that was suddenly far bigger and more complex than just two decades before, which both made the danger harder to see and spread the danger more widely – to everyone.

Looking back, the dangers of rising complexity were obvious. At a systemic level, the balance sheets of the world's countries, institutions and individual investors became fatter and more interconnected (see Part I). At the product level, financial instruments became more complex, largely thanks to the introduction of progressively more powerful computers into the portfolio-building process. Most large institutional investors, such as pension funds, were prohibited from investing in mortgages and other consumer loans. Entrusted with the accumulated retirement savings of whole industries, pension funds were only allowed to invest in assets that the major credit rating agencies (Standard & Poor's, Moody's and Fitch) deemed safe, and consumer debts were too small and risky to merit the agencies' attention. But what if sophisticated computer algorithms could construct big bundles from thousands of individual mortgages and debts – some more likely to default, some less – such that each resulting bundle met the agencies' thresholds for size and quality? This, essentially, is what mortgage lenders did: a process called securitization.[49] By securitizing mortgages and immediately selling them on to institutional investors, rather than holding those loans and default risks on their own books, mortgage lenders lost the incentive to scrutinize would-be homeowners' ability to repay. Mortgage quality declined, but neither the rating agencies nor the institutions that purchased these complicated products had the analytical powers or motivation to untangle this truth. Some funds insured themselves against the risk of default by buying insurance (called credit default swaps (CDSs)), but this practice only spread the danger to new sectors. Insurers were equally in the dark about the underlying mortgage risk, and pension funds were now *additionally* in the dark about the (in-)solvency of the insurance companies whose swaps they bought.[†] Like a pandemic pathogen, toxic debts originated in a small backwater (subprime mortgage lending) and spread quickly through intertwined balance sheets to threaten the global financial system.[50]

From the top down and bottom up, the financial sector's tangled complexity muddled the vision of those standing in its midst. Neither private- nor public-sector actors saw the accumulating danger. As a Bloomberg columnist observed in 2008, '[The CEO of Bear Stearns] plays bridge, and [the CEO of Merrill Lynch] golfs while their firms collapse, not because they don't care their firms are collapsing, but because they don't know that their firms are collapsing.'[51] In its 2007 Global Financial Stability Report, the International Monetary Fund concluded that 'weakness has been contained to certain portions of the subprime market, and is not likely to pose a serious systemic risk. Stress tests conducted by investment banks show that … most investors with exposure to subprime mortgages through securitized structures will not face losses.'[52]

[†] AIG, the largest such insurer, famously received over $180 billion in federal and state government money to bail it out of insurance claims that would have bankrupted it several times over.

Their concept of risk was linear; it ended at the margins of their own balance sheet, and they either did not see or did not take seriously the big picture that emerged when everyone's balance sheets were laid side by side.

Concentrations weaken our resilience

The second lesson is about how rising concentrations make failures in the financial system more likely to occur. Leading up to the financial crisis, concentrations were increasing at every level.

At the firm level, capital and resources were concentrated into the new securitized mortgage and debt products. At the turn of the century, these products were niche offerings; by the outbreak of the crisis, they had become the second-largest class of asset-backed securities sold in the United States each year. Subprime mortgages were first.[53]

Industry concentration was also on the rise. In the United States between 1990 and 2008, the market share of the top three banks quadrupled from 10 per cent to 40 per cent. In the UK in 2008, the top three banks owned 80 per cent of the market (up from 50 per cent in 1997).[54] The phrase 'too big to fail' entered public discourse to describe these behemoths. Their executives knew their respective governments would never let them go bust – the ensuing chaos would be too great. Their investment discipline weakened – a phenomenon economists aptly call 'moral hazard'. The biggest financial institutions began to take excessive risks, knowing that should things go seriously awry, taxpayers would bail them out. And, indeed, we did.

Concentration also rose at the level of whole economies, as booming financial sectors loomed ever larger in the total economic mix. In the UK, between 1990 and the start of the crisis, the size of the financial sector grew from less than 6 per cent to almost 10 per cent of total GDP, and to over one-fifth of London's economic output.[55] More perilous was Iceland's situation. At the dawn of the new millennium, Iceland, with just over 300,000 citizens, was a small fisheries economy. By 2008, after radical deregulation of the island's tiny finance industry turned Iceland into a haven for European investment, Iceland's banks had racked up $75 billion in debt – one-quarter million dollars for every man, woman and child in the country. When the financial crisis hit, Iceland's kroner plummeted, and a once simple but stable economy was crippled by the spiralling cost of servicing its foreign debts. Relative to the size of the host economy, it was, and remains, the biggest banking collapse in history.[56] Unemployment soared from zero to 10 per cent, and pensions were wiped out. The IMF bailed Iceland out – on the condition that Icelanders repay UK and Dutch investors a combined 6 per cent of total Icelandic GDP each year from 2017 to 2023. Iceland's financial sector became so big relative to the real economy that when it collapsed, so did the country.

Iceland also highlighted a rising regulatory concentration, as jurisdictions around the globe adopted a common policy of deregulation towards their domestic finance industries – a condition that Andy Haldane, in 2009 the executive director for financial stability at the Bank of England, described as a 'monoculture' that 'became, like plants, animals and oceans before it, less disease-resistant'.[57]

Each of these concentrations posed a genuine dilemma. Each one asked us to trade off legitimate private goals against poorly understood public dangers. What politician could afford to go against the deregulatory trend, when capital seemed so mobile, and loosening credit made voters feel so good? What financial firm could afford to stay out of a new market, when those entering it were profiting so highly? What person would not be tempted by the prospect of buying a house with little or no money down and building equity just by watching its value grow? All of which begs the question: Who, then, was to blame?

The financial crisis showed how difficult these dilemmas can be. Even if the risk of collapse had been more widely understood, it's not clear that we would have acted to prevent it.

Have we learned our lesson? Or will history repeat itself – again?

Taking nothing for granted

Infrastructure is vital. It is, literally, the *structure* that lies *below* (infra-) contemporary life, atop which we build our economies, corporations, cities, families and individual life plans. Infrastructure includes the transportation networks over which raw materials, goods and services, people and ideas move; the systems that supply energy, food and water to our populations; the communication channels that handle everything from remote monitoring of the electricity grid to broadcasting our *Pinterests*; and more.

This infrastructure is under threat, and that by itself is nothing new. Around the world, only a fortunate minority is served by public systems that reliably meet the demands placed upon them. For the global majority, however, the inadequacies of infrastructure are acute and make themselves painfully present in daily life. The same connective and developmental forces that boost health, wealth and populations are multiplying the demands upon lagging and aging infrastructure. Public belt-tightening in the wake of the financial crisis only exacerbates this strain, which is most acute in those areas most crucial to sustaining contemporary life: energy, water and food.

The World Economic Forum puts overall infrastructure investment needs at $100 trillion globally over the next twenty years.[58] It's a rich-world problem. The American Society of Civil

Engineers gives current US infrastructure an overall grade of D+. The country's rail and bridges are 'mediocre'; roads, drinking water and waste management systems are 'poor'; levees and waterways score somewhere between 'below standard' and 'unfit for purpose'.[59]

It's also (and more urgently so) a poor-world problem. By 2020, the developing world will need to double the aggregate $800–900 billion it currently spends on infrastructure each year to meet rapidly rising demands.[60] India, for example, suffers persistent and increasingly severe electricity shortages. In urban centres, the power switches off an average of three hours per day outside the monsoon season, and seventeen hours per day in it, and roughly 40 per cent of the rural population is entirely without electricity. In July 2012, the largest blackout in history left over 600 million people – 9 per cent of the planet's population – without power for more than two days.

Such crises are urgent and immense, but they are well understood. Our responses may be inadequate, but at least we know how to respond: in the last couple years, a half-dozen new multilateral infrastructure funds and facilities have been set up. However, the same complexities and concentrations that plague other social systems today also threaten infrastructure, and these risks are *not* well understood. Like all risks to basic social systems, they threaten severe consequences. But unlike traditional infrastructure risks, we do not have a clear idea how we should respond to them, and wealth and advancement offer little defence. The rich and the poor alike are made vulnerable.

Venice is sinking

This is the lesson that Venice learned during the Renaissance. Since the eleventh century, Venice had been the richest and most successful economy in Western Europe; by 1500, its citizens were the richest in the world on a per capita basis.[61] While most economies on the continent were occupied with primary industries – logging trees, raising cattle and grain, or mining useful stuff out of the ground – the Venetian economy was shockingly modern, dominated by trade and trade-related services. It was, in essence, an 'offshore bonded warehouse' (not unlike Singapore today) whose main resources were its location and its large pool of sophisticated merchants who understood supply and demand, consumer choice, on-time delivery and the importance of a supportive tax, legal and currency environment.[62] With its large merchant fleets, Venice was the world's leading naval power, with an undisputed monopoly over most Mediterranean trade, and the first European power to interact seriously and continuously with Islam.

Although Venice also produced fine glassware, silk, paper and other fine craft goods, the majority of Venice's wealth was invested in the trade of spices, which it imported into Europe via hundreds of middlemen and settlements along the Silk Roads and the Indian Ocean. See Figure 7.2. Today, pepper is an optional condiment we sprinkle in our food according to taste. But in an era without refrigeration, pepper, saffron and other spices made the difference between palatable and unpalatable meat. As the continent developed and demand for spices grew, so too did the profits of the Venetian spice trade and the importance of its Mediterranean transport infrastructure to the city-state's economy. A pair of external shocks exposed that same infrastructure as the republic's greatest vulnerability.

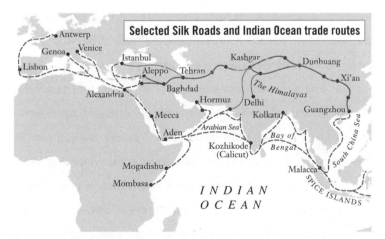

FIGURE 7.2 *The bulk of Venice's wealth was dependent on the world's longest supply chain.*

Source: Greg Prickman (2008). 'The Atlas of Early Printing: Trade Routes.' University of Iowa Libraries. Retrieved from atlas.lib.uiowa.edu; plus authors' analysis.

The first was the Ottoman advance into the Mediterranean. In 1453, the Turks captured Constantinople, which had stood as an unassailable bulwark against Islamic expansion into European waters for centuries. A series of naval incursions into the Mediterranean followed, culminating with the Battle of Zonchio in 1499. It was the largest naval battle in history up to that time, comprising over 350 ships and 55,000 men, and Venice's failure to win it marked the decisive shift from Venetian to Turkish dominance over the eastern Mediterranean.

From an Ottoman perspective, these events demonstrated the positive impact of new connections and economic development upon their own empire's reach and resources. The Ottomans married gunpowder from China with Hungarian-designed cannons to help assail Constantinople's walls. They harnessed European naval technology to build galleys – bigger, faster and, for the first time, cannon-wielding – to wrest control of the Mediterranean from the world's most experienced naval fleet. They adapted, rather than dismantled, Venice's trade practices and outposts, in order to help fund their empire-building. And they followed up each war with negotiations that reopened trade and exchange between East and West (at revised prices, of course).

The Turks could be negotiated with; geography could not. In the long run, therefore, the second shock was more devastating. In 1499, word reached Venice: three Portuguese *ships* had been sighted at the spice markets of India. Vasco da

Gama had found his sea route. 'At the receipt of this news, the whole city … was dumbfounded and the wisest thought it was the worst news ever heard', recorded Girolama Priuli, a Venetian senator and banker.[63] Venice's merchants knew instantly what it meant: Portugal would buy in bulk, ship direct, and cut out the hundreds of small middlemen and exorbitant taxes that lined the overland route Venice had constructed and maintained over the past seven centuries. In a single masterstroke, a competitor had rendered Venice's Mediterranean spice infrastructure obsolete.

Some consequences were immediate. The following year, prices in Venice plummeted against the expectation of much better terms on the Atlantic coast. Many German spice buyers decamped and moved their business to Lisbon. Eventually, the decline of the overland spice trade proved less precipitous than first feared, because the sea route offered its own dangers: storms, piracy and hostile settlements up and down Africa's West and East coasts. But it was no less inevitable. Cities and regions along the overland trade routes that had flourished as centres of commerce and culture since antiquity – Baghdad, Beirut, Cairo, Damascus, the Black and Red Seas – declined into relative backwaters. Venice herself did not so much decline as start to fall behind. Her economic lords struggled long and bravely, trying in turn to pivot towards shipbuilding, manufacturing and agriculture, but their city-state was too poorly located to compete against emerging ocean-going empires.

Venetians, like so many others, thought their long boom would last forever. They were unable to see the disruptive, non-linear shocks coming – the rise of Ottoman power and the discovery of more and better trade routes – to which their own accumulating trade success had made them so vulnerable. Venice prepared against neither, succumbed to both and dragged a once-thriving transcontinental network down with it.

Thailand is flooding

We have likewise accumulated concentrations in present-day supply chains and infrastructure that make us vulnerable to sudden, hard-to-foresee shocks. Despite its intuitive promise to help diversify risk, 'globalization' has reduced the variety of much of our investment and activity, as we all independently arrive at similar conclusions about how and where to minimize cost, maximize efficiency or achieve other common objectives.[64] It is only recently that we have begun to appreciate how our private pursuits of similar outcomes have increased our collective vulnerability to shock events.

As the Venetians demonstrated 500 years ago, supply chains are especially likely to accumulate concentrations. Private business moves fast in response to profit-making motives. In 1990, Thailand had modest electronics and automotive industries.[65] By 2010, spurred on by Thailand's accession to the

WTO in 1995, such manufactures accounted for 35 per cent of Thai GDP and 20 per cent of employment.[66] More than 40 per cent of global hard disk drive (HDD) assembly work and a large chunk of Japanese auto parts manufacturing had relocated to the Bangkok river valley.[67] Why? Because it offered low-cost labour, preferential government policies and convenient access to nearby Asian hubs. The more businesses that followed this logic into the valley, the stronger the lure of the logic became – which is why when violent tropical storms in late 2011 flooded the region, the consequences – which were deep in Thailand – were widespread. Direct flood damage and losses totalled $40 billion and temporarily forced over two million people out of work.[68] Indirectly, the shutdown of auto part exports forced Nissan and Toyota to halt or delay production in Malaysia, Vietnam, Pakistan, the Philippines, the United States and Canada.[69] The loss of electronics manufacturing capacity caused consumer prices to spike worldwide and hit tech stocks hard on Japan's Nikkei and New York's NASDAQ. With almost half the world's hard drive production underwater, global production of personal computers stalled. Across the Pacific in Santa Clara, California, Intel lost $1 billion of revenue in 2011's fourth quarter.[70] Thailand's HDD manufacturing recovered, but only temporarily. The 2011 floods helped hasten the tech industry's transition to the solid-state drives made by Thailand's neighbours, and since 2013 Thai HDD exports have been falling.[71]

A similar story unfolded when Iceland's Eyjafjallajökull volcano erupted in spring 2010, spewing a cloud of ash over Western Europe that shut down, for six days, all three major airport hubs that connect Europe to the rest of the world – London Heathrow, Frankfurt and Paris Charles de Gaulle. Almost 100,000 flights were cancelled, and the ensuing chaos – ranging from cancelled organ transplants in European hospitals to rotted flowers and fruit in Kenyan and Zambian warehouses – cost the world economy an estimated $5 billion.[72]

New social complexity and concentrations did nothing to raise the risk of a volcanic eruption actually occurring, but they raised its costs once it did occur.

Other big infrastructure failures have been more of our own making. In August 2003, the worst power failure in North American history hit the northeastern United States and Canada. It cast more than fifty million people into darkness for more than thirty hours, at a cost of some $6–10 billion.[73] Until that moment, few in government or the utilities had believed that a single outage on that scale was even possible. But US power consumption had jumped almost 30 per cent in a decade, not least due to the lighting up of the internet. Deregulation and privatization, begun in the early 1990s, had increased the number of parties plugged into the grid from hundreds to thousands. Emerging smart grid devices alongside aging power stations had complicated control systems. And greater use of renewable generation (which stops and starts according to the vagaries of sunshine and wind) had complicated load-balancing on the grid. Not surprisingly, a joint US–Canada task force concluded in the aftermath that the top two causes of the blackout were 'inadequate system understanding' and 'inadequate situational awareness'.[74]

Clearly, these episodes from our recent past have begun to sensitize us to systemic infrastructure risks. All told, in the first fifteen years of the twenty-first century, natural disasters taught some $2.5 trillion worth of lessons worldwide.[75] It is just as well we've had the chance to learn, because many other disasters loom. Throughout our global transportation networks, there exists much more variety, but far fewer ways to deliver it. Today, just the top thirty airports in the world encounter over 40 per cent of all international passengers and handle over two-thirds of all international freight.[76] The top ten seaports in the world touch fully 50 per cent of the global economy's container traffic.[77] The Strait of Malacca, the main lane between the Indian and Pacific Oceans, through which one-quarter of the world's traded goods and commodities now pass, is only 2.8 km wide at its narrowest point. The Gulf of Aden, connecting the Mediterranean Sea to the Indian Ocean via the Suez Canal, is equally significant, and almost as tight. A diminishing set of global platforms manufactures and delivers a startlingly large share of most everything we care about.

This is especially true of the internet, an entirely new source of systemic risk for the twenty-first century. The internet is so useful that we now use it for everything, and therein lies the danger. From a user perspective, the internet is an invisible field that connects us everywhere. But this user experience has a physical dimension – data centres and fibre-optic cables that concentrate our connectivity in dangerous ways. The same strait and canal choke-points through which the world's ships must pass are also the best routes along which to lay undersea cables. Every year in Africa, the networks of whole countries go dark when one of these threads is cut by a passing ship's anchor – or by an axe. In 2013, the Egyptian coastguard caught three men in a fishing boat who had pulled up, and were trying to hack through a Suez cable deliberately. Their target, the SEA-ME-WE 4 cable, is one of the principal data links between Europe, Africa and Asia. Cutting it would have choked networks on all three continents. It's also possible that some government agencies now possess 'kill switch' capabilities that can effectively shut down a target country's internet connections, by disabling essential servers, for example. That may explain why North Korea's internet briefly went dark in November 2014, only days after the US government had accused the country of hacking Sony Pictures in retaliation for a recently released satirical film about the North Korean regime.

Meanwhile, the complexity of network hardware and software is making it steadily harder to maintain reliable services. Google,

Microsoft, Amazon and Facebook operate around one million servers each, and downtime – due to glitches, natural disasters, equipment failure and human error – is a costly problem. Unexpected data loss and downtime cost businesses just under $2 trillion a year according to one global industry survey.[78] As we become more dependent on the internet, for example through wider adoption of cloud services, those costs will escalate.[79] And the exploitation of so-called 'zero-day' vulnerabilities – unknown bugs buried deep inside the code of widely distributed software or operating systems – threatens to interrupt services deliberately. Often, these bugs are fixed only after hackers have made use of them. In September 2014, a wave of attacks known as ShellShock exploited a core vulnerability in Mac and Linux operating systems to run malicious code on millions of computers. The bug had gone unnoticed for twenty years. Another zero-day vulnerability uncovered in November 2014, called Unicorn, had been present in every release of Microsoft Internet Explorer going back to 1995.[80]

The complexity of internet networks allows attacks like zero-day exploits to be performed with near-perfect anonymity. The most frequent kind of attack, distributed denial of service (DDoS), arranges to send dummy data requests to a victim's server from thousands of hijacked computers simultaneously, so that legitimate users can't get their own requests through. The internet was originally designed for sharing, not security, and perpetrators can hide in the open amidst the unwitting crowds they convene. Even when perpetrators are discovered – often overseas somewhere – limits of jurisdiction make it hard to bring them to justice.

Rare twenty years ago, today cybercrimes are ubiquitous: in our email, on the web, in social media, on mobile devices and on private networks. Their rapid spread has been enabled by maturing online marketplaces that supply cybercrime labour and tools, and that fence stolen goods. It is no longer a question of *whether* you will become a victim of cybercrime, but *when*. These crimes injure us personally, through the theft and ransom of identities, login information, webcam videos or Snapchat photos. They also use us to injure others, by making us unwitting accomplices in spam, phishing and email attacks, or by using our computers as web servers for malware and child pornography. And as more smart devices, from appliances to automobiles to the locks on our house, connect to the 'Internet of Things', the range of injuries that cybercriminals can cause us will only widen. In July 2015, some 1.4 million Jeeps were recalled when researchers proved they could exploit a bug to hack, and crash, the vehicles remotely over the internet.[81]

Cybercrime also steals intellectual property and other secrets from institutions. Every year, roughly one-half of small businesses, two-thirds of medium-sized companies and four-fifths of large enterprises worldwide are specifically targeted by a cybercrime.[82]

Keith Alexander, the director of the US National Security Agency until 2014, described cyberespionage activity as the 'greatest transfer of wealth in history'.[83] In the United States alone, where half of all cyberattacks originate and are committed, corporate losses from cyberespionage may range from $300 billion to $400 billion per year.[84] These attacks also harm customers and clients, by exposing their personal data and making them more vulnerable to identity theft. A 2014 survey found that 43 per cent of US firms, including the largest online service providers, retailers and banks, had suffered a data breach in the past year.[85] A hack at JPMorgan Chase & Co stole the bank records of seventy-six million households and seven million small businesses.[86] Public data networks are also at risk. Back in April 2007, Estonia, one of the world's earliest adopters of paperless government and internet banking, was brought to a sudden stop when its banks, telecom companies, media outlets and government ministries were all hit by simultaneous DDoS attacks. More recently, in mid-2015, personnel records of 21.5 million current and former employees of the US government, including 5.6 million fingerprint images, were stolen when the Office of Personnel Management was hacked – possibly by a foreign government aiming to recruit informants or identify spies.[87] Other highly sophisticated malware initiatives, likely state-sponsored, have likewise penetrated embassies, research institutes and other sensitive targets of governments around the world.[88]

The rising scale of critical infrastructure connected to the internet – including defence, chemical, food, transportation, nuclear, water, financial, energy and other systems – means that not just cybercrime, but cyberwarfare is now possible. In 2010, the Stuxnet worm sabotaged Iran's uranium enrichment infrastructure by infecting control systems and causing the uranium centrifuges to tear themselves apart.[89] (A similar worm had been aimed at North Korea's facilities, but failed to reach its target because of the country's extreme isolation.[90]) In 2014, a German steel mill suffered 'massive damage' after cyberattackers gained access to the plant's control systems and caused critical components to fail.[91] Many more such strikes are being attempted. The US Department of Homeland Security reports roughly 250 serious cyberattacks against critical public infrastructure per year, the majority in energy and key manufacturing sectors. The attacks range from from unauthorized access, to malware infections, to data theft (which may serve as reconnaissance for future attacks).[92]

Other cyber-assaults are less targeted, aiming instead to disrupt whole sectors of our digitized society. In 2017, one ransomware attack, WannaCry, crippled parts of the UK's National Health Service before going on to infect computers in 150 countries. A month later, another piece of ransomware, Petya, paralyzed airports, banks and government departments across the Ukraine.

With a growing range of state, criminal and other actors launching successful cyberattacks against supposedly secure critical national and business systems (including with the use of spyware allegedly stolen from the US National Security Agency), gone are the days when we could take any of our infrastructure for granted.

Nature as infrastructure

That includes nature. Natural infrastructure, like climate, is the clearest example both of how risks have changed since the first Renaissance and of how the lessons learned 500 years ago are relevant to us.

What's changed is the sheer scale of human activity, performed by a population that is seventeen times larger and with a level of technology that consumes far more energy per person.[93] A half-millennium ago, the forces of nature seemed unconnected to human industry. Humanity could alter the landscape by agriculture and forestry, for example, but mostly nature was taken as a given – a power beyond our influence, let alone control. Today, that's no longer the case. There's no longer a clear-cut division between human-made and natural disasters, because the scale of human activity is sufficient to measurably affect planetary habitats, species diversity, weather, temperature, atmosphere, even sea level.

The lesson – that connective and developmental forces generate challenges of complexity and concentration – is equally obvious. Take climate change, for example. Humanity's relationship with the earth's climate has become one of the most complex phenomena within all science. Natural factors that go into understanding this relationship include, among many others: solar cycles, the earth's orbital variations, atmospheric and ocean currents, cycles of carbon absorption and release by plant and animal life, and the absorptive capacities of different planetary surfaces. Onto such phenomena we next need to overlay the impact of human society: our accelerating production of greenhouse gases, land use, ozone depletion, agriculture, deforestation and so on. Then the hard work begins, to discover the interactions, feedbacks and non-linear tipping points within and between these two giant sets of variables. Cause and effect are very difficult to see. That's half of the reason why it's hard to mobilize strong public action to mitigate climate change – even when we suffer its consequences, like changing weather patterns, extreme hurricanes and other 'natural' disasters.

The second half of the reason is that climate change presents the paradigmatic concentration dilemma. It is a wholly unintended by-product of human initiative, adventurism, exploration, of connecting and cooperating – in short, of so much activity that we deem to be good. What are we to do, if in our individual pursuit of socially affirmed goals we contribute to an accumulation of carbon pollution that, as seems more and more certain, presents an existential threat?

* * *

Risk is flourishing, and the rising complexity and concentrations within our systems are to blame.

These two factors present different challenges. With complexity, the hardest part of solving a problem is seeing it. If we could see the cause–effect relations at work, we might protect ourselves with some mix of managerial and technocratic solutions – but we can't, so we don't.

If complexity strains our cognition, concentrations strain our judgement. Concentrations are the collective consequence of all our individual choices – choices guided by free will, by ambition, by our duty to loved ones. What do we do when our private actions increase the risk of collective shocks we never intended? Even when we can see the shock coming, there's no easy answer.

We can't avoid these strains. They are the other side of the tangled, rapidly developing age we've been born into, and they permeate our lives – including our relationships with one another.

8

Prophets and Bonfires

How the age we're in strains the bonds that hold us all together

Italy is at war – and famine finds new room;
The plague wins every shore – and spreads God's wrathful doom:
Such is the food of gloom – left for your blind,
Lost life, mankind – of faith as frail as glass.
Alas, alas, alas …

–GIROLAMO SAVONAROLA (1452–1498)[1]

Populist bonfires

He's a political outsider whose angry words have come to dominate public discourse. He's a gifted orator whose power to sway a crowd has been amplified by new media. He's a doomsayer who promises to banish the fear and anger that he himself has stoked in his audiences, and who cares little for rational argument because his opinions tap a deeper truth.

He is, of course, Girolamo Savonarola, the Dominican preacher who exploded from obscurity in the 1490s to shock the establishment across Renaissance Europe. Armed only with an apocalyptic message that lay blame for people's injuries and fears squarely upon the weakness of society's elites, he led a popular revolution to evict the Medici family from their lordship over Florence and install himself as de facto king.

The Republic of Florence was the intellectual and cultural heart of the European Renaissance. Home to Michelangelo and Machiavelli, its populace was among the most educated, wealthy and liberal on earth. But with public sermons and printed pamphlets, Savonarola mobilized those Florentines who felt left behind, economically or culturally, by a rapidly changing world. His daily sermons directed popular discontent towards leaders who, in his judgement, had gone morally soft, set bad policies and made stupid deals with foreign powers. He and his zealous supporters were a minority of the population, but they shouted loudest and gained control of the city's governing council. From that pulpit, Savonarola incited mass campaigns against liberal values. He renamed the city 'The Christian and Religious Republic of Florence' to emphasize who belonged and who did not.[2] He radicalized laws against homosexuality – or, as he described it, 'that accursed vice of sodomy for which you know Florence to be infamous throughout Italy. Make a law, I say, without pity, so that such persons are stoned and burned'.[3] And he bullied free-speaking politicians, artists and intellectuals into submission with public displays of intimidation.

The most famous public display took place in early February 1497. Savonarola and his fanatical followers gathered up all the hard evidence of liberal indulgence that they could lay their hands on: immoral books, heretical texts, nude paintings and sculptures, indecent perfumes, new musical instruments and baubles from far away. They piled them into a giant heap in Florence's central piazza, rising sixty feet high in seven tiers (to represent the seven deadly sins), then set fire to the lot in an act of arson that we still remember today: the Bonfire of the Vanities.

By 1494, and until his public execution four years later, this loudmouth prophet was easily the most powerful figure in Florentine politics.[4] The question on the lips of authorities everywhere – from the local Medici oligarchs to the pope in Rome – was how![5] Savonarola was, after all, only one man, speaking against wealthy elites and religious institutions that held all formal power. Plus, he was an outsider – literally. As a cleric *and* a non-citizen of Florence, he was doubly ineligible to hold public office, let alone rule.

It wasn't due to the newness of his campaign style. Public bonfires to burn away sin had been lit by Italian clergy before – by Bernardino da Siena in the 1420s, and more recently by Bernardino da Feltre in 1483.[6] Nor was Savonarola himself new.

He was a gifted orator who spoke against moral corruption in society, but the same could have been said of many preachers before him.[7]

In a previous time and place, such a man would have been denied power by reigning gatekeepers and ignored. Instead, Savonarola and his ideas somehow blasted those gates and enjoyed legitimacy and momentum completely out of proportion to his social position. In May or June 1490, when at the age of thirty-eight Savonarola first arrived in Florence to take up a teaching post at the sober Convent of San Marco, he was a mid-level friar from Ferrara with a small-but-rising reputation for giving stirring, apocalyptic speeches. Within a year, he was preaching from the most prestigious pulpit in the city, in the Duomo under Brunelleschi's dome, to crowds of 15,000.

Savonarola's success was, first, the failure of establishment elites to help the populace cope with anxieties brewing beyond their borders – many of which were well founded. The Ottoman Empire loomed like a dark cloud on the eastern horizon: the Turks had cut off Asia, occupied Greece and now terrorized Italian shores. The Medici patriarch Lorenzo 'the Magnificent', Florence's true kingpin and a symbol of the city's splendour, fell ill and died in 1492. His unimpressive heir, Piero 'the Unfortunate', inspired no confidence. In 1494, doubts about Piero were proven well founded, when Charles VIII of France invaded Italy and carried away a good deal of Florentine wealth in the deal Piero struck to buy peace. In a general way, Savonarola had predicted it all. The gravity of the threats the city faced called for strong leadership – moral and political – but 'O Florence, Florence, your cup is full of holes'. If the people did not wash away the sin that was corrupting their institutions and their own hearts, then God would send a new Flood to do it for them.

In part, his influence was due to his vigorous defence of traditional values deemed under assault by the runaway pace of change. Many Florentines, especially the creative classes, were inspired by a new, 'humanist' agenda: to elevate 'Man's' place in the Great Chain of Being by finding something *divine* within our artistic, scientific or political striving. Savonarola was horrified by it. By speaking and stoking that horror publicly, he gave his supporters permission to express their horror, too.

To them, promoting material beauty and secular achievement in society's hierarchy of values meant demoting religious ones like abstinence and penitence. The Virgin Mary was being painted as a beautiful, wealthy woman – an image that some men lusted after.[8] Pope Alexander VI (more widely recognized today by his family name, Borgia) was far too worldly. He had a penchant for mistresses, neglected his spiritual duties in order to chase temporal thrones, and lavished unearned favours on his family. 'The Church is teeming with abominations from the crown of her head to the soles of her feet!' Savonarola accused the pope and Florence's oligarchs of putting their own interests before those of the public they were sworn to serve, and thus failing to beef up Christian virtues at just the moment when the Devil was threatening them most.

Lest people forget, Savonarola preached, Heaven and Hell were real places. Salvation lay not in Man's attempts to rise above himself, but in obedience to God's moral laws and the hope for grace in the afterlife. Only in the spiritual Ark of Jesus Christ could people be spared from the coming Flood. For believers of this dogma, the culture of moral permissiveness that was taking root, in the Church and in society, needed a fierce opponent to uproot it immediately. Savonarola leveraged that conviction to radicalize traditional practices and infuse them with new meaning and urgency. Most importantly, he seized control of Florence's catechism schools and rewrote the curriculum. Under his guidance, they churned out gangs of fervent, ideologically bonded youth who would patrol the streets and enforce his moral programme with a mixture of harassment and violence.[9]

The third ingredient in Savonarola's shocking success was the advent of print. The friar's moral values may have been against the spirit of the times, but he was quick to adopt new technologies to push them. As best as history can remember, he was the first Italian politico to use the printing press as a mass propaganda tool.[10] He delivered fiery sermons to crowds of thousands, then reached thousands more with the printed version: not books, but short, one-sheet pamphlets that were quick to set up and cheap to produce.[11] Savonarola also invented the 'open letter' – addressed to all, intended for wide circulation and aimed at influencing public opinion.[12] His skilful use of these nascent media channels gave him dominance over the news cycle. He spread his narratives, stoked popular anxieties and built momentum behind them faster than complacent elites thought possible, until he and his followers became difficult, then dangerous, to resist.

Finally – and in an age of fragile faith, most importantly – he believed. Savonarola's most fervent follower was himself. God had appointed *him* the task of renewing the city. And as God's prophet, whatever words he spoke were true just because he spoke them.

That ecstatic arrogance was his greatest strength. The pope excommunicated him. Savonarola called it proof that the Devil had taken up residence in Rome. The preacher's imperviousness to attack seemed almost magical. It drew to his every sermon the usual horde of sensation-seekers, but also citizens who had lost faith and longed to have it restored by the sheer power of the man's reality-bending defiance. He promised Florentines a return to past glories, and he knew he could deliver – if only his enemies would stop trying to protect their own narrow agendas, and submit fully to his God-given mandate.

A second bonfire of vanity

Donald Trump, prophet and doomsayer. He may shock contemporary norms with the seeming originality of his power-taking, but through a Renaissance lens he is an obvious plagiarist. Ever since descending a gold-plated escalator to declare his candidacy for president of the United States, Trump has stolen his lines and stage directions from a populist playbook that is as old as print.

Shock should not be directed at the man and his methods, but at society's widespread failure to expect his arrival. We have seen the risks accumulating within our public health systems, economies, critical infrastructure and nature. Living amidst these upheavals, why would we imagine that our *social* systems should be invulnerable?

'Society' is people living together, and a social system is the bargain under which we do so, made firm by shared norms and values, and the institutions (governments, courts, media and the like) by which these shared thoughts take on concrete form. A Renaissance moment puts this entire bargain under stress. Yes, the forces at work reshaping society open magnificent new possibilities and terrifying new threats. But neither experience is uniform. There are big winners and big losers. The fortunate are spared; the unfortunate are struck down. New concentrations of prosperity and poverty develop, and these uneven outcomes challenge our settled notions of fairness and justice. At the same time, rising complexity makes it harder for us to sort out who or what caused the changes that worry us, so that once-clear notions of responsibility and accountability become blurred.

Fairness, justice, responsibility, accountability – these notions are the heart of the bargain that holds society together. They are always being tested, but this present age weakens their certainty at just the moment when the technologies to summon solidarity, or rally rebellion, are suddenly made more common and powerful.

A second Savonarola was always likely. The only question was which imitator would step into the role.

When resentments are left to pile up

A society full of broken promises is highly combustible – but no society starts that way. It takes time for leaders to heap up enough broken promises to make a proper bonfire.

In hindsight, it's obvious that Florentine elites took for granted how high they could build that heap and still count on their citizens' obedience. They let contradictions accumulate between the values they *professed* and the values they *expressed through their actions*, seemingly without serious consequence.

Only once Savonarola came along and demonstrated the public's flammability did elites recognize the error in their complacency. They – not God – had fuelled Savonarola's rhetoric. And they could have easily prevented him, had they taken their bargain with the populace more seriously.

After all, that world didn't promise the ordinary peasants who joined Savonarola's cause much to begin with. Most saw the wide gap in lifestyles between themselves and the nobility as part of the natural order. They remained stuck in a flat world roughly ten miles across, but why would they need to travel farther? They never sampled New World chilies, but why would they want to? They had little use for literacy and books, and few means to obtain either. They were happy to rely on God to fix the earth at the centre of creation, to set the sun in motion around it, and by His mercy to banish the demons of fever and infection that haunted them and their children.

For many ordinary people, *salvation* was the one promise they expected society to keep. But now even God's messengers, whose sole job was to bring God into their lives, were flaunting wealth and vice in their faces. The Church sold indulgences to the rich, while the poor were promised hell if they did not obey their lords. That was the final betrayal. The one institution in society whose mandate was to look out for their interests had been captured by elites looking out for their own. Popular disillusionment gave Savonarola the power to snatch away the vain possessions and secular authority of the rich and noble.

That disillusionment is being repeated.

Today, we measure well-being – and the institutions set up to care for it – in less spiritual and more material terms: income, education, life expectancy, as well as what we've come to recognize as the basic dignities owed to human beings, such as security, choice and self-expression. But even through our secular filter, sentiments of resentment echo. Today, as then, there is a wide, popular sense that the people and institutions at the top of society have become neglectful of the rest. Today, as then, there is a strong belief that those entrusted with the duty to care for the public's welfare are more focussed on enriching the few than saving the many. Today, as then, the popular mood is to feel betrayed, not lifted, by the age we're in.

And today, like then, complacent leadership has allowed these sentiments to pile up. By taking for granted the bargain that holds us all together, we have collectively failed, at too many moments of choice: to better translate wealth creation into well-being; to distribute society's gains and losses more widely, so that more individuals benefit; to forge fresh ties of belonging within and between communities wracked by rapid change.

Smothered sparks

In hindsight, these moments of failure are obvious. They stretch back to the dawn of this second Renaissance. 'It seems to have a relentless drive to extend its power'.[13] Savonarola might have used those words to criticize the papacy. Instead, they were spoken in 1999 by a prominent trade campaigner, Ronnie Hall, about the World Trade Organization (WTO).

The occasion, the 'Battle of Seattle', saw some 3,000 government ministers and negotiators from the WTO's then-135 member countries gather in Seattle to launch a new 'Millennium Round' of global trade talks.[14] They were met by 40,000–100,000 protesters who took to the streets around the conference site in protest against an institution that, contrary to its mandate to 'open trade for the benefit of all', was, in their view, promoting the interests of the rich at the expense of the poor and vulnerable. 'Opening trade' had in their minds become the WTO's euphemism for eliminating democratically installed protections for workers, society and the environment in order to help investors earn better returns on their capital.

That protest was smothered – by police armed with pepper spray, tear gas, stun grenades and ultimately rubber bullets. But discontent continued to smoulder. The Seattle meeting failed to kick off a new trade round. 'Anti-globalization' and 'fair trade' entered popular discourse. And most subsequent global governance gatherings – of the WTO, the World Bank, the International Monetary Fund (IMF), the G8, the G20, the World Economic Forum – were accompanied by mass social protest.

Then came the bursting of the dot-com bubble and the 9/11 terrorist attacks. Talk of 'globalization' abated and these crowds declined. Civil liberties were restricted and dissent became unpatriotic, especially in the United States. People's attention was drawn elsewhere. The apparent threat of multinational corporations diminished, and states and non-state militaries re-emerged as the principal villains in a colder, darker international system. In the meantime, rising returns to capital and stagnating wages in developed countries meant that, year by year, a larger and larger share of the money earned in these countries went to the already-rich.[15] As a result, from 2001 to 2007, total private wealth in North America and Europe – the total value of everyone's houses, investments and other assets, minus debt – doubled, from $75 trillion to almost $150 trillion[16] – and the richest 10 per cent of households held 65–70 per cent of it.[17] It was, for the developed world's capitalists, their best half-decade ever in dollar terms. Wage-earners muddled through.

Ignition

The breaking point, for households across the developed world, came in the aftermath of the global financial crisis. The immediate consequences of the crisis were bad enough. But then, having endured record foreclosures, unemployment and cuts to their pay and social benefits, the public discovered that the rich (whose investing activities had caused the crisis) hadn't shared in the pain. Across advanced economies, from 2007 to 2011, the incomes of the bottom 10 per cent of earners had fallen twice as fast as those of the top 10 per cent. In the United States, top incomes hadn't fallen at all. They'd actually come out ahead.[18]

The US social bargain has traditionally tolerated a wide wealth gap – to work hard and get rich is every American's right – but this was too much. From the end of the crisis through 2011, while the bottom 99 per cent (whose incomes had already fallen 12 per cent) were made even worse off, the incomes of the top 1 per cent recovered almost completely.[19] As a result, their share of the nation's accumulated wealth had actually grown, so that by 2011, the 1 per cent controlled 37 per cent of all American household wealth. That shook many Americans' settled notions of justice and fairness. The top 1 per cent weren't making money – they were transferring it, reverse-Robin Hood style, from everyone else's pockets into their own. Everyone else, it seemed, had paid dearly for the crisis: with bailout money that could instead have been spent on education, transportation or tax cuts; with their jobs (from 2008 to 2009, nine million Americans were forced out of work[20]) and even with their homes (from 2008 to 2013, banks foreclosed on 4.5 million homes – a 300 per cent jump over the previous five-year period[21]).

The ultra-rich had turned a profit.

Tough medicine can bring a people closer together, but not if privileged segments get to skip their doses. Disillusioned by the 'recovery' that wasn't (see Figure 8.1), in September 2011, several hundred people came together under the slogan 'We are the 99

FIGURE 8.1 *A big chunk of the US labour force lost their jobs (and still haven't found work).*

Source: *US Bureau of Labor Statistics (2015). 'Labor Force Statistics from the Current Population Survey: Employment-Population Ratio'. United States Department of Labor. Retrieved from data.bls.gov.*

per cent' and occupied New York City's Zuccotti Park, near Wall Street, in protest. What in another time and place might have remained an obscure act of civil disobedience instead found a discouraged global public willing to join in. Within a month, the Occupy movement had spread to over 950 cities in eighty-two countries across five continents.

The Occupy movement became a global brand, but it itself was inspired by popular uprisings in Europe and the Arab world. Unlike in the United States, the financial crises that unfolded in European countries like Spain, Greece, Ireland, Iceland and Italy were beyond the resources of their own governments to cope. So, they appealed to the European Union, the European Central

Bank and the IMF (the 'troika', as they came to be known) for help. The troika gave it – on condition that borrowing nations pass new budgets to tighten up public spending.

These 'austerity measures' did not go down well with a public that had already lost jobs and incomes in the banking crisis. The same entities who had tolerated reckless lending in the first place now demanded that governments privatize state assets, cut public salaries and pensions, and reduce public services so that international creditors could more reasonably expect to get repaid. In Greece, from 2010 onward, hundreds of thousands of people took part in the Indignant Citizens Movement – sit-ins and protests against this latest round of misery.[22] They were Greece's largest protests since revolts against their military junta in 1973. In Spain and Portugal, where youth unemployment soared above 40 per cent, the *Indignados* movement saw thousands more take to the streets, and millions visit protestors' camps, in a nationwide series of events beginning May 2011.[23] In Italy, a 2011 austerity plan was accompanied by a protest in Rome of some 200,000 people, as well as a new cabinet of unelected technocrats whose aim was to regain the trust of international lenders.[24] In late 2013, after Italy's longest ever post-War recession and with youth unemployment stuck at over 40 per cent, a nationwide Pitchfork movement comprising thousands of students, farmers, labourers and the unemployed made it clear that government had not regained *their* trust. In

March 2011, London saw its largest protest since the start of the Iraq War in 2003 – up to half a million people – after the UK government launched its own austerity plan to pay for its £1.5 trillion bailout of the British banking industry.[25] The announced cuts – which by 2020 will take public spending as a share of GDP down to levels last seen in the 1930s – coincided with news reports that billions of pounds of bailout money were being used to pay bankers' bonuses.[26] In June 2015, up to a quarter million more British marched through London to protest against a subsequent round of austerity measures.[27]

Mass disillusionment was a precursor to major political shifts, to both the left and right, across Europe. In 2012, France elected as its president the Socialist Party candidate, François Hollande, whose promise to tax 75 per cent of all earnings over €1 million won the hearts of a recession-weary public. (The super-tax expired in 2014.) Meanwhile, France's far right party, National Front, made historic gains in regional elections with its anti-EU, anti-immigrant, protectionist platform. Germany's Alternative für Deutschland, Denmark's People's Party, Sweden's Democrats and the People's Party of Switzerland all followed suit. In Spain, the anti-austerity Podemos ('We Can') party rose from non-existence in 2014 to become the country's second-largest by number of members, and by the end of the year had more 'likes' on Facebook than all other parties combined. In 2015, its popularity started to wane, in part due to the emergence of Ciudadanos ('Citizens'), 'the Podemos of the right', which won over Spanish voters with strong promises to stamp out government corruption.[28] The same year, Greeks voted the Coalition of the Radical Left (Syriza) into government, as their way of demanding better bailout terms from foreign creditors. With almost a third of citizens living below the poverty line, Greeks wanted assistance, not austerity.

And in the UK, the Conservative Party won a fresh majority from British voters in a tight 2015 election – a victory secured by adopting the far right's pledge to hold a public referendum on leaving the European Union. A few months later, Britain's defeated Labour Party elected, by a landslide, arguably the most left-wing leader in its history.[29]

All told, of the twenty-seven continental European Union leaders in office during the financial crisis, only one remained in power a few years later (Angela Merkel of Germany). The public's message was clear.

Fanning the flames

Protest and resistance can be positive forces that compel a more inclusive bargain to be struck. Instead, the distribution of gains and losses within our societies continued to worsen. Imagine ten people eating a pie. One person gets half the pie. Five people share the other half. The remaining four people get whatever crumbs are left over (in this case, 3 per cent). That is now, on average, the distribution of household wealth within the eighteen developed countries for which the best data is available.[30] (In the United States, one person gets four-fifths of the total pie.) Within developing countries, it's often hard to say who really owns what, but in general the gap between haves and have-nots is even wider.

Wealth is just one dimension of our social bargain with one another. Deep inequalities in health, education and opportunity also remain – and in many cases have worsened – among citizens. Across the United States, whites still live, on average, five years longer than blacks.[31] In Paris, people who live northeast of the Seine (the river that bisects the city) are only half as likely to have a university degree as those who live to the southwest.[32] In Australia, mature adults earning less than $20,000 per year are more than twice as likely to suffer from chronic illness – such as heart disease, diabetes or depression – as those earning more than $50,000.[33]

Yes, in aggregate terms this *is* the best time in history to be alive, but many of us have never felt that way. It certainly hasn't been the easiest. We as individuals have become ensnared in a transnational tangle of choices and burdens, enablers and obstacles, interdependencies and conflicts. Humanity's great gains have been accompanied by shocking upheaval and new vulnerabilities.

To date, this upheaval has made big winners of some: owners of capital; entrepreneurs who have grown into new markets;

and individuals whose low-cost labour or high-value skills give them a clear role in this tangle. But it has also made big losers of others: pensioners and home owners whose savings were decimated by unforeseen financial risks; middle-class workers whose jobs are now being done overseas by people escaping from poverty; other workers whose jobs stayed onshore but are being replaced by machines; farmers whose crops are failing due to climate change; citizens in countries where a small elite are siphoning the benefits of global integration off into foreign bank accounts.

Can we all become winners in this game? That was the lie we told one another, but honestly: no. At the macro level opportunity may be flourishing, but at the micro level our individual lives are full of practical constraints. Large parts of our societies are locked out of new jobs by advancing age, inadequate savings, heavy debt or soaring housing costs. Many of us are rooted to dying places, without the means or desire to. Others among us are rooted in place by duty—say, to care for ailing family members. Not everyone is able to sail for the New World with the elan that economic theory demands. That's why governments, businesses and all of us who are benefitting from our voyages must actively transport a share of the gains back to those left behind.

We missed many, many chances to do just that.

From bonfire to revolution

The political bonfire of our own time has been ignited. What happens now? What happens if we continue to fail one another – fail to better translate wealth into well-being; fail to distribute society's aggregate gains and losses more widely, so that more of us are *individually* lifted; fail to forge fresh ties of belonging?

The answer is clear: we break apart.

One complacent myth is that the fires will die and the old normal will return once the populists in power have been removed. That won't happen.

Savonarola himself was eventually removed – burned at the stake – by his political opponents in the very same square where he once lit his triumphant blaze. The fatal flaw with 'propheteering', the friar painfully discovered, is that governing is harder than pandering to people's fears. Reality pierced his veil of prophecy. Popular faith evaporated. He had made too many enemies: on the 'left', those who rejected his moral austerity; on the 'right', those who feared a trade war with the pope; and up high, those who feared for the privileges they had always enjoyed under the Medici. Even elites who had once supported Savonarola's agenda (not every noble was a fan of the Medici oligarchs) deserted him over his incapacity to rein in the messianic ego when prudence demanded.

Crucifying Savonarola was considered the expedient solution to remove the nuisance he had become. Reformist grumbles within the Church were shushed; populist urges in Florentine politics dissipated (and by 1512 the Medici were back in power). However, by his execution, the Church avoided confronting the one question that might have saved Europe a century of grief: What if Savonarola was not some lone cleric gone rogue, but, rather, the voice for a revolutionary mood that was already widely felt within the Church and among the public?[34]

Crisis of faith

In the years following Savonarola's death, it became increasingly clear that his strident indignation could not be unshouted. The mood of disillusionment he had tapped continued to spread, and to erode the bargain holding together not just Florence, but Europe itself. Pope Alexander died in 1503 and his successor, Julius II (1503–1513), 'The Warrior Pope', continued to lead the Church deeper into the worldly squabbles of his predecessor – often in full armour on horseback – and further away from its spiritual mandate to save the people. To devout Christians, the new pope on his Roman throne displayed a hunger for earthly power reminiscent of another Julius – Caesar. Led by his example, other high Church officials seemed more preoccupied with lording over the people than serving them in the manner Jesus had taught. They opted for ostentation over poverty. They interfered in the legal system on behalf of big donors. They spent – and sometimes whored – freely, but still managed to preach charity and virtue on Sundays.

The idea began to firm up in the minds of many that maybe the 'Catholic' Church (from the Greek *katholikos*, meaning 'universal') was a misnomer. If it couldn't represent their beliefs, then to reach God they might have to go around it.

The breaking point for one pious friar in Germany came in 1517 when he saw his local archbishop selling indulgences to wealthy sinners in order to fund his acquisition of a yet another Church office. In protest, on 31 October 1517, Martin Luther famously nailed his *95 Theses on Indulgences* to the doors of All Saints' Church in Wittenberg and unwittingly set in motion what came to be known as the Protestant Reformation.[35]

Like Savonarola, Luther began his career inside the Roman Church, as a friar and priest committed to austerity and moral perfection. Luther himself claimed to be following in Savonarola's footsteps.[36] But unlike Savonarola, Luther's critique extended not just to a particularly corrupt pope or oligarchy, but to the whole institution of the Church itself. Just the concept of any person standing between God and believers with the authority to judge their souls was, he deemed, corrupt – let alone when the priest charged money for the service. But the entire Church rested upon this idea of the priesthood as God's intermediaries. Ergo, it had to be wholly rejected.

In place of a super-state that served only to fatten its own hierarchy, Luther envisioned a thoroughly reformed Church, one that took the power to dispense God's forgiveness away from the priests and instead made it a private matter between God and sinners, and which, by replacing Latin with vernacular languages, made the Bible and the liturgy more accessible to laypeople so that they could start caring for their own souls.

The printed word, especially pamphlets, played a crucial role. Savonarola had discovered the persuasive power of print; Luther maximized it. It's possible that he was initially taken aback by how broadly it cast his *Theses*. As he wrote to a friend:

> I did not wish to have them widely circulated. I only intended submitting them to a few learned men for examination, and if they disapproved of them, to suppress them; or make them known through their publications, in the event of their meeting with their approval. But now they are being spread abroad and translated everywhere, which I never could have credited, so that I regret having given birth to them.[37]

But Luther, a prolific writer, was also quick to see the benefits. One-fifth of all pamphlets published in Germany between 1500 and 1530 bore his name. They served to spread his ideas to other opinion leaders quickly, keep them all in touch with each other's evolving thoughts and experiences, and broadcast a coordinated programme quicker, to a wider audience, than had ever been possible before.[38]

As with Savonarola's previous campaign, what in another time and place might have been dismissed as the rants of a political outsider instead found a receptive public who were willing, in their discouragement, to do something revolutionary. Only by this time, the object of revolution had widened from corrupt leaders to a corrupted *system*; to make things better the system itself had to be rejected. Savonarola's campaign was eventually snuffed out by the people whose power he threatened. Luther's new narrative kept spreading until it consumed them.

De-globalization (1.0)

The old narrative of a universal Church was broken. Battle lines began to be drawn between those who supported the papacy and those who supported Luther's bargain – which would strip Rome of its powers, dissolve some of them and return others to secular rulers.

Many of Europe's princes sided with Luther's more nationalist, 'Protestant' vision – for reasons that probably varied from sincere soul-searching to realpolitik. Significantly freed by Luther's theology from papal punishment, courts in England, Denmark, Sweden, Germany and Switzerland went their own way. They confiscated church property, seized church estates, and claimed for themselves powers of clerical appointment, public education, morality enforcement and poor relief. They did, however, face a backlash from the devout Catholics among their own people. New civil wars, this time fought over religion, flared up within, and spread across, Europe's states. From the 1520s until the end of the century, the continent counted fewer than ten years of complete peace. The half-century after that counted only two.[39]

The peasants and commoners who took part were fighting over more than religion. They were also punishing the ruling classes for years of exploitation, which Reformation rhetoric suggested they shouldn't have to suffer any longer. The Bible, which Luther urged people to read for themselves and which he caused to be translated into a language local peasants understood (German), introduced them to radical ideas about what society should be about, like rewarding honest labour and protecting the common good against the interests of the few. The nobility's ill treatment of commoners, which the latter had long put up with as the bargain they'd been born into, began to look grossly unfair – even ungodly. It was an explosive notion. From 1524 to 1525, perhaps a quarter-million peasants across the Holy Roman Empire took part in the 'Peasants War', the widest-scale public insurrection that Europe would ever see up until the French Revolution (some two hundred fifty years later). The war began innocently enough, as a not-uncommon dispute between tenant farmers and landlords over rising rents and legal burdens. But this time the landlords (Catholic monasteries and churches, mostly) were defensive, and the protestors were filled with fresh self-righteousness. It ended with tens of thousands of protestors killed, and thousands more tortured, by the Empire's soldiers.

Smaller, parallel revolutions played out across Western Europe: the Comuneros revolt in Spain (1520–1521) over oppressive taxes; the Grand Riot in Lyon (1529) over the rising price of wheat; the Revolt of the Straccioni ('rag people') in Tuscany (1531–1532) over exclusion from public offices; the 'Pilgrimage of Grace' (1536–1537) in England over religious reforms, food prices and new taxes. Reformation-inspired hostility to traditional authority, combined with rising unemployment, economic instability and a booming youth population, made it relatively easy to rally revolts all around Europe.[40] Their numbers magnified the scale and cost of these conflicts, and often radicalized what had begun as more moderate protests.[41]

The Catholic Church added to the climate of chaos and suffering with reactionary campaigns against the Reformation, such as the Roman Inquisition – set up in 1542 to stamp out heresy in Italy. Public authorities in other states, including England, France and the Netherlands, established similar tribunals and carried on their investigations throughout the sixteenth century and beyond. While not as deadly as popularly imagined (recent research has revised the scale of executions from millions down to thousands[42]), the Inquisitions terrorized and exiled whole communities and suffocated a great many traces of creative flourishing.

All told, over the sixteenth century, tens of thousands died, and hundreds of thousands were made homeless, as Europe rearranged its people into Catholic and Protestant halves, and communities that did not fit in, such as the Jews, Muslims and Roman (Gypsy) communities, were persecuted.. The revolution spawned the biggest refugee crisis that Europe had seen since the fall of the Roman Empire, and would ever see again until the First World War.[43] Wretched columns 'were repeatedly sent straggling along the roads of Europe', some driven by need to casual crime.[44] When, in 1526, the duke of Norfolk confronted such a crowd of English peasants and demanded to speak with their leader, they famously replied, 'Since you ask who is our captain, for sooth his name is Poverty, for he and his cousin Necessity, hath brought us to this doing'.[45] They filled the well-off with fear and alarm. Townspeople's first instinct, hardened by new medical understanding of immigrants' role in spreading disease, was to suppress and segregate. Great poor houses were built to hide vagrants from view. Anti-migrant laws spread across Western Europe, requiring alien beggars to leave town within a strict time limit (usually three days) or face a variety of punishments: jail, whipping or hard labour below decks on a merchant galley. But the migrant masses swelled too quickly – and state officers were too few – to make such laws stick.

How stable are the overall gains society makes, when accompanied by a break in popular faith? The Renaissance experience suggests: not very.

A new crisis of faith

The gains we've made over the past thirty years may not be stable, either. On the 500th anniversary of Martin Luther's Reformation, faith in the fundamental dogmas of the western world is again faltering.

Can capitalism really improve general economic welfare? The very short history of the twentieth century was the failure to find a better alternative. If we want to reap the broad benefits of a dynamic, competitive economic system, we need to celebrate, rather than demonize, the wealth it generates and accept the differences that it generates, too. That's the deal we've struck with one another. But the opening decades of the twenty-first century are testing how far we can stretch that bargain. In 1990, the three largest companies in Detroit were worth $36 billion to shareholders and employed 1.2 million workers. Today, the three biggest Silicon Valley firms are worth nearly thirty times more (over $1 trillion) but pay salaries to nine times fewer (less than 150,000) people.[46]

The creation of a few billionaires – and the loss of a few million jobs – is the price we must pay for technological progress and broader welfare gains. Or is it? Economists now realize that past a certain point, the social costs of rising inequality outweigh the incentive benefits of letting people hoard the wealth they create. Extreme inequality depresses economic growth.[47] (The logic is that when the rich get richer, they don't buy more stuff, because they already have everything; they just save and invest more. But if the poor get richer, they buy all the things they don't yet have – including, most importantly, better health for themselves and better schooling for their kids.) The very rich can also tilt the economic playing field in socially harmful ways by using their outsized wealth to influence policymaking. They can fix the rules to favour themselves and to discourage would-be competitors from innovating.

Therein lies the second doubt gnawing away the faith-foundation of our society. Can democracy still deliver 'rule by the people'?

In authoritarian states, the capture and corruption of public institutions by wealthy elites is plain to see. Russia's oligarchs won vast fortunes at taxpayers' expense in the early 1990s when, under the guise of market reform, state-owned infrastructure and natural resources were sold off to friends of the regime for pennies on the dollar. In China, more than one-third of all wealth is in the hands of the 1 per cent.[48] Corrupt officials, many now disgraced, have amassed private fortunes through their control of state assets and their authority to award licences and contracts without independent oversight. Angola, blessed with vast natural resources, is essentially a kleptocracy whose leaders 'live in an African version of St Tropez', as *The Economist* put it, while 90 per cent of residents in the capital, Luanda, have no running water.[49] The above are all examples of what economists call 'rent seeking' – making money by taking wealth away from others instead of creating it yourself.

But now this capture and corruption is becoming plain in democratic states. In the United States, too, the top 1 per cent hold more than one-third of all wealth.[50] Legislatures are demonstrating their enormous power to transfer wealth up or down the social ladder: by expanding or shrinking welfare programmes; by shifting the tax burden between rich and poor, between investors and wage-earners, or between corporations and private citizens; through the pricing and sale of state assets and public goods like railroads, postal systems, oil patches and wireless spectrum; by deregulating or re-regulating industries; by making it harder or easier for persons or corporations to clear their debts through bankruptcy; by deciding whether monetary policy should target low inflation or full employment.

In the United States' 2016 election cycle, presidential and congressional candidates raised and spent a total of over $7 billion.[51] Clearly, on assuming power, successful candidates (and their staffers) owe a lot to the lobbyists and other financial backers who paid for their campaigns. One of the most common demands lobbyists make is to ratchet back taxes, which squeezes public investment in education, health, welfare, infrastructure and shock preparedness. Lobbyists also push for deregulation, which can hasten the development of the complexities and concentrations seen in the last chapter, contributing to financial, environmental and other crises. And they seek to strengthen their intellectual property rights, extending the monopolies granted to them by patents and copyright to the point where these laws imprison, rather than release, creativity and innovation.

Back in the 1990s-era Battle of Seattle, protestors still had faith in democracy to set things right. It was the lack of democratic scrutiny over trade deals that frustrated them. But by the time they arrived in New York's Zuccotti Park to Occupy Wall Street, 'If Voting Made a Difference, It Would Already Have Made a Difference' and 'Error 404: Democracy not Found' were top-trending #slogans.

As it was for Martin Luther, so it is for many today: the distinction between corrupt leaders and a corrupt system has eroded until the only way forward now is to reject the whole religion. For them, through too many successive crises, no leader has convincingly demonstrated how our present politics and economics can accomplish anything but to magnify the gains of the winners at the cost of the losers.

The price of a broken bargain

There are reasons to believe that we will avoid the chaos that engulfed Luther's world. Democracy is a giant political innovation that separates our Renaissance moment from his. It gives us enormous adaptability to social stresses. (Very few lives have been lost in the protests that have washed over democratic countries since 2011.)

But this adaptability comes at a price: nothing important gets done unless the people stand together behind it. Consider for a moment what we – for lack of faith in traditional politics – are undoing, and are failing to do.

Europe's bold experiment of political and economic union – perhaps the war-prone continent's best hope of cementing a permanent post-national peace – is now plagued with uncertainty.

Through a Renaissance lens, upheaval to the political status quo in Europe readily foreseeable – and foreseen.[52] More surprising was the arrogant complacency displayed by Europe's elites, who dismissed such reversal as impossible. In 2015, when then-British Conservative Party leader David Cameron offered euro-sceptics a referendum on his country's EU membership in exchange for their vote, he repeated the elite conceit of a half-millennium prior. He failed to grasp that the whole narrative of a unified Europe becomes vulnerable once the narrative itself becomes the object of people's frustrations. Other EU leaders were guilty of the same arrogance when they rebuffed Cameron's pre-referendum efforts to negotiate a significantly different deal for Britain. Had they all looked to history – to a similar moment of similar stresses that had similarly been ignored – they might have stretched their imagination to encompass the future that has, now, arrived.

Now that the European Union's spell of permanence has been broken, the question is whether, and if so, how deeply it will split. Events like Brexit or Marine Le Pen's ascendancy to the final round of the French presidential elections stoke the spectre of an anti-EU, pro-nationalist gospel spreading across the continent, but Emmanuel Macron's electoral victory over Le Pen demonstrates that a pro-Europe platform can still sway continental hearts and minds.

With its present in flux, the Union's future is wide open. Europe's common currency, the euro, is mired in mud or a symbol of resiliency, depending on which pundit is speaking. Closer fiscal union among existing EU member states is either "on life-support" or "has a heartbeat". And with a queue of Balkan states waiting to join, expansions to the bloc are anyone's guess. One bold next step was to have been the admission of Turkey – which, up until the First World War, was still the Ottoman Empire. More than any other nation's, Turkey's inclusion would have broadened the European Union's horizon beyond its medieval Christian borders. Instead, more than ten years after recognizing the state's candidacy, the EU slammed the door in Turkey's face. The sting of that rejection helped boost the appeal of the country's authoritarian president, Recep Tayyip Erdoğan, and of his Who-needs-Europe-as-long-as-you've-got-me narrative.

The crisis of faith in a pan-European creed is echoed in political crises across advanced economies. The Development Round of WTO trade talks, meant to improve poor world access to rich-world markets, was stillborn in Seattle, then revived in Doha in 2001, but has agreed nothing for so long that most people don't know it is formally still ongoing. Rather than tackle the biggest issues on the global trade agenda (not least, perverse agricultural subsidies to rich world farmers), it has disintegrated into a patchwork of more modest bilateral and regional trade negotiations. Even those deals strain popular faith. Twenty-five years ago, the United States spearheaded NAFTA, and more recently the Trans-Pacific Partnership. Now the country's politicians believe that votes can be won more easily by trashing both. Americans, once the world's chief promoters of trade agreements, today rank among the French and the Italians as the most likely to say it destroys jobs and lowers wages (The Chinese have now become trade's loudest advocates—unsurprisingly. The emergence of their middle class has been made possible by three decades of export-driven growth.).[53]

The global migration of people is locked in tragedy. The United States builds a white-elephant wall to keep undocumented Mexicans out, amidst statistics showing that more Latinos now abandon the American dream each year than are drawn towards it. (The most direct beneficiaries of tougher border security are people smugglers, whose declining industry is made more valuable as a result.) Behind the fence, 11 million people remain trapped in an American half-life – quite welcome to contribute their unskilled labour, not welcome to access public services or call themselves members of the communities they live in. The European Union, which in recent years has been flooded with record numbers of new refugees from Syria, Afghanistan and other conflict countries, is split between those who quietly believe the long-term solution is for each member state to take in a mandatory quota each year, and those who loudly protest that this is exactly the sort of overreach that makes the EU a threat to national sovereignty.[54] While they debate, millions of refugees suffer in squalid camps and urban slums in Jordan, Lebanon and Turkey. Hundreds of thousands more attempt to bypass the camps, many suffering abuse and death at the hands of people smugglers, or drowning trying to cross the Mediterranean in makeshift boats. The 1951 UN Convention on Refugees, which defines refugees' rights and states' duties towards them, is badly in need of reform. Absent an updated global compact among stable, better-off countries to share fairly the duty to help people displaced by disaster, our response is going to be patchwork and poor each time disaster strikes. And it is only going to strike more often.

On arguably the greatest global threat today, climate change, vigorous action according to a common, inclusive and effective bargain has eluded humanity for decades. The 1997 Kyoto Protocol, a flawed but best-effort framework in which a subset of states bound themselves to cut their own carbon pollution, ended with most failing to follow through. At Copenhagen in 2009, world leaders opted not to bind themselves to a pain-sharing deal at all. The somewhat audacious hope that had pervaded the Kyoto conference – a pre-9/11, pre-global recession moment, when 'globalization' was still a good word – had been replaced with the sober realization by assembled world leaders that they possessed neither the will nor the popular support back home to make significant sacrifices for our common future.

That support has firmed up somewhat in recent years. Extreme weather events have worsened, and thick pollution in China's cities and elsewhere has heightened public anxiety over the health consequences of a fossil fuel economy.

The 2015 Paris Accord, in which 195 countries voluntarily committed to halt global warming at 'well below 2°C', is the result. By itself, the agreement was a giant achievement – one of the first times in history that scientific evidence persuaded virtually all the world's nations to agree on anything. That is a testament to the flourishing power of science, and to the new knotting together of a global awareness regarding the unintended consequences of progress.

The grave doubt now is: Will we all follow through? The United States, the world's second largest carbon emitter behind China, now says no. Other states will seize on that excuse to reduce or renege their own commitments. Other excuses are within easy reach. At Paris, key states balked at making the Accord legally binding, and its voluntary commitments do not begin until 2020. Meeting the sub-2°C target hinges upon states re-upping their commitments to cut carbon every five years after that – again, voluntarily. The target also assumes the mass deployment of better technologies to reduce carbon emissions (despite inadequate investment to date), and large-scale cash and technology transfers to the developing world (which so far have been, again, grossly inadequate). Have we forged a brave new bargain, or once again kicked the hardest choices down the road?

These are among the most ambitious political projects in the world today. And they are all on life-support. Other urgent global conversations are stillborn. We ought to agree how to redistribute the global use of antibiotics. In some (mainly rich) places, that means curbing antibiotic use, to slow down nature's development of antibiotic-resistant bugs. In other (mainly poor) places, it means figuring out how to make present antibiotics available to those most in need. At the same time, we ought to re-invigorate global efforts to develop new antibiotics before present defences fail.

And we ought to be working towards global compacts on research into human genetic modification and artificial intelligence. Both technologies are, in their own way, as significant as the nuclear arms race. No country can afford to forego their development unilaterally (for fear of losing strategic parity). But this logic of competition means that far more resources are being invested into making these technologies powerful than into making them safe.

Losing control of the narrative

We ought to be ... but we're not.

Such is the lament spoken everywhere by true believers of the old religion. A new 'ought' has emerged to challenge the narrative within which all the above was obviously good, urgent and important.

The gospel according to Trump

Rapid change (economic, social, demographic, geopolitical) has been forced upon all of us by liberal elites. The erosion we perceive in our personal well-being and in public values isn't due to external forces or to our own failure to adapt – despite what we've been told repeatedly in the past. It is, rather, due to failed leadership. For too long, our leaders have advanced their own far-flung interests and forgotten the public's immediate needs.

Trapped in their own bubbles, they don't understand how to lead us through this new, more contested world.

This new narrative proves seductive to many who feel threatened by the changes they perceive in their own lives and communities. It simultaneously: *explains why* they feel anxious and angry; *validates* those feelings as indignation – as righteous reaction to a betrayal of public trust; and *assigns blame* for our stresses onto others. Some scholars and commentators have labelled this narrative 'nationalism', but that confuses more than it clarifies. At its core is a much more basic appeal – loyalty.

The strength of this new narrative has been seen in the persistent popularity, and electoral wins, of far right and far left politicians who promise to make things better by undoing what the centre has done. It has been seen in once improper, now vote-winning, rants uttered by front-running politicians in the United States, UK, Italy and other big democracies against immigrants, trade partners and the moral weakness of centrist politicians.[55]

And it has been seen in the feebleness of the centre's reply. The loyalty narrative is stealing the voice from public figures who would defend established projects and norms, by making it very easy to brand them as *disloyal* for doing so. Through this loyalty narrative, to even speak of mitigating broad systemic risks (like climate change) while allowing members of the community to suffer specific injury or hardship is an act of betrayal. In the same vein, pushing projects to universalize values or build shared post-national identities is to compromise the security of one's own community. While 'the other' might achieve some fictitious legal 'equality' with us, they should never be equally trusted.

Seductive, but destructive

These are tribal accusations whose felt immediacy is difficult to confront with rational argument. That's why this new gospel will continue to challenge the old.

But it is not invincible. Rather, like the narrative it seeks to replace, the more widely it spreads, the more vulnerable it is to collapse under the weight of its own contradictions.

The old gospel of globalization transferred political power from the general public to elite technocrats. The coining of that omnipresent word (*global-ization*, the process of becoming global) was itself an act of public disempowerment. Within the guise of a *process* of economic development, the word obscured many important political *choices*: about how to go about creating wealth, and about how to share the rewards and risks that follow. The gospel taught that the public had little say over these matters; their preferences were constrained by inevitable economic laws and forces. To resist an inevitable *-ization* is irrational.

Global-*ism* (the *doctrine* of becoming global) would have been more honest packaging. To accept an *-ism* without critical inquiry – now that's irrational. The simple switch in language, from process to doctrine, would have shifted the burden of proof from those affected by the gospel to those who preached it.

Ultimately, this suppression of public choice proved self-defeating. When globalization yielded sharply uneven outcomes, those who felt left out or left behind had only the process to blame. If instead the narrative had been more forthright – making clear that the distribution of gains and losses was not merely an economic consequence, but also a political choice that had been made by somebody – then globalization's evangelists could have directed public frustration *inward* against those domestic choice-makers who were hoarding their lion's share. Instead, it is being directed outward at the traders and immigrants who are helping to generate gains in the first place.

The new, anti-globalization gospel deceives in the other direction. To those who are weary of being pushed around by unseen forces and processes beyond their control, it preaches the power of popular will to defy reality. Savonarola tried to burn away new art and literature; today's anti-intellectualism torches economic and science textbooks.

Then and now, some changes are hard to reject. Savonarola's greatest crime was that he gave his followers permission to try anyway. They put faith in his prophetic powers to save them. 'I announce this good news to the city: that she will be more glorious, richer, more powerful than she has ever been!' he proclaimed. But the preacher's self-belief could not overturn the military advantages of the French army that invaded Italy, nor cure people of the syphilis brought back to Europe from the New World, nor protect merchants from the shift in trade from the Mediterranean to the Atlantic.

Ultimately, today's populist narrative will prove self-defeating, too. US President Trump preaches a return to past glories. 'Make America Great Again'. But the past cannot be reconstructed. Humanity *is* transformed, in ways that we cannot undo, to which we can *only* adapt. Versus our grandparents' generation, the planet is twice as populous, teems with four times as many city dwellers, and boasts 3 billion more middle-class consumers. Likewise, our technology *is* transformed – and transforming. For all the attention that free-trade agreements and multilateral treaties get in our political discourse, they are mere conveniences that we have woven atop an irreversible entangling of the human condition.

To mitigate the biggest coming shocks to our well-being (be they environmental, biological, economic, social or technological) and to hold society together through these shocks will demand more public adaptation, not less. More social inclusion, not less. More science in policy-making, not less. More multilateral cooperation, not less. All this, in turn, requires a majority of citizens to empower public institutions with more, not less, trust to act on our behalf for the common good.

A call to loyalty that inspires citizens to lean on one another through a period of rapid change can be a farsighted act: we urgently need to weave such resilience into the social fabric of our communities. But a call to loyalty that dismisses everything and everyone else as irrelevant is wilful blindness. More than ever, our well-being depends not only upon the actions that we take, but upon those taken by others, in our own communities and around this tangled world. We need to care about *their* choices and actions – whoever 'we' and 'they' are.

Putting our immediate, narrow interests first can work to catapult political outsiders into power. It can work to restore our lost sense of control, or status. But it cannot give us the cures and jobs that others have to offer, nor can it spare us from calamities of which we did not approve.

Steering the second Renaissance

Whosoever owns the narrative will write the history of this age.

It is the defining contest of our time. Humanity is teeming with barely contained energy. This energy will either drive us all upwards or drive us apart, depending on how we channel it. The most sombre lesson of the first Renaissance is that if we choose the latter, everyone will pay a terrible price to put society back together again.

Thanks to a political technology called democracy, we may avoid the worst of the disintegration that Renaissance Europe endured. But if we cannot stop this rot in the trust-foundation of our social institutions, we do risk stagnation – not just of grand political projects, but of grand creative endeavours. Rather than attain the heights that this Renaissance age invites, we will merely muddle through. We will nurse cynicism in one another, and the environment of community and vitality in which genius flourishes will be undermined by growing division and apathy.

The latter, apathy, is especially pernicious. Public disorder, if it hits, hits us hard, but we recover – just as we can recover from tangible disasters. Towers that are torn down, we rebuild; that is the human spirit. But it is harder to replace the towers that are never erected because the energies of the neglected have been wasted, or the talents of the disheartened have been withdrawn.

Some already consider the fight for the guiding narrative lost. They have connected two dots labelled 'Brexit' and 'Trump' to extrapolate a future of ascendant economic nationalism, the dissolution of global governance arrangements and the twilight of cosmopolitan values.

But such expectations are just as narrow as the complacency that spawned this contest in the first place. In his own time, as a living witness to Savonarola's original Bonfire and its aftermath, Machiavelli's greatest fear was precisely such fatalism: that leaders and citizens would *drift* with, rather than *resist*, the momentum of their misfortunes.

The great service that Donald Trump, Brexit and similar populist mutinies in Germany, France, Greece, Brazil, Austria, the Philippines and other countries have performed is to shock more of us into recognizing our true predicament. In a growing number of countries, citizens are retaking control of the centre ground and fighting back against divisive and isolationist tendencies. As the electoral successes of Emmanuel Macron and his *En Marche!* party in France's 2017 elections showed, centrists can bypass traditional parties and media as effectively as extremists on the left or right. And centrists can channel anger against traditional authorities to push open markets and cooperative reforms.

We are coming to understand: voyaging through an age of discovery, there are no wise captains to guide citizen-passengers on an inevitable heading of rational progress. There's only us. We must all be pilots, and fight to steer the ship through unfamiliar waters.

Rebirth of a narrative

It is yet possible to regain control of this ship, and steer it towards the progressive possibilities of this age.

But not with the narratives that got us here.

'Globalization' is a political dead-end. It was never just a trend; it was always a test of faith. And we have failed it. Citizens' legitimate expectations for a greater share of opportunity and dignity went unmet for too long, and its cry now falls upon deaf ears.

'Globalism', which some advocates of the old gospel now rally around, is likewise apt to be ignored. It is far too late to swap -*ization* for -*ism* and expect the disillusioned to hear the difference. To a cynical ear, any explicitly pro-global agenda implicitly glorifies technocratic expertise and denigrates public wisdom.

Nor will people be galvanized by appeals to help build an 'open' world. 'Open' versus 'closed' is a false choice. The positive connotation of 'openness' is as deceptive in its own way as Trump's promise to put America First. We *are* tangled together. All our actions, in every sphere, defy the notion of borders. Neither open nor closed makes us safe. It is an absurd lens that simplifies away the very risks and complexities that we must start grappling with more seriously.

Having been knocked off their previous course, preachers of the old gospel cast about for a revised promised land: some new place that preserves the progress we've made along our present heading, but is fairer. Friendlier. More sensitive and just.

But citizens now hear all these grand sermons with heavy scepticism. How can revising our destination improve the conditions aboard ship? A new discourse of clarity and honesty is needed, in which tough choices are clearly stated, leaders are held accountable for their polemical promises, and pain is more widely recognized and shared.

For the luminaries of the first Renaissance, the destination towards which they rallied people was not a society that was richer or better run, but one that was *more fully human*. And what would vex them most about the populist gospel now burning through the ropes that bind us is not its ignorance of economic or scientific truth, but its fearfulness.

In their own age of new continents being discovered and old truths being ripped away, Michelangelo, Leonardo, Erasmus, Copernicus and others sought to conquer fear, and stoke virtue. Their narrative – which bound their diverse acts of individual genius together into one social, intellectual and artistic phenomenon – was that in order to navigate the storm they were living through, they had to resurrect and reinterpret for their own time the classical virtues: courage, civility, humanity, dignity. The range of futures before humanity seemed impossibly wide; the range of practices upon which thriving societies could be steered was narrow, and history had proved them so. To them, virtues were more than pretty words. They were social technologies – whose use or abuse would ultimately decide how history judged their generation's time at the tiller.

The present social and political climate only *feels* unprecedented. Seen through a Renaissance lens, the narrative we need now, and the actions we must take within it, are startlingly clear.

PART IV

THE CONTEST FOR OUR FUTURE

9

David

What to do

If people knew how hard I had to work to gain my mastery, it would not seem so wonderful at all.

TRADITIONALLY ATTRIBUTED TO MICHELANGELO

Michelangelo's *David* has endured many trials since his public unveiling in Florence's main square, more than 500 years ago. In 1511, his pedestal was struck by lightning. In 1527, he himself was struck (some say, by a chair thrown from an upper window), and his left arm broken off. (It was replaced in 1543.) An ill-considered attempt in 1843 to clean his marble skin (with a 50 per cent hydrochloric acid solution) did more harm in a day than the Florentine sun and rain had done over the previous three-and-a-half centuries. In 1873, accumulated weathering finally forced him to retreat from his prominent perch into a museum – the Accademia Gallery – where he languished in a crate for nearly a decade. When Mark Twain visited Florence in 1878, he 'found [the statue] in a board closet ... after a long hunt through uninteresting acres of picturesque'.[1] *David* was entombed again during the Second World War, this time in sand and brick to ward off bombs and theft.[2] Mercifully, he was spared both.

Today, Michelangelo's *David* is missing a few original fingers and toes, and his ankles are cracking from the strain of holding his pose for a half-millennium, but he's still with us. So, too, is much of the wisdom that humanity gained from the period in which he was born.

By his presence, *David* invites us to mine that wisdom – to find inspiration and illumination from the beauty and the ugliness that defined his own age of discovery. The present is not a repeat of the past, but nor does humanity reinvent itself with each new generation. Circumstances change; technologies change; but our deep nature remains more stable, and that is why we can peer back into history and bring back important lessons for the present.

Chief among them is the lesson that *David* himself embodies – *David*, who is, in the words of one art historian, 'human potential in its most vital form'.[3] He inspires us, and warns us, to stand like him: courageous. And ready, for the contest that has to be fought, and has to be won.

This contest, between flourishing genius and flourishing risk, defined his Renaissance, and it defines ours. Whether history remembers this moment as one of humanity's best or worst depends upon the courage with which we magnify the former and mitigate the latter.

Magnify flourishing genius

1. Welcome genius

I, for my part, cannot be different from what I really am.

Desiderius Erasmus (c. 1466–1536)[4]

It sounds obvious, but in practice we often do the opposite. Genius can be scary. It shows us a different way of looking at the world, and we might not like what we see. Copernicus used maths to show his world that they had their view of the heavens backwards. That was a dangerous truth. It seemed to challenge basic Biblical beliefs about the meaning of life. God set the earth at the centre of creation, and God set 'Man' as its custodian – both comforting thoughts. But if the earth were just the third rock from the sun, where would that leave *us*?

Of course, humanity was cruder back then; we are much more open to admitting science into our thinking today. That, too, is a comforting thought, but we have further to go than we think. For example, genetic research has shown conclusively that racism has very little scientific basis. There is far more genetic difference *within* 'races' than *between* them. Worldwide, three-quarters of a million people, including the two authors of this book, have submitted DNA swabs to the National Geographic's Genographic Project and got back personal proof of their shared African ancestry. But such evidence has not yet diminished the role of racial bias in our societies.

Some truths are so at odds with entrenched beliefs or established habits that we simply ignore them. Right now, we are in the process of ignoring much of what we've recently discovered about the global climate system, the global financial system, intergenerational poverty, heart disease and how investment into public education fuels economic growth. And most of us still don't wear sunscreen.[5]

We are all going to ignore many new truths in our lifetime. Try not to. Ultimately, reality is hard to reject. Healthy, successful people – and societies – are those that build upon it. So let go of comforting myths. In their place, champion critical thinking.

Digitization, like print before it, has amplified all speech equally, even if all speech is not equally worthy of an audience. In our newsfeeds, fact and opinion look much the same; in reality, they are two very different things. It's our constant job to separate the two, by demanding that opinions be backed by argument, by testing arguments for bias, and by asking what other views are out there. Those who did so in the first Renaissance helped usher in the next generations of free thinkers – including, from the mid-1500s to the mid-1600s, Galileo, Hobbes, Descartes, Locke, Leibniz and Newton. They, in turn, ushered in the Scientific Revolution and then the Enlightenment. New heights await, if we can muster the intellectual courage to climb them.

In a similar spirit, we must be open to new ideas. To make progress along the path of inquiry, we have to be ready to throw away our current views. Too often, we resist or suppress new ideas because they threaten vested interests. Copernicus' sun-centric theory wasn't the only *Aha!* idea to meet fierce opposition: Swiss scribes rallied against the printing press; Dutch guilds fought advances in shipbuilding; French paper makers burned machines that would have sped up pulp-making.[6] Likewise, today's fossil fuel industry is resisting the transition to alternatives; mainstream banks throw cold water on crowd-sourced lending; and taxi drivers cry foul over apps that help commuters buy rides from one another. Is every new idea a good one? No, but in a Renaissance moment that should be the default assumption – unless the idea directly harms people. Now, more than ever, society has the capacity to judge an idea, share it and spark a better one.[†] Let's applaud

---

[†]Recall that even dangerous mutations to the H5N1 flu were eventually made public. Better to put it out there and get people thinking about would-be vaccines, publishers rightly decided, than to one day be caught unawares.

experimentation, even with society's sacred cows – or some of the best discoveries of the twenty-first century might never happen.

Embrace geniuses

We cannot welcome genius unless we also welcome its harbingers.

Nobel laureates are an imperfect proxy, but nonetheless a clear indicator of what the world is missing. Of the 597 Nobel laureates named since the Nobel Prize was established in 1901 up until 1990, only ten went to people of African birth, twelve went to Latin Americans and twenty-two went to people born in Asia.[7] As we'd expect, since 1990, these regions have been far more successful at raising globally noteworthy achievers. Africa and Asia have, in the last twenty-five years, doubled their prize totals from the previous nine decades.[†] But the weight of these three regions among prizewinners (16 per cent of all prizes since 1990) is still far below their share of the world's population (in 2015, about 85 per cent and rising).[8] This skew mainly reflects the fact that modern science remains primarily a Western construct, and only a sliver of the top thinkers from other regions can find their way into a top-tier Western university. For the rest, it's going to take more time for their home countries

---

[†]Latin America, with three more, is stuck at its original pace.

to build local research engines that can support leading-edge academic breakthroughs.

But these national and social biases also reflect prejudices that follow individuals wherever they work. Would two scientists at the same university, one African, the other British, enjoy the same consideration for salary, promotion, laboratory space and research money? Sadly, the research suggests not.[9] Women face similar hurdles. Only 5 per cent of all laureates up to 2013 have been women. Tracing this outcome back to differences between the male and female brains is 'neurotrash'.[10] The blame lies squarely on stubborn social biases that from a young age, and at every step up the career ladder, turn women away from studying maths and science. Everywhere, men and women live side by side in roughly equal numbers, but even in the world's most educated countries, women make up only about one-third of researchers.

Diversity has been an essential ingredient in creative breakthroughs from Copernicus' revolutionary map of the heavens to the Human Genome Project's map of our genome. Prejudice, in any form, dampens diversity, and in so doing kills good ideas before they're even born. Now is the best time in history to end it. The rapidly growing acceptance in many countries of alternative sexual orientations, for example, not only strengthens communities, but also, we believe, enriches humanity's collective creative powers. And it challenges all of us to diminish prejudice in its many other forms. Clearly, we can.

Plump up public patronage

The chief patrons of creative genius during the first Renaissance were the Medici family. Fabulously wealthy, they loved art, and they loved funding the forerunners of artistic style. Whenever the experimental works of Ghiberti (painting and sculpture), Donatello (sculpture) or Brunelleschi (architecture) challenged convention, it was Medici patronage that made it mainstream.

Then and now, genius needs generous patrons. Whether in art or science, there's usually a big gap between the creator's vision and the public's focus and attention. Money is the filler.

Some patrons are stepping up. The XPrize 'innovation engine', which offers major cash awards to any who make 'radical breakthroughs for the benefit of humanity', is one right idea.[11] Another hope is the crowd. Some among it are willing to support science for science's sake. In 2010, there were about 100 crowdfunding platforms running; together, they raised just under $900 million for posted projects.[12] By 2015, over 1,250 platforms together raised an estimated $35 billion.[13] That's more than the global venture capital industry invests in an average year (about $30 billion), and is on pace to triple, at least, by 2020.[14] Crowdfunding allows a wide population to support discovery work, and scientists especially need to get better at extending that invitation as part of the research proposals they write.

But crowdsourcing has its limits. Even faced with the best proposals, the crowd seems unlikely to take much interest in research. Over 70 per cent of 2015 crowdfunding was in the form of short-term, person-to-person loans that lenders expect to be repaid, with interest.[15] And science is notoriously bad at keeping to a quick repayment schedule when it's camped out on the far northern frontier of human understanding. Research, especially basic research, aims to acquire new knowledge, often without any particular application in view. The payoffs are just too far off and too uncertain for those with a profit motive to get involved. That's why, although the private sector funds almost 70 per cent of *total* research and development work across the developed world, it funds only about 20 per cent of the *basic* research activity within that total.[16]

Instead, state funding – to which a much bigger crowd of citizens contributes yearly through taxes – lines up better with the costs and time horizon of doing fundamental science. Copernican revolutions are spun out of such science, and state money is the spinner. There is no real substitute. Unfortunately, in developed countries, state patronage is heading in the wrong direction, in two senses.

First, it has flattened. Across North America and Europe, but especially in the United States and the UK, austerity has taken a big bite out of government research budgets.[17] In real dollar terms, the US government spends less now on civilian R&D than it did ten years ago.[18]

Second, patronage has become too conservative. Scarce funds, together with rising public pressure to show value for money, are squeezing much of the adventure out of public grant-giving. Consider the US National Institute of Health (NIH), which by itself accounts for nearly half of all US federal non-defence research spending. More and more, small applications for safe, incremental studies, whose results are mostly known in advance, win approval instead of big boundary-pushing discovery work: in 2013 and 2014, the average size of NIH grants fell to its lowest level since 1999.[19] And more and more, experience wins over youthful ambition. Back in 1990, only 2 per cent of grant recipients were aged sixty-five or older; 11 per cent were thirty-six or younger. Today, the situation has reversed; among grant recipients, the over-65s outnumber the under-36 recipients two to one.[20] Partly, this trend is driven by the underlying science. Cutting-edge medical research increasingly needs to pull many disciplines together, and it is only later in their careers that researchers possess the necessary breadth to lead such efforts. But this emphasis on experience comes at a cost. Many discouraged young researchers are giving up on science altogether.[21]

Patronage has lost much of the bold spirit that once guided it. Public leaders need to summon it up again. They need to *spend more*. State patronage of research across the developed world ought to grow by at least 3 per cent per year. And they should *expect less*, in terms of immediate payback. A higher share – we suggest over one-third – of the annual increase in state patronage should be reserved for outstanding applicants at any career stage to do original, high-risk work of uncertain value. When, in 1508, Pope Julius II commissioned Michelangelo to paint the ceiling of the Sistine Chapel, he didn't tell the artist to put *The Creation of Adam* here and *The Flood* there; he (eventually) allowed Michelangelo 'to do as I liked'.[22] Then and now, autonomy is a key ingredient in most feats of genius.

2. Dare to fail

The greater danger for most of us lies not in setting our aim
too high and falling short; but in setting our aim too low, and
achieving our mark.

Traditionally attributed to Michelangelo

This was popular wisdom 500 years ago, and it is true again today. In his 2013 book *Mass Flourishing*, Nobel Prize-winning economist Edmund Phelps urged his readers to replace 'a palpable decline in vitalism – in "*doing*"' — with more experimentation, exploration, tinkering and guessing, so that we as individuals and society will not merely plod along, but thrive.[23] In an age of discovery, the balance between risk and reward tips in favour of taking bold action.

First, because there is suddenly so much new territory to explore. Our politics and our economics have opened the world's populations and markets. We have instruments to probe the fundamental particles of matter and the vastness of space. We are developing computing power to simulate creation's most complex mysteries, from the formation of galaxies, to the regulation of the climate, to how the brain produces consciousness. By 2020, the global middle class will number three billion people, and we will be able to connect with them all through the smart devices in our pockets.[24]

Second, because our entanglement accelerates and spreads the value we can create for ourselves and others, we cannot foresee the full benefits our actions may bring. Social media is full of examples. *Flappy Bird*, a crude mobile game produced in three days, went viral in 2013 and earned its Vietnamese creator an estimated $50,000 per day.[25] In 2014, the Ice Bucket Challenge raised over $100 million worldwide in just thirty days, and more than $220 million overall, for research into amyotrophic lateral sclerosis (ALS), as friends invited friends to dump cold water over their heads for charity.[26] If you were one of them, you should know: you made a difference. A year later, in August 2015, scientists at Johns Hopkins announced a major breakthrough towards finding a cure.[27]

Third, the costs of failure are plummeting. Open-source software and hardware, global online platforms for capital-raising, manufacturing and distribution, and 3D printed prototypes have cut the cost of bringing to life a widening range of ideas. What a decade ago was not possible, or could only be attempted in giant labs, now can be affordably built in a small room or office. Do-it-yourself biotech engineers have built a polymerase chain reaction (PCR) machine, a $30,000 piece of lab equipment essential for all DNA tinkering, for less than $600. You can buy one at openpcr.org (some assembly required). Artists can gauge their talent and global appeal with no more upfront investment than a smart phone, a Twitter account and a lot of friend-making. Twenty years ago, to write commercially successful software typically meant getting a computer science degree and then a job at a software company. Now, it can be done after a few months of playing around with the free developer kits put out by the big mobile platform makers. It should be no surprise that Apple's developer community doubled, from 4.5 to 9 million programmers, between 2012 and 2014.[28]

The reputational costs of failure are falling, too. Don't be too proud of your fame; don't be ashamed if your innovation flops. More and more, both are driven by network effects beyond your control – and are quickly crowded out of everyone's mind by whatever topic trends next. Attention is cheap. Knowing that frees you to make a brief fool of yourself as often as it takes to achieve what's important to you.

How to be bold

The first courageous act is to take a long-term, big-picture view. The news and social media give us awareness of events, but we ourselves need to give those events *perspective*. We've had some tough years recently. We will suffer through more instability and more shocks, and as more of humanity plugs into the same tangled systems, the shocks will come more quickly, from a widening range of sources, and get bigger. All of that biases us to be cautious, if not downright pessimistic. But, as Parts I and II of this book show, there is an equal or better case for optimism. It's got the stronger data behind it.

But it's also less told. The media we consume tends to under-report and obscure the broad positive shifts that underlie the present age. These shifts – to new heights of human health, wealth, education and entanglement – are slow-moving relative to our favourite television dramas, and they're expressed in statistics instead of celebrity tweets. The news also over-reports the bad stuff. From coverage of 9/11 through to the rise of the Islamic State and the outbreak of civil war in Syria, it can feel as if the twenty-first century has had an especially violent start. The year 2014 was in fact the bloodiest, by total battlefield deaths, since the end of the Cold War. But there's another side: seven other civil wars ended in 2014, and ten peace agreements were concluded and signed.[29] Direct war *between* states – historically, the deadliest kind – hasn't broken out again since the invasion of Iraq in 2003.

It takes courage to hold onto the big picture, and even more to confront a prevailing pessimism with the case for confidence. We need to find that courage. While consuming the news of the day, let's commit to read, watch and interact with those who gaze upon the longer term – this year, this decade and decades to come. Let's also discover voices from beyond our national borders, and from beyond our own field or industry. Being open to divergent ideas will help keep our eyes and ears open to the flourishing of genius underway.

From there, set out on a new voyage of discovery. Columbus sought Asia and found America. Likewise, this century will reward explorers who set out on paths whose final destination is uncertain. This has always been true, but the opportunities are rarely as rich as they are right now. If you are young, turn your back on the immediate paydays that your peers are chasing. Spend the next year chasing visions, learning from failure and gaining unique, defining experiences. You will be amply rewarded in later life. If you are older, apprentice this next generation. In return, they will teach you many new things, and invigorate your next big move.

The economic equivalent of courage is to invest. Companies have been hoarding cash and treasuries have been tightening belts for several years now, because the global economic outlook remains uncertain. That's the short-term reality. But the bigger powers at work – global entanglement and human development – present great opportunities for those who align with them.

Now is the time to turn the tap back on and get ahead of overcautious competitors who lack your insight into the bigger picture. Companies and entrepreneurs that are showing the way include: IBM, which in 2014 announced a five-year plan to bet 10 per cent of its net income on post-silicon computer chips;[30] Google (Alphabet), whose recent long-term bets include a new quantum artificial intelligence lab, self-driving cars and research into anti-aging drugs;[31] and Elon Musk, a co-founder of PayPal whose moonshots include SpaceX (a space transport firm whose eventual goal is to colonize Mars) and Tesla (whose diverse aims include the mass-market adoption of electric cars, household battery packs to store renewable energy, and a 600-mile-per-hour hyperloop to transport people between Los Angeles and San Francisco).

Dare citizens to fail

Academic researchers and think tanks debate endlessly how to make public taxes, laws and regulations better. In truth, there is no one right answer. This is a values question as much as an empirical one, and around the world the policy response should draw on the values citizens cherish as well as the evidence.

But in a Renaissance age, asking the right policy *question* is at least as important as finding the right policy answer. It's not only 'How can government work better?' but also 'How can government *make people bolder*?' The same public systems that serve us also shape our behaviours. Wise governments will incentivize citizens to seize the opportunities in front of them.

Reform taxes. Our taxes pay for the goods that government delivers. But how those taxes are collected sharply shape social behaviour.

1. Shift the tax base upward. Progressive taxes (where the rich pay a higher percentage) embolden society by giving the poor more cash to work with and the rich more reason to reinvest theirs. For starters: close tax loopholes for individuals and multinationals alike, end deductions that mainly benefit the rich, and tax land (of which the poor have little or none) more heavily. The latter will also spur property speculators to develop more and hoard less.

2. Use taxes to discourage public bads (like congestion, pollution and fatty foods). Taxing income discourages work; taxing carbon emissions incentivizes people to find clever ways to reduce them.

3. Remove perverse energy and agricultural subsidies. They benefit the few, distort trade and are environmentally disastrous. Energy subsidies cost the world's taxpayers $5.3 trillion dollars (or 6.5 per cent of global GDP) in 2015; agricultural subsidies in the

OECD cost their citizens $600 billion.[32] Ending these subsidies would free up funds for bold investments in infrastructure, education and health, and raise incentives for renewable energy and sustainable farming – all at current tax levels.

4. Raise inheritance taxes. Knowing that we can't hoard as much wealth for our descendants will spur us to invest it in the present and reduce inequality across generations.

Strengthen the social safety net. Most people leap at the opportunity to get a job or switch to a better one. That much is clear from the rapid growth since the 1990s (especially among the bottom third of wage-earners) of part-time, freelance and other non-standard work arrangements – jobs that tend to pay less and offer fewer benefits, but are jobs nonetheless.[33] By accepting, or creating, non-standard work, people help the overall economy to flex and adapt to technological and market change. That can be good for everyone. But these individuals also endure weaker on-the-job training and a greater risk of slipping into poverty. They and their families shouldn't have to bear those costs alone — not least because society as a whole suffers when their productivity lapses. To support people's risk-taking in new, flexible labour markets, we need to solidify funding for unemployment and social security benefits, and widen eligibility rules to recognize new varieties of work.

Rebalance intellectual property (IP) protections. From the very first patent in Venice in 1486 to today, the reason why the law secures IP has been two-fold: to reward you for your innovation *and* to speed up the next one by giving the rest of us access to your ideas. Over the past twenty years, the balance has tipped in favour of the former. In most jurisdictions, copyright now endures for too long (up to seventy years, depending on the nature of the work), and patents are awarded too easily and too broadly. Progress in everything from art to biotech and software is slowed by this IP thicket. Bottom-up initiatives like the Creative Commons licence (creativecommons.org) have helped recalibrate copyright somewhat, but much more is needed. For starters, exemptions for academic research and non-commercial 'fair use' should be expanded. Licensing systems should be bolstered to make IP harder to squat on and easier to commercialize. Too many inventions are locked in the safes of large pharmaceutical and technology companies, which stifles innovation and slows the arrival of drugs that might improve, even save, millions of lives. At the same time, IP protections need to be extended to those whose claims have long gone unrecognized – to indigenous peoples, for example, so that they can go to court to stop the free plunder of their traditional medicines or music.

Simplify regulations. The IP thicket is slow going; the regulatory thicket can be well-nigh impassable. Research shows that as rules for setting up a new company increase, start-up activity falls.[34] In general, the more rules regulators make, the harder it is for society to follow them, and the more creative resources get wasted on compliance. Armies of lawyers are required simply to navigate regulations, greatly raising the barrier to entry for start-ups and small firms. This wastage is rising rapidly, as regulators try to tame the present moment's complexity with complicatedness. The total amount of paperwork required by the 2010 Dodd–Frank Act, US lawmakers' 848-page response to the 2008 financial crisis, passed 30,000 person-years in 2014.[35] By one estimate, that's more time wasted filling forms than it would have taken to catalogue every species on the planet.[36]

Lawmakers and regulators need to resist this tendency. In uncertain times, proven rules of thumb applied by highly experienced supervisors serve as well as (or better than) sophisticated models – and cost society far, far less.[37] Recruit the wisest people, pay them accordingly and empower them to set and surveil smart, succinct rules.

3. Find your Florence

During the fifteenth and early sixteenth centuries, Florence was quite unlike anywhere else in the Western world. Its location in the heart of Italy made it a major crossroads for trade and finance, and a front line for exchange with the East. While much of Europe subsisted on gruel, Florentines walked through markets hawking eggplant and asparagus from Armenia, bananas from Egypt, chickpeas from Turkey, spinach from Persia and, later, chilli pepper, chocolate and corn from the Americas. Intellectually, too, they lived in a world apart. The Florentine population boasted the highest rate of literacy in the wider Western world, with more than 30 per cent of citizens able to read and write at a time when perhaps fewer than 10 per cent of Europeans could sign their own name. More than three-quarters of Florence's youth received schooling, and social mobility – a fantasy amidst the rigid hierarchy that defined much of Europe – was a real possibility for a person possessed of superior skill, talents or knowledge. Ordinary burghers became powerful politicians, humble merchants embarked on great trading ventures and sharp-minded paupers received scholarships to become accomplished secretaries of the state.[38]

Culturally, Florence was likewise renowned. The Medici were based there and pumped money into project after project to aggrandize themselves and their city-state. The place gave birth to Donatello, Brunelleschi, Leonardo da Vinci, Michelangelo, Machiavelli and other innovators, and throughout the Renaissance boasted more artistic masters per capita than anywhere else in Europe. The settled artist population was amplified by a constant stream of migrants – travelling masters, apprentices, apprentice-wannabes – who came to spot the latest trends, learn new techniques and share their passion. One of the first great works of Renaissance art – the *Duomo*, capped by Brunelleschi's dome – was raised in Florence's central square, and to this day many of the age's greatest masterpieces reside in the city's museums.

Place matters

It's tempting to think that place matters much less than it used to. Vital inputs – materials, capital, people and ideas – now circulate globally. Through the digital medium, we can access information, communicate with one another and work from anywhere. Surely, the more entangled the world becomes, the less our physical location matters.

In fact, the opposite is true. When it comes to working genius, *where* you choose to plant yourself matters more than ever, for two reasons: craft and concentration.

Craft

Knowledge circulates ever more freely, but probe beneath knowledge and within every domain you will find a more profound, and far stickier, expertise – what the economist Brian Arthur terms *deep craft*.[39]

Craft was what made Florence a magnet for artists in the first Renaissance; not knowledge, which increasingly was being made available to everyone, everywhere through the medium of print, but a *set of knowings* that formed within and were bound within a tight community of practice. That set included: knowing which experiments were likely to work and which ones not; knowing which novelties to ignore as passing fads and which ones might add lasting value; knowing whom to consult to get past this or that artistic or technical obstacle; knowing whom to petition, and how, to secure scarce resources.

Such tacit understandings are taken for granted by any skilled practitioner, but hard for her to put into words if asked. Consequently, deep craft tends to stay in the place where it originates. It imparts extra momentum, enthusiasm and odds of success to creative activity in that privileged place. All boundary-pushing artists of the Renaissance, if they had the means, made the pilgrimage to Florence to profit from the wisdom that soaked its workshops, market squares and palazzi.

The lure of deep craft was very strong then, but it is much stronger now. Our science, technology and systems are far more advanced. Whether you mix music, write code, engineer robots or estimate economic growth, the mysteries at the leading edge are deeper and take longer to learn, the range of disciplines that must come together to make a breakthrough is wider, and the universe of possible solutions is so vast that only a well-honed intuition can keep you on a productive path. All this multiplies the unspoken knowings that separate the able from the adept, and makes the craft harder to transfer to other places.

Seek the physical place where people from all over go to share your passion. Commit a real chunk of time – a year, for starters – to being there, connecting there and creating something there.

Concentration

If you haven't yet found your passion, or if it defies simple definition, the best place to look for it is in one of the world's great or growing cities.

Part II highlighted the environmental conditions that help genius to flourish: a rich and varied flow of ideas, many well-educated brains, and private and social incentives that focus the latter upon creative work. Inevitably, big cities meet these conditions best.

Part III explained why that's the case, and it's the other reason why place matters now more than ever: concentration. Creative inputs don't flow evenly everywhere. Set them into global motion, and they very quickly *pool* in those places that boast advantages along the remaining dimensions of difference: geography, climate, infrastructure, government policy or the hard-to-define 'buzz' bred by the crowds and complexity of a big city.

In the first Renaissance, which cities ranked among the great was obvious. Paris was the largest city in the Western world.[40] Rome was eternal, the religious hub of Western Christendom. All roads led to it. Florence oozed Medici-financed magnificence. Constantinople, the jewel of the East – renamed Istanbul – sparkled anew under the fresh patronage of its sultans. The emerging centres – Seville, glistening with New World silver, innovative Antwerp, plus Lisbon, Madrid, London and Amsterdam – were becoming Asian and Atlantic gateways.

Today, cities are still the beating heart of civilization – even more so. Home to over half of humanity, cities hold most of our wealth, attract most of our investment and generate more than four-fifths of global economic activity.[41] The hundred largest cities in economic terms make up 40 per cent of global GDP by themselves. The best known among them – New York, San Francisco, London, Paris, Singapore, Tokyo – are the Florence, Rome and Constantinople of today. And while their lights shine brightest, in sheer numbers they are dwarfed by the hundreds of new Sevilles, Antwerps and Amsterdams. Each one, from India's textile capital, Surat, to Brazil's Porto Alegre (city-host of the inaugural World Social Forum), is a portal to new and exciting experiences.

These cities are all places of stress and conflict. (During the first Renaissance, Florence's homicide rate soared.[42]) But they are also the crossroads where creative resources exist in the greatest abundance and where developmental and connective forces collide – literally in the streets – to generate constant newness. They are the crucibles of innovation and opportunity, and worth not just visiting, but living in.

Build a new crossroads

In our role as citizens, vested with the power and the responsibility to shape our own communities, the task is not to find our Florence, but to re-create it. Some of Florence's appeal derived from natural factors – its central location, for example. Most of it was built. We can repeat that achievement.

The first step is to strengthen our communities' physical or digital foundations for exchange. Very few cities in the world have the geographical good fortune or state backing to raise a new global hub, as Dubai and Shanghai are doing. But where brute strength is unavailable, good governance and good citizenship can accomplish much. In the early days of the internet, local operators in Amsterdam foresaw the benefits of building a shared, neutral hub where everyone's networks could join up and trade traffic. Today, the city is the world's largest internet exchange point, where 650 network operators from every continent connect. The world-class data infrastructure has made Amsterdam a European hotspot for technology firms, but also for financial institutions and others for whom fast, reliable network access is a competitive advantage.

Toronto, meanwhile, has established itself as one of the world's busiest crossroads for people. Over half of the city's residents are immigrants, making it the most open city on earth in per capita terms.[43] Its success at absorbing 100,000 new foreigners per year, every year, is rooted in a well-oiled infrastructure of municipal programmes, such as a Newcomer Strategy that coordinates hospitals, schools and service organizations, and an Immigration Portal that helps immigrants to access public benefits like health care, affordable housing and childcare, and language education. What they give back to their host city more than makes up for the cost.[44] In 2015, *The Economist's* Safe Cities Index ranked Toronto 'the best place to live' in the world – confounding those who want to argue that immigration is a bad thing.[45]

Other big cities showing how to become new global crossroads through deliberate design include Mumbai (global offshore services), Lagos (African trade and finance) and Tel Aviv (technology). Smaller cities, if well run, can become major intersections at a niche or regional level. Copenhagen may never challenge New York or London for traditional financial flows, but it is rapidly becoming a hub for crypto-currencies. Per capita, more Bitcoins are used in Scandinavia than anywhere else.[46] Regina, a small city in the middle of the Canadian Prairies, in 2010 opened one of Canada's largest inland ports, a 1,700-acre Global Transportation Hub, to interconnect North America's major rail and trucking networks. A city in the middle of nowhere is equidistant from everywhere, and as global trade volumes swell, such places can make themselves essential nodes to help balance loads across different transportation systems.

Accommodate newcomers

Diversity cannot thrive in places where not everyone can afford to live. Property prices are rising faster than incomes in many of the world's big and upcoming cities.[47] London prices jumped 20 per cent in 2014 alone.[48] Those who cannot afford to buy now watch the dream of home ownership move further and further away. Meanwhile, increasing rents and time spent commuting can squeeze out the benefits that lure people to the city in the first place. To foster human flows, cities need to increase the density and supply of housing, expand affordable housing (not least for young people) and prevent speculators from cornering the market.

Cities also need higher-up policy support to flourish as crossroads for people. A vice chairman of General Electric, one of the world's largest corporations whose slogan is 'Imagination at Work', remarked in 2014 that 'All innovation now involves collaboration between societies.' When a national government wields immigration policy to insulate its society from others, every creative ambition within its borders suffers.

Unfortunately, that has been the recent trend across the developed world. In the United States, eleven million undocumented immigrants are trapped in an American half-life – able, in seven out of ten cases, to find low-skilled work,[49] but unable to access public services or pay the taxes that would make them full members of their host communities.[50] High-skilled immigrants are also being turned away. In 2004, the annual visa quota for skilled temporary workers in the United States was slashed from 195,000 to 85,000,[51] making it much harder for foreign students to linger in the country past graduation.[†] This dampened innovation almost immediately. In the decade 1995–2005, 52 per cent of Silicon Valley tech start-ups were founded or co-founded by immigrants. Since then, that figure has fallen to 42 per cent.[52] Would-be entrepreneurs still come to America to fill their heads with ideas (more than half of the 150,000 students who each year earn advanced maths, science and engineering degrees from US universities are foreign-born), but more and more are returning home to set up their companies (and create the associated jobs and wealth).[53]

Even if the intention behind tighter immigration controls is to help citizens during a time of economic distress, the overall results are the opposite. In 2013, the non-partisan US

[†]To be precise, the quota is 65,000 visas, plus another 20,000 reserved specifically for holders of advanced degrees awarded by US universities.

Congressional Budget Office estimated that failing to reform current immigration laws could cost the US economy over 5 per cent in lost growth over the next twenty years, and nearly $900 billion in missed tax revenues.[54] In the UK, research shows that halving annual migrant inflows could cause the UK economy to contract by some 10 per cent over the next fifty years, due to an aging and shrinking native labour force.[55] More to the point here, poor immigration policies dampen cities' efforts to create a cosmopolitan buzz, and raising higher walls wastes public money that could be better spent on municipal roads, airports, fibre and other windows to the world. (From 2005 to 2014, America's population of undocumented immigrants nudged up only 10 per cent, from an estimated ten million to eleven million.[56] Nonetheless, annual federal spending on immigration enforcement grew 80 per cent, from $10 billion to $18 billion – surpassing all other federal law enforcement agencies combined.[57]) It is past time to reverse anti-immigrant trends.

* * *

The above half of the agenda is asking a lot of ourselves, and of our politics. Most people and places will have a hard time harnessing anything close to the potential that this age offers. Those who do will be the change-makers, and host the creative hubs, of the twenty-first century.

Mitigate flourishing risk

The first Renaissance also imparted wisdom to help us cope with flourishing risk.

1. Make new maps

Learned people in the first Renaissance completely changed their mental map of the world to suit the new challenges they faced. We still have some way to go.

The chief obstacle to a more accurate idea of our earth is the language we use to group countries and people. In this book, for example, we cannot avoid talking about the 'developed' and 'developing' worlds, about 'rich' and 'poor' countries, or about 'advanced' and 'emerging' economies. So much data, analysis and opinion are trapped in these simple dichotomies that it is hard to say anything about the state of the world today without reference to them.

But they are all misleading.

First, they suggest that the 'developed', 'advanced' and 'rich' countries have reached some sort of stable endpoint in the human story. No idea could be more wrong than that – both because political, economic and social innovation continues to transform them all, and because every advanced country faces immense challenges that have yet to be worked out.

Second, they suggest that 'developed' countries are at the core of world affairs, whereas the 'developing' are at the periphery. Hardly. By 2014, so-called 'emerging' markets accounted for a larger share of world GDP (57 per cent) than the advanced economies.[58] And the biggest developing countries, like China and India, have a more important role to play in, say, solving climate change than many developed ones.

Third, these dichotomies suggest that the countries within each grouping are broadly similar. That, too, is bogus. Within each group can be found diametric differences in governance and regime (from democracies to absolute monarchies), economy and population size (China's economy is almost as large as all other developing economies put together) and resource endowments. Malawi is land-locked; its neighbour Mozambique enjoys vast offshore gas reserves.

Our mental maps have to evolve. No simple dichotomy can describe the political, economic, social and environmental variety across the world today. When we use one, we risk blurring the very issues that matter most, and worsening the cognitive blind spots that Chapter 7 warned against. An immediate improvement would be to think about the world in two dimensions instead of one, with the absolute size of countries along one axis and some measure of per capita development along the other. But, as Mercator discovered when making his famous map, there is no one best way to project a round sphere onto a flat surface. However we do it, some parts will always be distorted.

Our labelling, too, needs to improve. Christian, Muslim, Jew, Hindu, Buddhist and atheist are crude identifiers that often do more to isolate us than to help us find one another. Islamic democracies in Turkey, Senegal, Indonesia and elsewhere, and Buddhist ethnic cleansing in Myanmar, belie our attempts to colour-code people based on faith.

If we can keep these errors in mind, while also attempting to draw more precise conceptions of the globe, we'll navigate the twenty-first century better.

2. Admit risk

Venice's greatest mistake was complacency in the face of increasingly clear vulnerabilities. We are in danger of repeating it.

Our own complacency has two roots: lack of awareness and lack of urgency. How to tackle the first is straightforward: political leadership, public education and social media campaigns have all proven effective. Take one of the biggest issues in the world today: climate change. In 2014, about the same time that the United Nations' Intergovernmental Panel on Climate Change released an updated report on the increasing likelihood of 'severe, pervasive and irreversible impacts', surveys showed that climate change ranked somewhere between twelfth (in Europe) and fourteenth (in the United States) on people's list of worries.[59] By mid-2015, in the build-up to the United Nations Climate Change Conference in Paris, it had risen to third and sixth, respectively. And survey respondents across sub-Saharan Africa and Latin America (regions especially vulnerable to climate change) rated it the top global threat they could see – far ahead of global economic instability, Iran's nuclear programme or the rise of the Islamic State.[60] So we know how to put things on the global public's radar.

But raising urgency is far more difficult.

'Should' is a long way from 'Will'

It's obvious what we *should* do. When faced with high and uncertain risks, humanity has always had two general coping strategies available: robustness and resiliency. The idea of the first is to strengthen each part so that it is less likely to fail. The idea of the second is to diversify, so that when one part does fail the whole can still function. Today, this is the language of systems theorists, but we all know it intuitively. So did Columbus. He had no idea what dangers he was sailing into, so he built the hulls of his ships extra thick, and he sailed a fleet of three of them together.

This wisdom still works. It has, for instance, guided regulators' response to the global financial crisis. In the years since, they have required banks to hold more capital in reserve against their own lending activities (making each bank more robust).

They have also set up new processes to improve multilateral surveillance, restrict speculative money flows and diversify the emergency funds available to stricken states (making the overall banking system more resilient).

The same wisdom tells us that we *should* add some fat back into our companies' inventories, diversify supply chains and diversify the strategies available to management by hiring more executives whose names don't end in the same 'MBA'.

We *should* identify the overburdened nodes in public infrastructure – in power grids, ports and levees – and upgrade them to withstand a hard-hitting century. Through either regulation or incentives, we should spread out critical infrastructure – like internet exchanges, financial hubs and transport control centres – geographically, and away from vulnerable zones. (In an ideal world, we'd even spread out ourselves. We'd move away from hurricane-prone coastlines and floodplains, and from sunny but water-scarce deserts.)

We *should* help poorer countries – the places where new pandemics like H5N1 are most likely to erupt – to strengthen their public health systems, and we should build and maintain a global 'rapid reaction force' that can swoop in and contain an outbreak when local efforts fail. We should reinvest in the World Health Organization, whose current budget of about $2.2 billion per year is only that of a single, big-city hospital.[61]

We *should* put in place carbon taxes, which would discourage fossil fuel use and slow climate change, and should help save our shared global assets or 'global commons' – the oceans, polar regions and, especially, rain forests, which are a giant carbon sink and home to 50–75 per cent of Earth's biodiversity.[62]

We *should* invest heavily in the world's poor and the young so that they can take part in the global gains being made around them, by providing free preschool, primary and secondary schooling and direct cash transfers to female heads of poor households – conditional upon their children attending school and getting vaccinated. All this should be paid for by more progressive income taxes, harder-to-avoid corporate taxes and a shift from universal to means-tested welfare programmes. We should aggressively liberalize migration, which would reinvigorate aging advanced economies and increase the positive spillover of rich-world incomes, knowledge, skills and institutions to the poor.

Foresight is no one's responsibility

The problem is, for the most part we don't – and won't – do the things we know we ought to. The banking industry deserves no credit for its reforms. Those were made in hindsight, after the shock had already struck and the damage had been done.[†] We

---

[†] The reforms are also incomplete. Global banking has become more concentrated, not less, since the crisis. Most countries' big banks are still 'too big to fail' and take risks they shouldn't because they know from recent experience that their government (i.e. taxpayers) will bail them out if they bet wrongly.

can always be trusted to make some changes after a deep and painful crisis.

But can we do so *before*? Clear hindsight is a bitter reminder of how hard it is for us to take preventive steps. The reason is that everywhere we might look for leadership on these matters, we instead find people and institutions that are obliged to repeat the same behaviours that make us vulnerable.

Governments, both authoritarian and democratic, are obliged to keep their own supporters and citizens happy. People want government to solve their clear and immediate concerns: the economy, the debt, unemployment, welfare, crime. In comparison, as Chapter 7 showed, most major risks we face present a genuine dilemma between promoting private goods (choice, consumption, profit, efficiency) and accepting public bads (such as pollution, inequality and the occasional calamity). The complexity of how the former cause the latter makes it hard to convince the public to spend tax dollars or swallow tough trade-offs. The unevenness of costs and benefits across geographies (costs borne here, benefits felt there) and generations (costs borne today, benefits enjoyed by the as-yet-unborn) makes it nearly impossible.

Companies are obliged to keep their owners happy. Some owners, like pension funds, focus on long-term financial health, but most look for shorter term profits – and in the short run, risk prevention rarely delivers a return on investment. The system-wide benefits, while real, appear nowhere on a single company's financial statements. The costs do. On the other hand, reliable ways to boost short-term profits include: concentrating production in lower cost hubs; making freer use of the global commons (air, rivers, forests, oceans); or avoiding domestic taxes by shifting profits overseas.

Finally, as individuals, we are obliged to develop into the best people we can be and to provide the best life we can for our loved ones. For most of us, these duties weigh more heavily than other, wider concerns we might recognize. Yes, other things also matter to us, and that's why some of us drive electric cars or cycle to work, support socially responsible businesses, and volunteer or give to charity. But we all have a very hard time denying ourselves and our families goods that everyone else freely consumes. How many of us are willing to give up air travel for the sake of the atmosphere? Who among us is willing to forego the use of antibiotics to slow the emergence of resistant bugs, or to relocate away from the coast to help make their country more resilient against hurricanes? How much income are we willing to forego to prevent rare catastrophes from happening, or to help the excluded feel included?

If the dangers were clear and immediate, then maybe we would be willing to make a sacrifice. But the causal link between our personal lives and the systemic threats our lives generate is so complex, it's hard to know how much – if any – difference our own choices make. Regardless, it would seem that the concentrations built up by so many people making free-but-similar choices overwhelm any positive impact our lone sacrifice might have. Like Venetian merchants a half-millennium before us, the most rational-seeming choice is to keep our heads down, follow the crowd, do right by our families and wait for some technology or policy to change social behaviour en masse – probably in reaction to the next big shock.

The biggest step towards a safer twenty-first century is to admit to ourselves that this is how a lot of society runs; this is how many of us approach life. Every day in which we do not actively map new connections, we become more lost in their complexity. Every day we do not actively diversify social wealth, corporate suppliers, public infrastructure and our mental attention, they become more concentrated. All of us, whether we realize it or not, have already suffered injury from our inaction against these risks – be it financial loss, diminished health or lost opportunity. But we choose to let these risks accumulate because we cannot seem to do otherwise.

3. Stoke virtue

As though the maker and moulder of thyself, thou mayest fashion thyself in whatever shape thou shalt prefer.

Giovanni Pico della Mirandola, Oration on the Dignity of Man[63]

Is our inability to change before it's too late simply the tragic human condition, or can we rise above it?

Chapter 4 began by observing that one of the most important thought projects of the first Renaissance was to prove that, indeed, we can. Humanists, from Petrarch to Erasmus and Machiavelli, began to revise the medieval notion of 'Man's' fixed place in the Great Chain of Being, and embraced the possibility that we could reshape ourselves through our own will and actions.

The instrument of our self-shaping, they proposed, was virtue. Virtue, the Greek Aristotle had explained, was just that quality of character to act as one *should*, even when doing so is difficult, or unpopular, or upsets vested interests. For fifteenth- and sixteenth-century humanists in search of a practical response to the moral decay they saw around them, virtue had two important features. First, it is learned by doing. We cannot be taught the virtues. They are habits of thought and action, and the only way to gain them is to go out and try to do virtuous things. Eventually a habit is formed, and virtue becomes our new nature. Second, virtue is infectious; it can become endemic to a place. Our virtuous actions don't just shape us; they shape society around us by helping to produce a tradition in which such behaviour becomes meaningful and common. The more people who govern their own actions by a particular virtue, the more it becomes a norm that governs others.

By exploiting these features, Renaissance humanists stoked virtue in the world around them, and strove to make it commonplace in their own time. For inspiration, they drew upon the already well-known lives of the saints, and upon exemplars from ancient Greece and Rome. Architects revived the classical sense of harmonious proportion. Artists revived the classical conceptions of beauty. Politicians revived Cicero's habits of rhetoric, rational argument and civic participation.

Humanists had a harder time promoting classical virtues of social and political leadership – wisdom, fairness, civility, courage – as the crises and conflicts of their time attest. But they had the right idea. Today's social scientists don't often invoke 'virtue', but they do talk a lot about norms. Nudging behavioural norms is a powerful way to reshape outcomes in complex systems. Top-down control fails because the technocrats in charge cannot possibly know enough to get their directives right (and even if they do, the directives are hard to enforce). Bottom-up efforts fail because they depend on people to change their own behaviour out of reflective, long-term self-interest, and too few people act consistently for the long term. But norms are internalized habits of action that directly regulate our own behaviour and infect others around us. Take the widespread increase in obesity, for example. Mandating that everyone lead a healthier lifestyle is unworkable. Relying on individuals to take better care of themselves has only produced the present epidemic. But take an obese person and put him into a healthy community, and research shows that that person is likely to get fit.

The difference between a norm and a virtue is that the former can shape our behaviour without us even being aware of it, whereas the latter is a habit that we deliberately choose to cultivate. There are many helpful habits that, if we choose to cultivate them, will help us to better weather the risks (and seize the opportunities) we face today. Some are classic, others contemporary. But three – honesty, audacity and dignity – stand out.

Honesty

In the developing world, an estimated $1–2 trillion per year is siphoned away from public treasuries by corrupt officials and cosy monopolists, facilitated by global investors and financial firms in the developed world.[64] In advanced economies, scandals like the five-year diesel emissions fraud uncovered at Volkswagen in 2015, or the twenty-year Libor rate-fixing swindle conducted by London banks until 2012, remind us that people everywhere may cheat when given the incentive and opportunity. And whistle-blowers remind us that the problem includes government officials, who may be influenced by lobbyists to put the few ahead of the many, or by powerful bureaucracies to put, say, data collection ahead of citizens' privacy rights.

Such deceptions cost everyone. Direct financial losses stand out because they are quantifiable. But, in addition, important public objectives, like cleaner air and safer consumer goods, are thwarted; protected resources, like bluefin tuna or rare hardwoods, are strained; new policy agendas, like the one laid out here, are denied the tax revenues they need; and people's rights – to privacy, but also to fairness and even life – can be abused.

Headline-making misbehaviours elicit predictable top-down responses: we improve oversight, and maybe toughen punishments, to deter wrongdoers from committing similar crimes again. Such responses are necessary, but incomplete. They don't grapple with the deeper truth: the 'wrongdoer' often isn't a person, but, rather, a shared culture in which putting a private interest before a public good, or duty, is sometimes deemed okay. When even iconic companies like Volkswagen choose to deceive millions of customers and regulators worldwide rather than shoulder their share of a global burden, it is a worrying sign to all of us that society's ethics may not be strong enough to reliably do the right thing in the face of even greater stresses to come.

We urgently need to stoke honesty in society, from the bottom up. Honesty breeds trust – perhaps *the* essential attribute of a more robust, resilient humanity. There are two ways everyone can help it grow.

The first is to **share our data**, because the more we share, the fewer harmful secrets we can keep from one another. Governments can join the open data movement and make taxpayer-funded databases available to taxpayers (see data.gov or data.gov.uk). Corporations can sign up with data-sharing initiatives like the Extractive Industries Transparency Initiative, Publish What You Pay and Transparency International to make decisions that impact public goods known to the public. Individuals can be more forthcoming to the right professionals about experiences of sexual and labour exploitation, and mental and physical health problems, to help society to see better when and where it's breaking down.

The second thing we can do is to **improve the quality of our data**, because inconsistent, incomplete, disorganized facts can blind our awareness as surely as secrecy. No one really knows how many tax dollars are lost to crime, or species lost to urban development. No one knows exactly how many migrants there are in the world, where they're coming from and going to; every country keeps its own, inconsistent statistics. Sometimes, the problem is that we 'know' too much. In the run-up to the 2007–2008 financial crisis, bank managers and regulators were inundated with industry data. What they lacked was the ability to compare it, distil it and extract from it the information that would have made the system's fragility plain. Governments: start up WorldStat, a new multilateral agency, to improve practices of data collection and analysis, especially in the developing world.[65] Industries: standardize your risk assessments, so that it's easier to compare with one another and build a more accurate picture of industry-wide threats. Individuals: upload your location-based awareness of neighbourhood issues through public data apps like *SeeClickFix* or *Nextdoor*.

The more transparent we all are, the less likely we will be to rely upon suspicions, stereotypes and misinformation, and the easier it will be for us to trust one another. Every act of openness and honesty helps.

Audacity

I certainly believe this: that it is better to be impetuous than cautious ...[66]

Niccolò Machiavelli

Audacity is an ancient virtue. *Audentis Fortuna iuvat* ('Fortune favours the bold'), Virgil wrote in his first-century BC epic, *The Aeneid*.[67] In his own time, Machiavelli agreed, although the luck he had in mind was the ill variety. For him, Fortune was 'one of those destructive rivers that, when they become enraged, flood the plains, ruin the trees and buildings, raising the earth from one spot and dropping it onto another'.[68] In the face of her fury, he deemed audacity to be the one virtue above all others whose absence would be most bitter.

Amidst chaos and uncertainty, the most prudent course is often to take risks. Why? Because while boldness helps us to flourish, it also helps us to endure. Impetuous initiative is what kicks people out of the bad habits that ill fortune exploits. (When disaster strikes, people 'should not blame Fortune, but rather their own indolence'.[69]) Audacity is what produces new discoveries that force people to update their awareness and keep pace with a rapidly shifting world. It is what stokes the public's confidence in their leaders, and gives them hope that the latter can guide them through the storms ahead.

Today, we need more of all these things that boldness brings – but especially the confidence and hope. Current sentiments of anti-globalization, Euro-scepticism and protectionism are the inevitable public response to short-term and small-minded initiatives in the face of big shocks and long-term worries. At this point, only audacious actions will convince an increasingly sceptical public that our growing entanglement can be made to serve positive ends, rather than just exposing us all to greater stress and danger.

Go first. Not everyone will see the imperative to act when you do, and you can no longer wait for them. The opportunity costs are too great for your initiative to be held back by those who lack the vision or mandate to take part. Make it a habit to gather together the like-minded and get started. Through crowd launchpads like solutions.thischangeseverything.org, individuals and communities can find hundreds of ways to make a real difference. Business groups such as the B Team, the World Business Council for Sustainable Development and the UN Global Compact offer industry a similar opportunity to challenge indolence and do good. Leading companies need to lead.

Much of what needs to be done can be done by 'coalitions of the working' – groups of influential citizens, companies, cities or countries that get the issue, get the urgency and by their coordinated actions generate momentum that pulls the laggards along.[70] The C40 cities initiative (c40.org), originally comprising forty megacities (now sixty-nine) around the world, is a good template. Member cities commit to take practical actions to cut greenhouse gases and share best practices among themselves. Many global challenges can be met when a few big players get together like this. These challenges include climate change – over half of the world's carbon emissions are produced by just four countries (China, the United States, India and Russia) – and finance, in which the top thirty-odd banks can make or break the health of the global banking system.

Burn, responsibly. To adopt new behaviours is to replace old ones, and that is never easy. Social habits – of consumption, of distribution, of investment – are reinforced daily by the benefits we get from them. Leading by doing and other positive example-setting is not always enough to make society abandon established practice, vested interests or sunk costs. Sometimes, it takes a fire from below.

To stand and speak against abuses of authority or bad practice is hard, but to remain silent is timid and unworthy of us. 'You are not only responsible for what you say, but also for what you do not say', Martin Luther is reputed to have taught. Humans are by nature social creatures, the Greek philosopher Aristotle instructed, and that means we express our values publicly. If, instead, we retreat into a kind of cloistered virtue, taking refuge inside our own personal monastery to avoid confrontation with global developments, we are denying ourselves a fundamental part of being fully alive.

Moreover, we deny our duty as citizens. For Cicero in ancient Rome and the Renaissance humanists who revived his ideas, citizenship – by which they meant serving society in order to make it stronger – was the whole point of the virtuous life.[71] 'We are not born, we do not live for ourselves alone; our country, our friends, have a share in us.'[72] The twenty-first century needs each of us to acknowledge that share.

Citizenship is also what separates the conscientious fire-setter from the indiscriminate arsonist. Girolamo Savonarola and Martin Luther, though agents of great upheaval, were first and foremost devout members of the Christian community. Both began their careers as friars, and both took a revolutionary turn only after they decided that the institutions of Christian authority had strayed from their purpose. Without doubt, Luther's Reformation weakened the temporal power of the Catholic Church, but it also hastened a Counter-Reformation that aimed to train priests better, fight corruption and refocus its leaders on spiritual matters. Other impassioned reformers, like Desiderius Erasmus and Thomas More, famously stayed loyal to their church but changed it from within by stubbornly demanding that it hold itself to its own professed standards.

We, too, must become advocates of the virtues that are lacking in our communities. For starters, we can punish misbehaviour through social media. With our voices and our votes, we can call for the establishment of tougher anti-corruption agencies and stronger antitrust policies so that the public can 'follow the money'. We can demand stronger civil oversight of public and state security.

And we can demand civility — of ourselves and others — in our dealings with one another.

But also, **demand more from the rich**. The Medici spent huge sums on public works, partly out of generosity, but also under social pressure. In a Christian world that professed the virtues of charity and poverty, possessing huge wealth put one on shaky moral ground. The rich needed a new virtue to legitimize their outsized fortunes, and patronage was it. By funding art, architecture and scholarship, they sought to convince society that great fortunes could be a good thing – *if* put to good use. Gradually, they succeeded. Eulogies at fourteenth-century funerals commended the renunciation of worldly goods; by the fifteenth and sixteenth centuries, they praised industry and acquisition.[73]

Today, the onus is again on the wealthy to justify their hoards, although the underlying morality is increasingly secular. No fortune is wholly earned by its possessor's own efforts. Parents, teachers and luck all play a big part along the way – as do publicly provisioned goods like knowledge, technology, markets and infrastructure. Digitization, by multiplying the market reach of a single good idea, yields a 'winner-take-all' effect (think Facebook, Uber or Airbnb) that only widens the gap between what one justly earns and what one accumulates.[74]

The evidence says that the rich haven't done nearly enough to make that gap acceptable to the societies they live in. Since the turn of the century, total global private wealth has more than doubled; the number of millionaire households worldwide has more than tripled (from 5.5 million to 16.3 million); and the latter – despite making up only 1.1 per cent of households globally – have concentrated more than half of all private wealth into their own hands.[75] Global private *giving* is harder to quantify, but it certainly hasn't kept pace. For example, from 2008 to 2011, when global wealth swelled by some $22 *trillion*, annual philanthropy destined for the developing world from twenty-three major developed countries plus Brazil, Russia, India and China nudged up only $4 *billion* (from $55 billion to $59 billion per year).[76]

Some among the rich do recognize the debt they owe to society. Efforts like the Giving Pledge, a public vow by participating billionaires to give more than half their wealth away, are helping shift norms of private patronage in the right direction.

But too many still do not fully recognize this debt, and it will take pressure from the rest of society to help them do so. Reserve your respect for givers. 'What's your plan to give back?' should be the first question we all ask the newly minted rich. Name and (if they won't give back) shame society's oligarchs, whose great wealth is too often the result of a government handout or bad regulation. Ultimately, if the rich won't give more, then demand more progressive tax reforms.

Dignity

Dignity is the practice of respecting and exploring one's full potential as a human being. For the humanists of the first Renaissance, this exploration was a sort of meta-virtue that underlay their whole philosophy. They recognized that some habits of thought and action are humanizing, in that they expand the worth and variety of our potentials and values, while others are literally de-humanizing, because they reduce the human experience down to just one or a few ends – like money or fame or economic growth.

Of all the virtues we can strive to revive, dignity is the most personal and has the greatest power to reshape the human condition. The present age is falling into the dangerous habit of commodifying our lives and focusing on material possessions and status symbols rather than deeper, shared values. Within our increasingly rational and secular value systems, we are discounting the long term. We are discounting the liberal arts. (Since 1990, the number of bona fide liberal arts schools in the United States has fallen by 40 per cent.[77]) We are discounting community, tradition and sometimes even the sanctity of life – as evidenced by the nearly 4,000 Syrian refugees who were allowed to drown or go missing in 2015 as they attempted to cross the Mediterranean into Europe.[78] Humanity's highest purposes simply don't *weigh* upon our thoughts, individual or collective, as much or as consistently as they should. In short, we are eroding the nobility and beauty of being alive. Is it any wonder that many of us feel cut off?

To build a more inclusive world, and one in which the long term matters more, we all need to widen and deepen our habitual appreciation of what makes life worth living.

Don't just get an education. Make one. More, better education for all must be a top priority. The returns on education peak in a Renaissance age: society's need for educated people mushrooms, and the opportunities to deploy one's education, for personal and social enrichment, multiply. The faster the world changes, the faster we need to learn – and re-learn, as the 'truths' we once lived by expire.

The flip side is that the penalty for missing out on education and training has never been higher. Because the returns on education are so great, differences in educational attainment are one of the biggest factors widening the achievement gap, between countries and within them, in our lifetime.

For society, this means: improve access urgently for those the present system is failing. Most countries already give this notion plenty of good rhetoric, but for the acid test, follow the money. Market prices reflect social priorities; in most disadvantaged places, teachers' salaries are far lower than they should be. To undervalue teachers' contributions now is a perilous error.

For individuals, this means: consume as much learning as we can, all our lives. To develop dignity takes active study, Renaissance humanists believed. The key word is *active*. Like Tycho Brahe and his self-study of astronomy, we each need to take our education into our own hands. Julius Yego, a Kenyan javelin thrower, couldn't find a coach for his sport because, as he said, 'everybody in Kenya is a runner'. So, 'my coach is me, and the YouTube videos'. By 2012, Yego's achievements on the field had attracted some of the world's best coaches, and in 2015, he won gold at the World Athletics Championships.[79]

As for formal schooling, in the past twenty years enrolment at all levels has leapt worldwide, but at the same time the idea of what education means has eroded. 'Get the degree', we tell our kids, and that's good advice, but by itself it's dehumanizing. Parents should add, 'While you're at it, come up with an original answer to a question that interests you.' Too much focus on the

CV-building aspect of education can diminish *us* and make *it* boring. If Renaissance humanists were alive today, their first order of business would probably be to reverse the recent decline in humanities and liberal arts curriculums.

Otherwise, we risk treating education like a product you buy and consume. And that's not what it is. Education is more like a game. It takes effort – and a lot of practice with other earnest players – to learn how to play it well. For those who succeed, the line on the CV is the least valuable take-away. They've worked out their own unique angle on life, and the world is full of questions just waiting for their uncommon answer.

Think *and*, not *or*. Self-help literature often harps on the power of focus, but if we consistently prune our own curiosities in order to 'get ahead', then that, too, is dehumanizing. We are capable of knowing at least something about each branch of knowledge and endeavour, Renaissance humanists believed, and as we widen the things we comprehend, we become somehow 'bigger' on the inside. Hopefully, this book – which has deliberately spanned history, geography, politics, economics, science and art – has helped you to get in touch with that innate satisfaction.

Be warned: curiosity is costly. Society values specialists highly and consistently; generalists have to cope with more uncertain pay and prestige. Productivity can also suffer. Over forty years, Leonardo da Vinci painted fewer than two dozen works because he spent so much time developing new varnishes and sketching new machines.

But it can also pay off. A Renaissance is an age for polymaths – for 'Renaissance Men' and 'Renaissance Women'. Virtually none of the greats we remember from the first Renaissance worked in just one field. Art informed science: Leonardo's hand and eye for detail helped revolutionize the study of anatomy. And science informed art: Leonardo's study of anatomy helped him to make breathtakingly lifelike drawings. Today, again, the world sorely needs such people, imbued with unquenchable curiosity and feverish imagination. The more knowledge we create, the harder the task of figuring out how it all fits together. The greatest contributions – and rewards – will be for those of us who do.

Seek difference. The point is not simply to visit different places and read different things; it's to accumulate new perspectives. We may think we do this already, but most often we don't, not really. We visit new spaces, but do we learn to see them through local eyes? If every business trip follows the same script – airport–taxi–hotel–office–artisanal café–taxi–airport – then the answer is no.

In Renaissance Europe, the best seeker was probably Desiderius Erasmus (c. 1466–1536). Born in Holland, Erasmus was orphaned by plague at the age of seventeen. He immersed himself in books, mastered Latin and, by about the age of twenty-five, landed a job as personal secretary to a bishop in northern France. By 1495, he had worked his way inland to the University of Paris, and he divided the next thirty years between France, Italy, Belgium, England and Switzerland.

But his farthest travels were between his ears. By the age of forty, he had lived the breadth of European intellectual life – from stodgy scholastic learning to the new Italian influences – and made it his life's work to share the richness and common links of his learning. In Belgium, he helped set up the Collegium Trilingue for the study of Hebrew, Latin and Greek. (He mastered Greek in his spare time.) He turned down prestigious academic posts and instead made his living as a public intellectual who saw the big picture more clearly than most. He corresponded regularly with over 500 political and intellectual leaders (thousands of his letters survive in museums and private collections around the world). And he wrote books: in education, religion, classical Latin and Greek, poetry and many other genres. He was the most prolific and influential writer of his time.[80]

We can all borrow from his example to live well in our second Renaissance. First, learn new languages. Yes, we can make ourselves understood almost anywhere in English, but people talk about what's important to *them* in their native tongue. Second, step into the communities you visit. Ride the public transport and walk through the parks; read the local headlines and Twitter feeds; watch local films. Third, regularly set aside your own reasoning and get curious about how other people think. If you've never watched Fox or Sky News, do. If that is all you watch, change channels. Across our 24/7 media world, the news is much the same; the perspectives are quite different. Why are climate sceptics sceptical? What drives religious extremism? Why do mainland Chinese support Communist Party rule? The more we can get inside others' viewpoints – even those we're absolutely convinced are wrong – the richer our own values and insights will become.

Love art. Today, we tend to see art as a rarefied form of entertainment. Music and film are for the masses, but painting, sculpture, ballet and poetry are either luxury goods or a way to signal sophistication on a date night. 'Artists' are those few people who do art full-time, and most of us cannot imagine choosing so impractical a career.

It's time to re-raise art's place in our daily lives. The creation or appreciation of art for its own sake is one of the most dignifying habits we can adopt, because in each instance we set aside our economic, rational selves, and we prioritize emotions and ideals instead. Renaissance humanists believed the great works of Roman literature were written with such power and beauty that they could fill us with virtue through their eloquence alone. That may be a bit over-romantic to modern sensibilities, but what art does do is remind us that the intangibles matter. From there, we're better able to reconnect with the values and aspirations we haven't left time for recently, and to see the bigger picture.

* * *

Most people will not try to cultivate the above virtues. They will continue to be driven by the most immediate rewards and stressors that this age presents, and take a free ride on the virtuous efforts of others. But that does not matter, so long as *you* cultivate them. Through your actions, you will nudge prevailing norms and lure others to join in a new habit of being, one that brings *should* closer to *will*. We all share this opportunity to reshape the human condition, but ultimately it's up to you.

Goliath

The present age is a second Renaissance.

It is a contest between flourishing genius and risk.

How history records it – that depends on all of us.

The manifesto of the first Renaissance, Mirandola's *Oration on the Dignity of Man*, ended with a call to action:

> Let some holy ambition invade our souls, so that, dissatisfied with mediocrity, we shall eagerly desire the highest things and shall toil with all our strength to obtain them, since we may if we wish.[81]

It was a call repeated over and over by the luminaries of that age. 'There is no greater harm than that of time wasted'. 'People of accomplishment rarely sit back and let things happen to them.

They go out and happen to things'. Tradition attributes these words to Michelangelo and Leonardo da Vinci, respectively. In his conclusion to *The Prince*, Machiavelli urged the rulers of Italy that 'everything has converged for your greatness. The rest you must do yourself'.[82]

They all saw the moment they lived in for what it was: a clash of creative and destructive forces that would ultimately reshape humanity and the whole world. By the lives they led, they made clear their belief that hand in hand with recognition of this contest came the urgent responsibility to join it.

That, too, is once again true. Goliath is waiting.

NOTES

Chapter 1: To Flounder or Flourish

1 United Nations Department of Economic and Social Affairs (2014). *World Urbanization Prospects: The 2014 Revision Highlights*. New York: United Nations.

2 Greenhalgh, Emily (2015). '2014 State of the Climate: Earth's Surface Temperature'. *National Oceanic and Atmospheric Administration*. Retrieved from www.climate .gov.

3 Internet Live Stats (2015). 'Internet Users'. Retrieved from www.internetlivestats.com/internet-users.

4 Pew Research Center (2010, 9 November). 'Public Support for Increased Trade, except with South Korea and China. Fewer See Benefits from Free Trade Agreements'. *Pew Research Center Global Attitudes and Trends*. Retrieved from www.people-press.org.

5 Rasmus, Jack (2015, 21 September). 'Global Corporate Cash Piles Exceed $15 Trillion'. *TelesurTV*. Retrieved from www.telesurtv.net/english/opinion; Dolan, Mike (2014). 'Analysis: Corporate Cash May Not All Flow Back with Recovery'. *Reuters*. Retrieved from www.reuters.com.

6 Bost, Callie and Lu Wang (2014, 6 October). 'S&P 500 Companies Spend Almost All Profits on Buybacks'. *Bloomberg*. Retrieved from www.bloomberg.com.

7 da Vinci, Leonardo (1452–1519) (1955). 'Chapter XXIX: Precepts of the Painter – of the Error Made by Those Who Practice without Science'. In *The Notebooks of Leonardo Da Vinci*, edited by E. MacCurdy. New York: George Braziller.

8   Machiavelli, Niccolò (1469–1527) (1940). 'Discourses on the First
     Ten Books of Titus Livius, Third Book, Chapter XLIII: Natives of
     the Same Country Preserve for All Time the Same Characteris-
     tics'. In *The Prince and the Discourses*, edited by C. E. Detmold, M.
     Lerner, L. Ricci and E. Vincent. New York: The Modern Library.

9   Pettersson, Therese and Peter Wallensteen (2015). 'Armed Conflicts,
     1946–2014'. *Journal of Peace Research* 52(4): 536–550.

10   Huizinga, Johan (1959). 'The Problem of the Renaissance'. In *Men
     and Ideas: History, the Middle Ages, the Renaissance (Essays by Johan
     Huizinga)*. New York: Meridian Books.

11   Brotton, Jerry (2002). *The Renaissance Bazaar: From the Silk Road to
     Michelangelo*. Oxford: Oxford University Press.

12   Hale, J. R. (1985). *War and Society in Renaissance Europe, 1450–1620*.
     London: Fontana Press.

13   Frankopan, Peter (2015), *The Silk Roads: A New History of the World*.
     London: Bloomsbury

14   Asian Art Museum (2015). 'The Invention of Woodblock Printing in
     the Tang (618–906) and Song (960–1279) Dynasties'. Retrieved from
     education.asianart.org.

Chapter 2: The New World

1   Cardano, Girolamo (1501–1576) (1931). 'Chapter XLI: Concerning
     Natural Though Rare Circumstances of My Own Life'. In *The Book
     of My Life (De Vita Propria Liber)*, edited by J. Stoner. London: J. M.
     Dent.

2   Brotton, Jerry (2012). *A History of the World in Twelve Maps*. London: Al-
     len Lane.

3   Goldin, Ian (2016). *Development: A Very Short Introduction*. Oxford:
     Oxford University Press.

4 UNDP (2010). *The Real Wealth of Nations: Pathways to Human Development*. Human Development Report 2010. New York: United Nations, p. 6.

5 Economist Intelligence Unit (2016). *Democracy Index 2015: Democracy in an age of Anxiety*. London: *The Economist*. Retrieved from www.eiu.com/democracy2015.

6 World Trade Organization (2015). 'Members and Observers'. Retrieved from www.wto.org/english/thewto_e/whatis_e/tif_e/org6_e.htm.

7 'Bread and Circuses'. *The Economist* (8 August 2015). Retrieved from www .economist.com.

8 Rhodes, Neil and Jonathan Sawday (2000). *The Renaissance Computer: Knowledge Technology in the First Age of Print*. London: Routledge, p. 1; Brotton, *A History of the World in Twelve Maps*.

9 Brant, Sebastian (1458–1521) (1498). *Varia Carmina*. Basel: Johann Bergmann, de Olpe, f. l VIII r-v.

10 Eisenstein, Elizabeth L. (1980). *The Printing Press as an Agent of Change*. Vol. 1. Cambridge: Cambridge University Press, p. 46.

11 Foresti, Giacomo Filippo (1434–1520) (1492). *Supplementum Chronicharum*. Venice: Bernardinum riçium de Nouaria.

12 Ruggiero, Guido (2002). *A Companion to the Worlds of the Renaissance*. Oxford: Blackwell, p. 335.

13 Ibid., p. 95.

14 Ibid., p. 183.

15 Whitlock, Keith (2000). *The Renaissance in Europe: A Reader*. New Haven, CT: Yale University Press, p. 301.

16 Ibid., p. 302.

17 Man, John (2002). *The Gutenberg Revolution: The Story of a Genius and an Invention That Changed the World*. London: Review, p. 224.

18 World Bank Databank (2014). 'Internet Users (per 100 People)'. *World Development Indicators*. Retrieved from data.worldbank.org.

19 World Bank Databank (2015). 'Mobile Cellular Subscriptions (per 100 People)'. *World Development Indicators*. Retrieved from data.worldbank.org.

20 International Telecommunications Union (2014). 'Key ICT Indicators for Developed and Developing Countries and the World'. Retrieved from www.itu.int /en/ITU-D/Statistics/Documents/statistics.

21 Ibid.; International Telecommunications Union (2014). 'Mobile Broadband Is Counted as 3G or Above'. Retrieved from www.itu.int/en/ITU-D/Statistics/Documents/statistics.

22 IDC (2014). 'The Digital Universe of Opportunities: Rich Data and the Increasing Value of the Internet of Things'. *EMC Digital Universe*. Framingham: IDC. Retrieved from www.emc.com/leadership/digital-universe/2014iview/index.htm. Plus authors' estimates.

23 TeleGeography (2015). *The Telegeography Report*. Retrieved from www.telegeography .com.

24 Snyder, Benjamin (2015). 'Gmail Just Hit a Major Milestone'. *Fortune*. Retrieved from www.fortune.com; Quigley, Robert (2011). 'The Cost of a Gigabyte over the Years'. *The Mary Sue*. Retrieved from www.themarysue.com/gigabyte-cost-over -years.

25 Cisco (2015). *The Zettabyte Era: Trends and Analysis*. San Jose, CA: Cisco Systems Inc.

26 Internet Live Stats (2015). 'Internet Users'. Retrieved from www.internetlivestats .com/internet-users.

27 Manyika, James, Jacques Bughin, et al. (2014). *Global Flows in a Digital Age*. New York: McKinsey & Co.

28 International Telecommunication Union (2015). *ICT Facts & Figures: The World in 2015*. Geneva: ITU; International Energy Agency (2014). 'World Energy Outlook 2014 – Electricity Access Database'. *OECD/IEA*. Retrieved from www.worldenergyoutlook.org.

29 International Telecommunication Union, *ICT Facts & Figures*.

30   Dennis, Sarah Grace, Thomas Trusk, et al. (2015). 'Viability of Bioprinted Cellular Constructs Using a Three Dispenser Cartesian Printer'. *Journal of Visualized Experiments* 103: e53156.

31   Dredge, Stuart (2015). 'Zuckerberg: One in Seven People on the Planet Used Facebook on Monday'. *The Guardian*. Retrieved from www.theguardian.com.

32   BBC News (2011). 'Facebook Users Average 3.74 Degrees of Separation'. *BBC*. Retrieved from www.bbc.co.uk.

33   Gates, Bill (1995). *The Road Ahead*. London: Viking, pp. 4–5.

Chapter 3: New Tangles

1   Emmer, Pieter (2003). 'The Myth of Early Globalization: The Atlantic Economy, 1500–1800'. *European Review* 11(1): 37–47.

2   Ruggiero, Guido (2002). *A Companion to the Worlds of the Renaissance*. Oxford: Blackwell, p. 288.

3   Maddison, Angus (2001). *The World Economy: A Millennial Perspective*. Development Center Studies. Paris: OECD, p. 64.

4   Ruggiero, *A Companion to the Worlds of the Renaissance*, p. 287.

5   Casale, Giancarlo (2003). 'The Ottoman "Discovery" of the Indian Ocean in the Sixteenth Century: The Age of Exploration from an Islamic Perspective'. Retrieved from webdoc.sub.gwdg.de.

6   Krugman, Paul (1995). 'Growing World Trade: Causes and Consequences'. *Brookings Papers on Economic Activity* 1: 331.

7   United Nations Conference on Trade and Development (2015). 'Merchandise: Total Trade and Share, Annual, 1948–2014'. *UNCTADStat*. Retrieved from unctadstat.unctad.org.

8   United Nations Conference on Trade and Development (2015). 'Services (BPM5): Exports and Imports of Total Services, Value, Shares

and Growth, Annual, 1980–2013'. *UNCTADStat*. Retrieved from unctadstat.unctad.org.

9   Containerisation International (1992). *Containerisation International Yearbook*. London: National Magazine Co.; World Shipping Council (2015). 'Top 50 World Container Ports'. Retrieved from www.world-shipping.org/about-the-industry/global-trade.

10   International Civil Aviation Organization (1991). 'Air China Took Delivery of Its First Wide-Body Freighter'. *ICAO Journal* (July): 16.

11   United Nations Statistics Division (2015). 'GDP and Its Breakdown'. *National Accounts Main Aggregates Database*. Retrieved from unstats.un.org.

12   Trading Economics (2015). 'Bangladesh Exports 1972–2015'. Retrieved from www.tradingeconomics.com/bangladesh/exports.

13   'Creaming Along'. *The Economist* (16 June 2011). Retrieved from www.economist .com.

14   India Brand Equity Foundation (2015). 'Indian IT and ITES Industry Analysis'. *IBEF*. Retrieved from www.ibef.org.

15   Eichengreen, Barry and Poonam Gupta (2012). *Exports of Services: Indian Experiences in Perspective*. New Delhi: National Institute of Public Finance and Policy, p. 11.

16   United Nations Conference on Trade and Development (2015). 'Goods and Services (BPM5): Exports and Imports of Goods and Services, Annual, 1980–2013'. *UNCTADStat*. Retrieved from unctadstat.unctad.org.

17   Statista (2015). 'International Trade: Monthly Value of Exports from China'. Retrieved from www.statista.com/statistics/271616/monthly-value-of-exports -from-china.

18   China Statistics Press (2015). 'China's Exports & Imports, 1952–2014'. *China Statistical Yearbook*. Retrieved from www.stats.gov.cn.

19   United Nations Conference on Trade and Development (2015). 'Merchandise: Intra-Trade and Extra-Trade of Country Groups by

Product, Annual, 1995–2014'. *UNCTADStat*. Retrieved from unctad-stat.unctad.org.

20 Hillsberg, Alex (17 September 2014). 'How & Where iPhone Is Made: Comparison of Apple's Manufacturing Process'. *CompareCamp*. Retrieved from comparecamp.com/how-where-iphone-is-made-comparison-of-apples-manufacturing-process.

21 Davidson, Nicholas (20 January 2014). *Overseas Expansion and the Development of a World Economy (Lecture)*. Oxford: University of Oxford.

22 Denzel, Markus (2006). 'The European Bill of Exchange'. *International Economic History Congress XIV*. Retrieved from www.helsinki.fi/iehc2006/papers1/ Denzel2.pdf.

23 de Maddalena, Aldo and Hermann Kellenbenz (1986). *La Repubblica Internazionale Del Denaro Tra XV E XVII Secolo*. Bologna: Il Mulino.

24 Goldthwaite, Richard (2009). *The Economy of Renaissance Florence*. Baltimore: Johns Hopkins University Press.

25 Ehrenberg, Richard (1928). *Capital and Finance in the Age of the Renaissance: A Study of the Fuggers and Their Connections*. London: Jonathan Cape, p. 238.

26 Roxburgh, Charles, Susan Lund, et al. (2011). *Mapping Global Capital Markets 2011*. McKinsey Global Institute. New York: McKinsey & Co., p. 32.

27 Manyika, James, Jacques Bughin, et al. (2014). *Global Flows in a Digital Age*. New York: McKinsey & Co.

28 Chomsisengphet, Souphala and Anthony Pennington-Cross (2006). 'The Evolution of the Subprime Mortgage Market'. *Federal Reserve Bank of St. Louis Review* 88(1): 31–56.

29 Manyika, Bughin, et al., *Global Flows in a Digital Age*.

30 International Monetary Fund (2015). 'Summary of International Transactions'. *IMF Balance of Payments*. Retrieved from data.imf.org.

31 United Nations Conference on Trade and Development (2015). 'Inward and Outward Foreign Direct Investment Flows, Annual, 1970–2013'. *UNCTAD Stat*. Retrieved from unctadstat.unctad.org/wds.

32 Jin, David, David C. Michael, et al. (2011). 'The Many City Growth Strategy'. Boston: Boston Consulting Group . Retrieved from www.bcgperspectives.com.

33 Wheatley, Jonathan and Sam Fleming (1 October 2015). 'Capital Flight Darkens Economic Prospects for Emerging Markets'. *The Financial Times*. Retrieved from www.ft.com.

34 Osler Hampson, Fen (30 October 2012). 'Canada Needs a Foreign Investment Plan Based on Fact, Not Fear'. *iPolitics*. Retrieved from www.ipolitics.ca/2012/10/30/breaking-out-of-the-investment-igloo.

35 United Nations Conference on Trade and Development, 'Goods and Services (BPM5); International Monetary Fund, 'Summary of International Transactions'.

36 United Nations World Tourism Organization (2015). *UNWTO Tourism Highlights* (2015 Edition). Madrid: UNWTO.

37 World Bank Databank (2015). 'Air Transport, Passengers Carried'. *World Development Indicators*. Retrieved from data.worldbank.org.

38 Manyika, Bughin, et al., *Global Flows in a Digital Age*.

39 International Civil Aviation Organization (1991). 'Comparison of Traffic at the World's Major Airports, 1989 versus 1980'. *ICAO Journal (July)*; International Civil Aviation Organization (2013). 'Forecasts of Scheduled Passenger and Freight Traffic'. Retrieved from www.icao.int/sustainability/pages.

40 Boeing (2015). *Current Market Outlook 2015–2034*. Seattle: Boeing Commercial Airplanes Market Analysis.

41 Ibid.

42 Acemoglu, Daron, Simon H. Johnson, et al. (2002). *The Rise of Europe: Atlantic Trade, Institutional Change and Economic Growth*. Boston: Massachusetts Institute of Technology.

43 Lynch, Katherine (2003). *Individuals, Families, and Communities in Europe, 1200–1800: The Urban Foundations of Western Society.* Cambridge: Cambridge University Press, p. 30.

44 Elliott, J. H. (1963). *Imperial Spain: 1469–1716.* London: Edwin Arnold Ltd., p. 177.

45 United Nations Department of Economic and Social Affairs, Population Division (2014). *World Urbanization Prospects: The 2014 Revision.* New York: United Nations.

46 Ibid.

47 United Nations Population Fund (2007). *Growing up Urban: State of World Population 2007, Youth Supplement.* New York: United Nations.

48 China National Statistics Bureau (1990). *Fourth National Population Census.* Beijing: Department of Population Statistics.

49 Shenzhen Government Online (2015). 'Overview: Demographics'. Retrieved from english.sz.gov.cn/gi.

50 United Nations Department of Economic and Social Affairs, Population Division, *World Urbanization Prospects.*

51 Ibid.

52 MacCulloch, Diarmaid (2003). *Reformation: Europe's House Divided, 1490–1700.* London: Allen Lane, pp. 60, 648–649.

53 Frankel, Neil A. (2008). 'Facts and Figures'. *The Atlantic Slave Trade and Slavery in America.* Retrieved from www.slaverysite.com/Body/facts%20and%20figures.htm.

54 World Bank (2013). 'Bilateral Migration Matrix 2013'. *Migration & Remittances Data.* Retrieved from econ.worldbank.org.

55 Manyika, Bughin, et al., *Global Flows in a Digital Age.*

56 Eurostat (2015). 'Non-National Population by Group of Citizenship, 1 January 2014'. *Eurostat.* Retrieved from ec.europa.eu/eurostat.

57 Goldin, Ian (2012). *Exceptional People: How Migration Shaped Our World and Will Define Our Future.* Princeton: Princeton University Press.

58 United Nations Department of Economic and Social Affairs (2013). 'Total International Migrant Stock, 2013 Revision'. *UN Population Division*. Retrieved from esa.un.org/unmigration; Pew Research Center (2014). 'Origins and Destinations of the World's Migrants, from 1990–2013'. Retrieved from www.pewglobal.org.

59 Dustmann, Christian and Tommaso Frattini (2014). 'The Fiscal Effects of Immigration to the UK'. *The Economic Journal* 124(580): 593–643.

60 Goldin, *Exceptional People*.

61 Ibid.

62 Ibid.

63 Kosloski, Rey (2014). *The American Way of Border Control and Immigration Reform Politics*. Oxford: Oxford Martin School.

64 Miles, Tom (25 September 2015). 'UN Sees Refugee Flow to Europe Growing, Plans for Big Iraq Displacement'. *Reuters*. Retrieved from www.reuters.com.

65 Spate, O. H. K. (1979). *The Spanish Lake: The Pacific since Magellan*. Canberra: Australian National University Press, pp. 15–22.

66 Ibid.

67 Thrower, Norman J. W. (2008). *Maps and Civilization: Cartography in Culture and Society* (3rd Edition). Chicago: University of Chicago Press, p. 63.

68 Wightman, W. P. D. (1962). *Science and the Renaissance*. Edinburgh: Oliver & Boyd, p. 143.

69 Puttevils, Jeroen (2016). *Merchants and Trading in the Sixteenth Century: The Golden Age of Antwerp*. New York: Routledge.

70 Kohn, Meir (2010). 'How and Why Economies Develop and Grow: Lessons from Preindustrial Europe and China'. Hanover, NH: Dartmouth College Department of Economics. Retrieved from ssrn.com/abstract=1723870.

71 Manyika, Bughin, et al., *Global Flows in a Digital Age.*

72 Macaulay, James, Lauren Buckalew, et al. (2015). *Internet of Things in Logistics.* Troisdorf, Germany: DHL Trend Research and Cisco Consulting Services. Retrieved from www.dpdhl.com.

73 Seoul Metropolitan Government (2015). 'Seoul Transportation: People First'. *Seoul Solution.* Retrieved from www.seoulsolution.kr.

74 Bernhofen, Daniel M., Zouheir El-Sahli, et al. (2013). 'Estimating the Effects of Containerization on World Trade'. Nottingham: Centre for Research on Globalisation and Economic Policy. Retrieved from www.nottingham.ac.uk/gep.

75 World Maritime News (19 February 2015). 'Global Container Volumes Rise'. *World Maritime News.* Retrieved from worldmaritime-news.com.

76 Schneider, Friedrich, Andreas Buehn, et al. (2010). 'Shadow Economies All over the World: Estimates for 162 Countries from 1999 to 2007'. *Policy Research Working Paper 5356.* Development Research Group, Poverty & Inequality Team, Washington, DC: World Bank.

77 Naim, Moses (2005). *Illicit: How Smugglers, Traffickers and Counterfeiters Are Hijacking the Global Economy.* London: Random House.

78 Pimentel, David (2005). 'Update on the Environmental and Economic Costs Associated with Alien-Invasive Species in the United States'. *Ecological Economics* 52: 273–288.

79 Intergovernmental Panel on Climate Change (2014). *Climate Change 2014: Synthesis Report.* Geneva: IPCC.

80 Anderson, Benedict (2006). *Imagined Communities: Reflections on the Origin and Spread of Nationalism.* London: Verso.

81 W3 Techs (2015). 'Usage of Content Languages for Websites'. Retrieved from w3techs.com/technologies/overview/content_language/all.

82 Internet World Stats (2014). 'Internet World Users by Language'. *Usage and Population Statistics.* Retrieved from www.internetworldstats.com/stats7.htm.

Chapter 4: Vitruvian Man

1   Ramus, Peter (1569). *Scholarum Mathematicarum, Libri Unus Et Triginta*. Basel: Per Eusebium Episcopium, & Nicolai fratris haeredes, Preface.

2   della Mirandola, Pico (1463–1494) (2012). *Oration on the Dignity of Man: A New Translation and Commentary*, translated by F. Borghesi, M. Papio and M. Riva. Cambridge: Cambridge University Press.

3   Peterson, David S. (2004). 'Religion and the Church'. In *Italy in the Age of the Renaissance: 1300–1550*, edited by J. Najemy. Oxford: Oxford University Press, p. 76; *Britannica* (2014). 'Giovanni Pico Della Mirandola'. *Britannica*. Retrieved from www.britannica.com.

4   Hendrix, John (2003). *History and Culture in Italy*. Oxford: University Press of America.

5   Wheelis, Mark (2002). 'Biological Warfare at the 1346 Siege of Caffa'. *Journal of Emerging Infectious Diseases* 8(9): 973.

6   Ruggiero, Guido (2002). *A Companion to the Worlds of the Renaissance*. Oxford: Blackwell.

7   Bartlett, Robert (1993). *The Making of Europe: Conquest, Colonization and Cultural Change 950–1350*. London: BCA.

8   Najemy, John (2006). *A History of Florence, 1200–1575*. Oxford: Blackwell, pp. 97–100.

9   Lis, Catharina and Hugo Soly (1979). *Poverty and Capitalism in Pre-Industrial Europe*. Hassocks, UK: Harvester Press.

10 Ruggiero, *A Companion to the Worlds of the Renaissance*.

11 Ibid.

12 The Maddison Project (2013). 'Maddison Project Database'. Retrieved from www.ggdc.net/maddison/maddison-project/home.htm.

13 Geremek, Bronislaw (1994). *Poverty: A History*. Oxford: Blackwell.

14 World Bank Databank (2014). 'Life Expectancy at Birth, Total (Years)'. *World Development Indicators*. Retrieved from data .worldbank.org.

15 'Global Health: Lifting the Burden'. *The Economist* (15 December 2012). Retrieved from www.economist.com.

16 Deaton, Angus (2013). *The Great Escape: Health, Wealth, and the Origins of Inequality*. Princeton: Princeton University Press.

17 Banerjee, Abhijit V. and Esther Duflo (2006). 'The Economic Lives of the Poor'. *MIT Department of Economics Working Paper No. 06–29.* Cambridge: Massachusetts Institute of Technology, Abdul Latif Jameel Poverty Action Lab. Retrieved from economics.mit.edu.

18 World Bank Databank (2015). 'GDP Per Capita (Constant LCU)'. *World Development Indicators*. Retrieved from data.worldbank.org.

19 World Bank Databank (2015). 'GDP Per Capita (Constant 2005 US$)'. *World Development Indicators*. Retrieved from data.worldbank.org.

20 United Nations (2015). 'Goal 1: Eradicate Extreme Poverty & Hunger'. *Millennium Development Goals and Beyond 2015*. Retrieved from www.un.org/millenniumgoals/poverty.shtml.

21 World Bank (17 April 2013). 'Remarkable Declines in Global Poverty, but Major Challenges Remain'. Retrieved from www.worldbank.org/ en/news/press-release/2013/04/17/remarkable-declines-in-global-poverty-but-major-challenges -remain.

22 Trading Economics (2015). 'China Average Yearly Wages'. Retrieved from www.tradingeconomics.com/china/wages.

23 World Bank (2015). 'World Development Indicators: Women in Development'. *2015 World View*. Retrieved from wdi.worldbank.org.

24 'Hopeless Africa'. *The Economist* (11 May 2000). Retrieved from www. economist.com.

25 Schneidman, Witney and Zenia A. Lewis (2012). *The African Growth and Opportunity Act: Looking Back, Looking Forward*. Washington, DC.: Brookings Institution.

26 World Bank Databank (2015). 'Sub-Saharan Africa (Developing Only)'. *World Development Indicators*. Retrieved from data.worldbank.org.

27 African Development Bank Group (2014). 'ADB Socio-economic Database: National Accounts'. *ADB Data Portal*. Retrieved from dataportal.afdb.org/default.aspx.

28 de Ridder-Symoens, Hilda (1996). *A History of the University in Europe*. Cambridge: Cambridge University Press.

29 von Eulenburg, Franz (1904). *Die Frequenz Der Deutschen Universitaten Von Ihrer Grundung Bis Zur Gegenwart*. Leibzig: B.G. Teubner.

30 Ralph, Philip Lee (1973). *The Renaissance in Perspective*. New York: St Martin's Press.

31 Roser, Max (2015). 'Literacy'. *OurWorldInData.org*. Retrieved from ourworldindata.org/data/education knowledge/literacy.

32 United Nations (2015). 'Goal 2: Achieve Universal Primary Education'. *Millennium Development Goals and Beyond 2015*. Retrieved from www.un.org/millenniumgoals/education.shtml.

33 World Bank Databank (2015). 'Primary Enrollment Rate; Primary Completion Rate'. *Education Statistics All Indicators*. Retrieved from databank.worldbank.org.

34 World Bank (2012). *World Development Report 2012: Gender Equality and Development*. Washington, DC: World Bank.

35 World Bank Databank (2014). 'School Enrollment, Primary, Female (% Net); School Enrollment, Secondary, Female (% Net)'. *World Development Indicators*. Retrieved from data.worldbank.org.

36 World Bank, *World Development Report 2012*, p. 106.

37 World Bank Databank (2014). 'School Enrollment, Tertiary (% Gross)'. *World Development Indicators*. Retrieved from data.worldbank.org.

38 UNESCO (2014). 'Enrolment in tertiary education'. *UNESCO Institute for Statistics Database*. Retrieved from data.uis.unesco.org.

39 Hultman, Nathan, Katherine Sierra, et al. (2012). *Green Growth Innovation: New Pathways for International Cooperation*. Washington, DC: Brookings Institution.

40 World Bank, *World Development Report 2012*, p. 14.

41 UNICEF (2015). *Levels and Trends in Child Mortality*. New York: UNICEF.

42 Ibid.

43 World Health Organization (2012). *World Health Statistics 2012*. Geneva: WHO.

44 World Health Organization (2014). *Global Status Report on Noncommunicable Diseases 2014*. Geneva: WHO.

45 Dwyer, Terence, PhD. (1 October 2015). 'The Present State of Medical Science'. Interviewed by C. Kutarna, University of Oxford.

46 Human Mortality Database (2014). *Global Population and Mortality Data*. Retrieved from www.mortality.org.

47 Goldin, Ian, editor (2014). *Is the Planet Full?* Oxford: Oxford University Press.

48 Goldin, Ian and Kenneth Reinert (2012). *Globalization for Development*. Oxford: Oxford University Press.

49 Vietnam Food Association (2014). 'Yearly Export Statistics'. Retrieved from vietfood.org.vn/en/default.aspx?c=108.

50 Bangladesh Garment Manufacturers and Exporters Association (2015). 'Trade Information'. Retrieved from bgmea.com.bd/home/pages/TradeInformation#.U57MMhZLGYU.

51 Burke, Jason (14 November 2013). 'Bangladesh Garment Workers Set for 77% Pay Rise'. *The Guardian*. Retrieved from www.theguardian.com.

52 Goldin and Reinert, *Globalization for Development*.

53 Industrial Development Bureau (2015). 'Industry Introduction-History of Industrial Development'. *Ministry of Economic Affairs*. Retrieved from www.moeaidb.gov.tw/external/view/en/english/about04.html.

54 Kim, Ran (1996). 'The Korean System of Innovation and the Semi-conductor Industry: A Governance Perspective'. *SPRU/SEI-Working Paper*. Paris: OECD.

55 IC Insights (2015). *Global Wafer Capacity*. Scottsdale: IC Insights.

56 World Bank, *World Development Report 2012*.

57 World Bank (2015). 'Migration and Remittances: Recent Developments and Outlook'. *Migration and Development Brief 22*. Washington, DC: World Bank.

58 Dayrit, Manuel M. (2013). *Brain Drain and Brain Gain: Selected Country Experiences and Responses*. Singapore: Asia Regional World Health Summit.

59 Statistics Canada (2011). 'Data Tables (Ethnic Origin)'. *National Household Survey*. Retrieved from www12.statcan.gc.ca.

60 Goldin and Reinert, *Globalization for Development*, Chapter 7.

61 World Bank (2011). *World Development Report 2011: Conflict, Security and Development*. Washington, DC: World Bank.

62 Zakaria, Fareed (2008). *The Post-American World*. London: Allen Lane.

63 World Bank, *World Development Report 2011*.

64 Ibid.

65 Goldstone, Jack A. (1991). *Revolution and Rebellion in the Early Modern World*. Berkeley: University of California Press.

66 Lis and Soly, *Poverty and Capitalism in Pre-Industrial Europe*.

67 Geremek, *Poverty*.

68 Jütte, Robert (1994). *Poverty and Deviance in Early Modern Europe*. Cambridge: Cambridge University Press.

69 Goldstone, *Revolution and Rebellion in the Early Modern World*.

70 Davidson, Nicholas (2014). *Overseas Expansion and the Development of a World Economy*. Lecture. Oxford: University of Oxford.

71 Ruggiero, *A Companion to the Worlds of the Renaissance.*

72 Kukaswadia, Atif (2013). 'What Killed the Aztecs? A Researcher Probes Role of 16th Century Megadrought'. *Public Health Perspectives.* Retrieved from blogs.plos.org/publichealth/2013/07/30/guest-post-what-killed-the-aztecs/; Hunefeldt, Christine (2004). *A Brief History of Peru.* New York: Facts on File Inc., p. 52.

73 Ruggiero, *A Companion to the Worlds of the Renaissance.*

74 Milanovic, Branko (2012). 'Global Income Inequality by the Numbers: In History and Now'. *Policy Research Working Paper 6259.* Washington, DC: World Bank Development Research Group.

75 Oxfam (2017). *An Economy for the 99%.* Oxford: Oxfam International.

76 United Nations Department of Economic and Social Affairs (2014). 'Access to Sanitation'. *International Decade of Action 'Water for Life' 2005–2015.* New York: United Nations. Retrieved from www.un.org/waterforlifedecade/sanitation.shtml; International Energy Agency (2015). 'World Energy Outlook 2014–Electricity Access Database'. *OECD/IEA.* Retrieved from www.worldenergyoutlook.org; Food and Agricultural Organization of the United Nations (2015). *The State of Food Insecurity in the World.* Rome: FAO.

77 UNDP (2010). *The Real Wealth of Nations: Pathways to Human Development.* Human Development Report 2010. New York: United Nations; World Health Organization (2014). 'The Top 10 Causes of Death'. Retrieved from www.who.int/mediacentre/factsheets/fs310/en/index3.html; World Health Organization (2015). 'Chronic Diseases and Health Promotion'. Retrieved from www.who.int/chp/en.

78 Barro, Robert J. and Xavier Sala-i-Martin (1992). 'Convergence'. *Journal of Political Economy* 100(2): 223–251; Deaton. *The Great Escape*; Pritchett, Lant (1997). 'Convergence, Big Time'. *Journal of Economic Perspectives* 11(3): 3–17.

79 Kharas, Homi (9 January 2015). 'The Transition from "the Developing World" to "a Developing World"'. *Kapuscinski Development Lectures.* Retrieved from www .brookings.edu.

80 World Bank Databank (2015). 'GDP Per Capita (Constant 2005 US$)'. *World Development Indicators*. Retrieved from data.worldbank .org.

81 Deaton, *The Great Escape.*

82 United Nations Development Program, *The Real Wealth of Nations.*

83 Goldin, Ian and Mike Mariathasan (2014). *The Butterfly Defect*. Princeton: Princeton University Press.

84 Thomas, Saji and Sudharshan Canagarajah (2002). *Poverty in a Wealthy Economy: The Case of Nigeria*. IMF Working Paper. Washington, DC: International Monetary Fund; World Bank Databank (2015). 'Poverty Headcount Ratio at $1.25 a Day (PPP) (% of Population)'. *World Development Indicators*. Retrieved from databank.worldbank. org. Changes over time in how researchers measure poverty make long-term rate comparisons contentious, but the overall direction in Nigeria's case is clear.

85 US Census Bureau (2015). 'Table F-3. Mean Income Received by Each Fifth and Top 5 Per Cent of Families'. *US Population Survey*. Suitland, MD: Economics and Statistics Administration. Retrieved from www. census.gov.

86 Goldin and Mariathasan, *The Butterfly Defect.*

87 United Nations Development Program, *The Real Wealth of Nations.*

88 International Telecommunications Union (2013). *Measuring the Information Society*. Geneva: ITU.

89 Goldin and Reinert, *Globalization for Development.*

90 MacMillan, Margaret and Dani Rodrik (2011). 'Globalization, Structural Change and Productivity Growth'. *National Bureau of Economic Research Working Paper Series, #17143.*

91 Berenger, Jean (1990). *A History of the Habsburg Empire, 1273–1700*. New York: Routledge, p. 79.

92 Goldin and Mariathasan, *The Butterfly Defect.*

93   Munich RE NatCatSERVICE (2015). 'The 10 Deadliest Natural Disasters'. *Significant Natural Disasters since 1980*. Retrieved from www.munichre.com.

94   United Nations High Commission for Refugees (2015). 'Facts and Figures about Refugees'. Retrieved from www.unhcr.org.uk/about-us/key-facts-and-figures.html.

95   World Bank (2014). 'Somalia Overview'. Retrieved from www.worldbank.org/en /country/somalia/overview.

96   Baker, Aryn (14 March 2014). 'The Cost of War: Syria, Three Years On'. *Time Magazine*. Retrieved from www.time.com; El-Showk, Sedeer (2014). 'A Broken Healthcare System: The Legacy of Syria's Conflic'. *Nature Middle East*. Retrieved from www.natureasia.com.

97   Dobbs, Richard and Shirish Sankhe (2010). *Comparing Urbanization in China and India*. New York: McKinsey & Co.

98   'Africa Rising: A Hopeful Continent'. *The Economist* (2 March 2013). Retrieved from www.economist.com.

99   Leke, Acha, Susan Lund, et al. (2010). *What's Driving Africa's Growth*. New York: McKinsey & Co.

100 World Bank Databank (2015). 'Life Expectancy (Years)'. *World Development Indicators*. Retrieved from data.worldbank.org.

101 United Nations Development Program, *The Real Wealth of Nations*.

102 United Nations Development Program (2014). *Sustaining Human Progress: Reducing Vulnerabilities and Building Resilience*. Human Development Report 2014. New York: United Nations.

Chapter 5: Copernican Revolutions

1   Contopoulus, G. (1974). *Highlights of Astronomy, Volume 3: As Presented at the XVth General Assembly and the Extraordinary Assembly of the IAU*. Boston: D. Reidel Publishing Company.

2 Sobel, Dava (2011). *A More Perfect Heaven: How Copernicus Revolutionized the Cosmos*. London: Bloomsbury.

3 Copernicus, Nicolaus (1473–1543) (1995). 'Introduction, Book 1'. *On the Revolutions of the Heavenly Spheres*, translated by C. Wallis. New York: Prometheus Books.

4 Ferguson, Niall (2011). *Civilization: The West and the Rest*. London: Allen Lane; Mokyr, Joel (1990). *Twenty-Five Centuries of Technological Change*. London: Harwood Academic.

5 OECD (2015). *In It Together: Why Less Inequality Benefits All*. Paris: OECD Publishing.

6 'Workers on Tap'. *The Economist* (5 January 2015). Retrieved from www.economist.com.

7 Costandi, Moheb (19 June 2012). 'Surgery on Ice'. *Nature Middle East*. Retrieved from www.natureasia.com.

8 Dwyer, Terence, PhD. (1 October 2015). 'The Present State of Medical Science'. Interviewed by C. Kutarna, University of Oxford.

9 National Human Genome Research Institute (1998). 'Twenty Questions about DNA Sequencing (and the Answers)'. *NHGRI*. Retrieved from community.dur.ac.uk/biosci.bizhub/Bioinformatics/twenty_questions_about_DNA.htm.

10 Rincon, Paul (15 January 2014). 'Science Enters $1,000 Genome Era'. *BBC News*. Retrieved from www.bbc.co.uk.

11 Regalado, Antonio (24 September 2014). 'Emtech: Illumina Says 228,000 Human Genomes Will Be Sequenced This Year'. *MIT Technology Review*. Retrieved from www.technologyreview.com/news.

12 GENCODE (15 July 2015). 'Statistics about the Current Human Gencode Release'. *GENCODE 23*. Retrieved from www.gencodegenes.org.

13 Noble, Denis (2006). *The Music of Life*. Oxford: Oxford University Press.

14 Venter, Craig, Daniel Gibson, et al. (2010). 'Creation of a Bacterial Cell Controlled by a Chemically Synthesized Genome'. *Science* 329(5987): 52–56.

15 Liang, Puping, Yanwen Xu, et al. (2015). 'CRISPR/Cas9-Mediated Gene Editing in Human Tripronuclear Zygotes'. *Protein & Cell* 6(5): 363–372.

16 Persson, Ingmar and Julian Savulescu (2012). *Unfit for the Future: The Need for Moral Enhancement*. Oxford: Oxford University Press.

17 Bohr, Mark (2014). '14 nm Process Technology: Opening New Horizons'. *Intel Developer Forum 2014*. San Francisco: Intel.

18 Turok, Neil (2012). *The Universe Within: From Quantum to Cosmos*. Canadian Broadcasting Corporation Massey Lectures. London: Faber&Faber.

19 Dattani, Nikesh and Nathaniel Bryans (2014). 'Quantum Factorization of 56153 with Only 4 Qubits'. *arXiv:1411.6758 [quant-ph]*.

20 Korzh, Boris, Charles Ci Wen Lim, et al. (2015). 'Provably Secure and Practical Quantum Key Distribution over 307 km of Optical Fibre'. *Nature Photonics* 9: 163–168.

21 Campbell, Peter, Michael Groves, et al. (2014). 'Soliloquy: A Cautionary Tale'. Conference paper. Ottawa: IQC/ETSI 2nd Quantum-Safe Crypto Workshop.

22 Drexler, K. Eric (2013). *Radical Abundance: How a Revolution in Nanotechnology Will Change Civilization*. New York: PublicAffairs.

23 Nature.com (2015). Citation searches performed at www.nature.com/search.

24 American Chemistry Council Nanotechnology Panel (2014). 'The Nano Timeline: A Big History of the Very Small'. Retrieved from nanotechnology.americanchemistry.com/Nanotechnology-Timeline.

25 Kuo, Lily (17 August 2015). 'A New "Drinkable Book" Has Pages That Turn Raw Sewage into Drinking Water'. *Quartz Africa*. Retrieved from www.qz.com.

26 Luef, Birgit, Kyle Frischkorn, et al. (2015). 'Diverse Uncultivated Ultra-Small Bacterial Cells in Groundwater'. *Nature Communications* 6(6372): 1–8.

27 New York University (3 June 2010). 'Chemist Seeman Wins Kavli Prize in Nanoscience'. *NYU*. Retrieved from www.nyu.edu/about/news-publications/news.

28 Arthur, Brian (2010). *The Nature of Technology*. London: Penguin.

29 Rabelais, Francois (1490–1553) (1608). 'Chapter 8: How Pantagruel, Being at Paris, Received Letters from His Father Gargantua, and the Copy of Them'. In *Five Books of the Lives, Heroic Deeds and Sayings of Gargantua and His Son Pantagruel, Book Two*. Lyon, France: Lean Martin.

30 Mokyr, *Twenty-Five Centuries of Technological Change*.

31 Sobel, *A More Perfect Heaven*.

32 Ibid.

33 Freely, John (2014). *Celestial Revolutionary: Copernicus, the Man and His Universe*. London: I. B. Tauris.

34 Arthur, *The Nature of Technology*.

35 da Vinci, Leonardo (1452–1519) (1955). 'Volume 1, Chapter X: Studies and Sketches for Pictures and Decorations'. In *The Notebooks of Leonardo Da Vinci,* edited by E. MacCurdy. New York: George Braziller.

36 Lipscy, Richard, Kenneth Carlaw, et al. (2005). *Economic Transformations, General Purpose Technologies and Long-Term Economic Growth*. Oxford: Oxford University Press.

37 Swetz, Frank (1989). *Capitalism and Arithmetic: The New Math of the 15th Century*. Chicago: Open Court Publishing Company.

38 Arnold, Thomas (2002). 'Violence and Warfare in the Renaissance World'. In *A Companion to the Worlds of the Renaissance*, edited by G. Ruggiero. Blackwell Reference Online: Blackwell.

39 Lee, Alexander (2013). *The Ugly Renaissance*. London: Hutchinson.

40 Mokyr, Joel (1990). *The Lever of Riches: Technological Creativity and Economic Progress*. Oxford: Oxford University Press, p. 79.

41 Brynjolfsson, Erik and Adam Saunders (2010). *Wired for Innovation: How Information Technology Is Reshaping the Economy*. Cambridge, MA: MIT Press.

42 Partnership for a New American Economy (2012). *Patent Pending: How Immigrants Are Reinventing the American Economy*. Partnership for a New American Economy. Retrieved from www.renewoureconomy.org.

43 Manyika, James, Jacques Bughin, et al. (2014). *Global Flows in a Digital Age*. New York: McKinsey & Co.

44 Castelvecchi, Davide (15 May 2015). 'Physics Paper Sets Record with More Than 5,000 Authors'. *Nature: International Weekly Journal of Science*. Retrieved from www .nature.com/news.

45 NobelPrize.org (2015). 'List of Nobel Prizes and Laureates'. Retrieved from www .nobelprize.org/nobel_prizes.

46 United Nations Conference on Trade and Development (2015). 'Merchandise: Intra-Trade and Extra-Trade of Country Groups by Product, Annual, 1995–2014'. *UNCTADStat*. Retrieved from unctadstat.unctad.org.

47 BBC News (27 November 2006). 'Star Wars Kid Is Top Viral Video'. *BBC*. Retrieved from www.bbc.co.uk.

48 Stark, Chelsea (22 July 2015). 'PewDiePie's Youtube Success Puts Him on the Cover of "Variety"'. *Mashable.com*. Retrieved from mashable.com.

49 Whitehead, Tom (9 January 2015). 'Paris Charlie Hebdo Attack: Je Suis Charlie Hashtag One of Most Popular in Twitter History'. *The Telegraph*. Retrieved from www.telegraph.co.uk.

Chapter 6: Cathedrals, Believers and Doubt

1 Gallichan, Walter M. (1903). *The Story of Seville*. London: Dent.

2   Pettegree, Andrew (2010). *The Book in the Renaissance*. New Haven: Yale University Press.

3   Lowry, Martin (1974). *Two Great Venetian Libraries in the Age of Aldus Manutius*. Manchester: John Rylands University Library of Manchester.

4   Staikos, Konstantinos (2000). *The Great Libraries: From Antiquity to the Renaissance (3000 B.C. To A.D. 1600)*. New Castle, DE: Oak Knoll Press; Febvre, Lucien and Henri-Jean Martin (2010). *The Coming of the Book: The Impact of Printing, 1450–1800*. London: Verso.

5   Barker, Nicolas (1989). *Aldus Manutius: Mercantile Empire of the Intellect, Volume 3*. Los Angeles: University of California Research Library; Davies, Martin (1995). *Aldus Manutius: Printer and Publisher of Renaissance Venice*. London: British Library.

6   Lowry, Martin (1979). *The World of Aldus Manutius: Business and Scholarship in Renaissance Venice*. Oxford: Blackwell.

7   Ibid.

8   Ibid.

9   Staikos, *The Great Libraries*.

10   Davies, *Aldus Manutius*.

11   Nesvig, Martin Austin (28 October 2011). 'Printing and the Book'. *Oxford Bibliographies*. Retrieved from www.oxfordbibliographies. com.

12   W3 Techs (2015). 'Usage Statistics and Market Share of Apache for Websites'. Retrieved from w3techs.com/technologies/details/ws-apache/all/all.

13   Statista (2015). 'The Most Spoken Languages Worldwide (Speakers and Native Speaker in Millions)'. Retrieved from www.statista.com/statistics/266808/the -most-spoken-languages-worldwide.

14   Lewis, M. Paul, Gary Simons, et al. (editors) (2015). *Ethnologue: Languages of the World* (18th Edition). Dallas: SIL International. Retrieved from www.ethnologue.com.

15 Hale, Scott A. (2014). 'Global Connectivity and Multilinguals in the Twitter Network'. SIGCHI Conference on Human Factors in Computing Systems. Toronto.

16 Wikipedia (2015). 'List of Wikipedias'. Retrieved from en.wikipedia. org/wiki/List_of_Wikipedias.

17 Kemp, Simon (2014). 'Social, Digital and Mobile Worldwide in 2014'. Retrieved from wearesocial.net/blog.

18 Manyika, James, Jacques Bughin, et al. (2014). *Global Flows in a Digital Age*. New York: McKinsey & Co.

19 Ibid; United Nations Conference on Trade and Development (2015). 'Merchandise: Intra-Trade and Extra-Trade of Country Groups by Product, Annual, 1995–2014'. *UNCTADStat*. Retrieved from unctadstat.unctad.org.

20 von Ahn, Luis (2011). 'Massive-Scale Online Collaboration'. *TEDTalks*. Retrieved from www.ted.com, plus authors' estimates.

21 Ibid.

22 Duolingo (2015). 'About Duolingo'. Retrieved from www.duolingo. com/press.

23 Pinkowski, Jennifer (28 March 2010). 'How to Classify a Million Galaxies in Three Weeks'. *Time*. Retrieved from content.time.com.

24 CERN (2015). 'Computing: Experiments at CERN Generate Colossal Amounts of Data'. Retrieved from home.web.cern.ch/about/computing.

25 Langmead, Ben and Michael C. Schatz (2013). 'The DNA Data Deluge'. *IEEE Spectrum*. Retrieved from spectrum.ieee.org/ biomedical/devices/the-dna-data -deluge.

26 Jet Propulsion Laboratory (27 October 2013). 'Managing the Deluge of "Big Data" from Space'. NASA. Retrieved from www.jpl.nasa.gov/news.

27 SciTech Daily (24 September 2013). 'Researchers Publish Galaxy Zoo 2 Catalog, Data on More Than 300,000 Nearby Galaxies'. *SciTech Daily*. Retrieved from scitechdaily.com.

28 van Arkel, Hanny (2015). 'Voorwerp Discovery'. Retrieved from www. hannysvoo -rwerp.com.

29 Smith, A., S. Lynn, et al. (December 2013). 'Zooniverse-Web Scale Citizen Science with People and Machines'. *AGU Fall Meeting Abstracts 1*: 1424.

30 Bonney, Rick, Jennifer L. Shirk, et al. (2014). 'Next Steps for Citizen Science'. *Science* 343(6178): 1436–1437.

31 Schilizzi, Richard (20 March 2013). *Big Pipes for Big Data: Signal and Data Transport in the SKA*. STFC Knowledge Exchange Workshop. Manchester: University of Manchester.

32 Lee, Alexander (2013). *The Ugly Renaissance*. London: Hutchinson.

33 Sobel, Dava (2011). *A More Perfect Heaven: How Copernicus Revolutionized the Cosmos*. London: Bloomsbury.

34 Gordon, Robert J. (2012). 'Is US Economic Growth Over? Faltering Innovation Confronts the Six Headwinds'. *National Bureau of Economic Research Working Paper No. 18315*. Retrieved from www.nber. org/papers/w18315.

35 Ibid.

36 Thiel, Peter (2011). 'What Happened to the Future?' Retrieved from www.foundersfund.com/the-future.

37 Phrma.org (2015). *2015 Pharmaceutical Industry Profile*. Washington, DC: PhRMA. Retrieved from www.phrma.org/profiles-reports.

38 European Federation of Pharmaceutical Industries and Associations (2014). 'The Pharmaceutical Industry in Figures'. Brussels: EFPIA. Retrieved from www.efpia.eu.

39 Abbott, Alison (2011). 'Novartis to Shut Brain Research Facility'. *Nature in Focus News* 480: 161–162.

40 Pew Research Center (2014). 'Inequality and Economic Mobility'. *Economies of Emerging Markets Better Rated during Difficult Times*. Global Attitudes Project. Washington, DC: Pew Research Center.

41 Merali, Zeeya (20 July 2015). 'Search for Extraterrestrial Intelligence Gets a $100-Million Boost'. *Nature*. Retrieved from www.nature.com/ news.

42 United Nations Development Programme (2010). *The Real Wealth of Nations: Pathways to Human Development*. Human Development Report 2010. New York: United Nations.

43 'In Search of the Perfect Market'. *The Economist* (8 May 1997). Retrieved from www.economist.com.

44 Young, Anne L. (2006). *Mathematical Ciphers: From Caesar to RSA*. Providence, RI: American Mathematical Society.

45 Brynjolfsson, Erik and Andrew McAfee (2014). *The Second Machine Age: Work, Progress, and Prosperity in a Time of Brilliant Technologies*. New York: W.W. Norton & Company.

46 Chen, Yan, Grace Young, et al. (2013). 'A Day without a Search Engine: An Experimental Study of Online and Offline Searches'. *Experimental Economics* 14(4): 512–536; Brynjolfsson and McAfee, *The Second Machine Age*.

47 Metcalfe, Robert (4 December 1995). 'Predicting the Internet's Catastrophic Collapse and Ghost Sites Galore in 1996'. *InfoWorld*.

48 Arthur, Brian (2010). *The Nature of Technology*. London: Penguin.

49 Mansfield, Harvey (1998). *Machiavelli's Virtue*. Chicago: Chicago University Press.

50 Arthur, *The Nature of Technology*.

51 Brynjolfsson and McAfee, *The Second Machine Age*.

52 EvaluatePharma (2015). 'World Preview 2015, Outlook to 2020'. London: Evaluate Group. Retrieved from info.evaluategroup.com.

53 Lloyd, Ian (2015). 'New Active Substances Launched during 2014'. *Pharma R&D Annual Review 2015*. Citeline. Retrieved from www. citeline.com.

54 Mullard, Asher (2015). '2014 FDA Drug Approvals'. *Nature Reviews Drug Discovery* 14: 77–81.

55 Ward, Andrew (22 July 2015). 'Eli Lilly Raises Hopes for Break-through Alzheimer's Drug'. *Financial Times*. Retrieved from www.ft.com.

56 World Health Organization (April 2015). 'Malaria'. *Fact Sheet No. 94*. Geneva: WHO. Retrieved from www.who.int/mediacentre/factsheets.

57 Mora, Camilo, Derek P. Tittensor, et al. (2011). 'How Many Species Are There on Earth and in the Ocean?' *PLOS Biology* 9(8): e1001127.

58 Smith, Dennis A., editor. (2010). *Metabolism, Pharmacokinetics, and Toxicity of Functional Groups: Impact of the Building Blocks of Medicinal Chemistry in Admet*. London: Royal Society of Chemistry.

59 Guicciardini, Francesco (1483–1540) (1969). *The History of Italy*, translated by S. Alexander. New York: Macmillan.

60 Bartlett, Kenneth R. (2011). *The Civilization of the Italian Renaissance: A Sourcebook* (2nd Edition). Toronto: University of Toronto Press.

61 Mallet, Michael and Christine Shaw (2012). *The Italian Wars, 1494–1559: War, State and Society in Early Modern Europe*. Harlow, UK: Pearson.

62 Wimmer, Eckard (2006). 'The Test-Tube Synthesis of a Chemical Called Poliovirus: The Simple Synthesis of a Virus Has Far-Reaching Societal Implications'. *EMBO Reports* 7: S3–S9.

63 von Bubnoff, Andreas (2005). 'The 1918 Flu Virus Is Resurrected'. *Nature* 437: 794–795.

64 Takashi, H., P. Keim, et al. (2004). 'Bacillus Anthracis Bioterrorism Incident, Kameido, Tokyo, 1993'. *Emerging Infectious Diseases* 10(1): 117–120.

65 Doornbos, Harald and Jenan Moussa (28 August 2014). 'Found: The Islamic State's Terror Laptop of Doom'. *Foreign Policy*. Retrieved from www.foreignpolicy .com.

66 Levy, Frank and Richard Murnane (2004). *The New Division of Labor: How Computers Are Creating the Next Job Market*. Princeton: Princeton University Press, p. 20.

67   Frey, Carl and Michael Osborne (2013). *The Future of Employment*.
     Oxford: Oxford Martin School. Retrieved from www.oxfordmartin.
     ox.ac.uk; Schwab, Klaus (2016). *The Fourth Industrial Revolution*.
     Geneva: World Economic Forum.

68   Berger, Thor and Carl Frey (2014). *Industrial Renewal in the 21st
     Century: Evidence from US Cities*. Oxford: Oxford Martin School.
     Retrieved from www.oxfordmartin .ox.ac.uk.

69   Gunn, Steven (2010). 'War and the Emergence of the State: Western
     Europe 1350–1600'. In *European Warfare 1350–1750*, edited by F. Tal-
     lett and D. Trim. Cambridge: Cambridge University Press, pp. 50–73.

70   Sands, Philippe (23 May 2014). 'No Place to Hide: Edward Snowden,
     the NSA and the Surveillance State by Glenn Greenwald – a Review'.
     The Guardian. Retrieved from www.theguardian.com.

71   Gallagher, Ryan (25 August 2014). 'The Surveillance Engine: How
     the NSA Built Its Own Secret Google'. *The Intercept*. Retrieved from
     firstlook.org/theintercept.

72   Machiavelli, Niccolò (1469–1527) (1532). *Florentine Histories*. Rome:
     Antonio Blado. Second Book, Chapter 22.

Chapter 7: The Pox Is Spreading, Venice Is Sinking

1   Tognotti, Eugenia (2009). 'The Rise and Fall of Syphilis in Renais-
     sance Europe'. *The Journal of Medical Humanities* 30(2): 99–113.

2   Ibid.

3   Allen, Peter Lewis (2000). *Wages of Sin*. Chicago: University of Chicago
     Press.

4   Ibid.

5   Hale, J. R. (1985). *War and Society in Renaissance Europe, 1450–1620*.
     London: Fontana Press.

6 Tognotti, 'The Rise and Fall of Syphilis in Renaissance Europe'.

7 Ibid.

8 Calvin, John (1509–1564) (1574). 'Sermon 141 on Job 36'. In *Sermons of Master John Calvin, Upon the Book of Job*. London: George Bishop.

9 Phillips, Tony (2014). 'Near Miss: The Solar Superstorm of July 2012'. *NASA Science News*. Retrieved from science.nasa.gov/science-news/science-at-nasa/2014/23jul_superstorm.

10 Tognotti, 'The Rise and Fall of Syphilis in Renaissance Europe'.

11 French, Roger, Jon Arrizabalaga, et al., editors. (1998). *Medicine from the Black Death to the French Disease*. Aldershot: Ashgate.

12 World Health Organization (2014). 'Factsheet No. 211: Influenza (Seasonal)'. Geneva: WHO. Retrieved from www.who.int/mediacentre/factsheets/fs211/en.

13 Goldin, Ian and Mike Mariathasan (2014). *The Butterfly Defect*. Princeton: Princeton University Press.

14 World Health Organization (2003). 'Agenda Item 14.16: Severe Acute Respiratory Syndrome (SARS)'. *Fifty-Sixth World Health Assembly*. Geneva: WHO.

15 Brilliant, Larry (February 2006). 'My Wish: Help Me Stop Pandemics'. TedTalks. Retrieved from www.ted.com.

16 Lee, Jong-Wha and Warwick J. McKibbin (2004). 'Estimating the Global Economic Costs of SARS'. In *Institute of Medicine Forum on Microbial Threats: Learning from SARS: Preparing for the Next Disease Outbreak: Workshop Summary*, edited by S. Knobler, A. Mahmoud and S. Lemon. Washington, DC: National Academies Press; World Health Organization (2003). 'Chapter 5: SARS: Lessons from a New Disease'. *The World Health Report*. Geneva: WHO.

17 World Health Organization (2015). 'Severe Acute Respiratory Syndrome (SARS)'. *Emergencies Preparedness, Response*. Geneva: WHO. Retrieved from www.who.int/csr/sars/en.

18 Roberts, Michelle (2014). 'First Ebola Boy Likely Infected by Playing in Bat Tree'. *BBC News*. Retrieved from www.bbc.co.uk.

19 Centers for Disease Control and Prevention (2015). 'Outbreaks Chronology: Ebola Virus Disease'. Atlanta: CDC. Retrieved from www.cdc.gov/vhf/ebola/outbreaks/history/chronology.html.

20 Fink, Sheri (3 September 2014). 'Cuts at WHO Hurt Response to Ebola Crisis'. *The New York Times*. Retrieved from www.nytimes.com.

21 (14 November 2014). 'The Toll of a Tragedy'. *The Economist*. Retrieved from www.economist.com.

22 Centers for Disease Control and Prevention (2015). '2014 Ebola Outbreak in West Africa – Case Counts'. Atlanta: CDC. Retrieved from www.cdc.gov/vhf/ebola/outbreaks/2014-west-africa/case-counts.html.

23 Blas, Javier (19 November 2014). 'World Bank Dramatically Reduces Projection of Ebola's Economic Toll'. *The Financial Times*. Retrieved from www.ft.com.

24 World Bank (2014). 'Health Expenditure Per Capita (Current US$)'. *World Development Indicators*. Retrieved from data.worldbank.org.

25 World Health Organization Global Health Observatory (2014). 'Density of Physicians (Total Number per 1,000 Population, Latest Available Year)'. *Global Health Observatory Data Repository*. Retrieved from apps.who.int/gho/data.

26 BBC News (7 October 2014). 'Ebola Outbreak: Liberia "Close to Collapse" – Ambassador'. *BBC*. Retrieved from www.bbc.co.uk.

27 Callimachi, Rukmini (18 September 2014). 'Fear of Ebola Drives Mob to Kill Officials in Guinea'. *The New York Times*. Retrieved from www.nytimes.com.

28 United Nations Conference on Trade and Development (2015). 'Intra-Trade of Regional and Trade Groups by Product, Annual, 1995–2014'. *UNCTADStat*. Retrieved from unctadstat.unctad.org.

29 Grepin, Karen (2015). 'International Donations to the Ebola Virus Outbreak: Too Little, Too Late?' *British Medical Journal (BMJ)* 350: 1–5.

30 Gire, Stephen, Augustine Goba, et al. (2014). 'Genomic Surveillance Elucidates Ebola Virus Origin and Transmission during the 2014 Outbreak'. *Science* 345(6202): 1369–1372.

31 World Health Organization (26 September 2014). 'Experimental Therapies: Growing Interest in the Use of Whole Blood or Plasma from Recovered Ebola Patients (Convalescent Therapies)'. *Ebola Situation Assessment – 26 September 2014.* Geneva: WHO. Retrieved from www.who.int/mediacentre/news/ebola/26-september-2014/en.

32 Gaidet, Nicolas, Julien Cappelle, et al. (2010). 'Potential Spread of Highly Pathogenic Avian Influenza H5N1 by Wildfowl: Dispersal Ranges and Rates Determined from Large-Scale Satellite Telemetry'. *Journal of Applied Ecology* 47(5): 1147.

33 International SOS (8 February 2015). 'Pandemic Preparedness: H5N1 Affected Countries'. Retrieved from www.internationalsos.com/pandemicpreparedness; International SOS (5 April 2013). 'Pandemic Preparedness: H5N1 in Birds'. Retrieved from www.internationalsos.com/pandemicpreparedness.

34 Ibid.

35 Arnold, Jeffrey L. (2002). 'Disaster Medicine in the 21st Century: Future Hazards, Vulnerabilities, and Risk'. *Prehospital and Disaster Medicine* 17(1): 3–11.

36 International SOS (2 February 2015). 'Pandemic Preparedness: Avian Flu'. Retrieved from www.internationalsos.com/pandemicpreparedness.

37 World Health Organization (2015). 'HIV/AIDS'. *Global Health Observatory Data Repository.* Retrieved from apps.who.int/gho/data.

38 UNAIDS (2002). 'Fact Sheets: Twenty Years of HIV/AIDS'. Retrieved from library.unesco-iicba.org/English/HIV_AIDS.

39 World Health Organization, 'HIV/AIDS'.

40 Ibid.

41 Goldin and Mariathasan, *The Butterfly Defect.*

42 Brockmann, Dirk, Lars Hufnagel, et al. (2005). 'Dynamics of Modern Epidemics'. In *SARS: A Case Study in Emerging Infections*, edited by Angela McLean, Robert May, et al. Oxford: Oxford University Press, pp. 81–91.

43 Liu, Yi-Yun, Yang Wang, et al. (2015). 'Emergence of Plasmid-Mediated Colistin Resistance Mechanism MCR-1 in Animals and Human Beings in China: A Microbiological and Molecular Biological Study'. *The Lancet*. Retrieved from dx.doi.org/10.1016/S1473–3099(15)00424–7.

44 Schoenberger, Erica (2014). *Nature, Choice and Social Power*. London: Routledge, p. 95.

45 Dattels, Peter and Laura Kodres (21 April 2009). 'Further Action Needed to Reinforce Signs of Market Recovery: IMF'. *IMF Survey Magazine*. Retrieved from www.imf.org/external/pubs/ft/survey/so/2009/RES042109C.htm.

46 World Bank (September 2009). 'Impact of the Financial Crisis on Employment'. Retrieved from go.worldbank.org/9ZLKOLN0O0.

47 United Nations Development Programme (2010). *The Real Wealth of Nations: Pathways to Human Development*. Human Development Report 2010. New York: United Nations.

48 Parts of our discussion of systemic risk in the financial sector draw upon prior work by Goldin and Mariathasan in *The Butterfly Defect*.

49 Gorton, Garry B. and Andrew Metrick (2009). 'Securitized Banking and the Run on Repo'. *National Bureau of Economic Research Working Paper No. 15223*. Retrieved from www.nber.org/papers/w15223.

50 Goldin and Mariathasan, *The Butterfly Defect*.

51 Lewis, Michael (26 March 2008). 'What Wall Street's CEO's Don't Know Can Kill You'. *Bloomberg*. Retrieved from www.bloomberg.com.

52 International Monetary Fund (2007). 'Global Financial Stability Report: Market Developments and Issues'. *World Economic and Financial Surveys*. Washington, DC: IMF, p. 7.

53 Thompson, Anthony, Elen Callahan, et al. (2007). 'Global CDO Market: Overview and Outlook'. *Global Securitization and Structured Finance 2007*. Frankfurt: Deutsche Bank.

54 Goldin and Mariathasan, *The Butterfly Defect*.

55 Kosmidou, Kyriaki, Sailesh Tanna, et al. (2005). 'Determinants of Profitability of Domestic UK Commercial Banks: Panel Evidence from the Period 1995–2002'. *Money Macro and Finance (MMF) Research Group Conference 2005*. Retrieved from repec.org/mmfc05/paper45.pdf; Maer, Lucinda and Nida Broughton (2012). *Financial Services: Contribution to the UK Economy*. London: House of Commons Library, Economic Policy and Statistics.

56 'Cracks in the Crust'. *The Economist* (11 December 2008). Retrieved from www.economist.com.

57 Haldane, Andrew G. (28 April 2009). 'Rethinking the Financial Network'. Speech given to the Financial Student Association, Amsterdam. Retrieved from www.bankofengland.co.uk/archive/Documents/historicpubs/speeches/2009/speech386.pdf.

58 Green Growth Action Alliance (2013). 'Required Infrastructure Needs'. *The Green Investment Report*. Geneva: World Economic Forum.

59 American Society of Civil Engineers (2013). 'Grade Sheet: America's Infrastructure Investment Needs'. Reston, VA: ASCE. Retrieved from www.infrastructurereport-card.org.

60 Bhattacharya, Amar, Mattia Romani, et al. (2012). 'Infrastructure for Development: Meeting the Challenge'. Policy brief. Seoul: Global Green Growth Institute. Retrieved from www.gggi.org.

61 Bolt, J. and J. L. van Zanden (2014). 'The Maddison Project: Collaborative Research on Historical National Accounts'. *The Economic History Review* 67(3): 627–651.

62 Crowley, Roger (2011). *City of Fortune: How Venice Won and Lost a Naval Empire*. London: Faber&Faber.

63 Ibid.

64 'When the Chain Breaks'. *The Economist* (15 June 2006). Retrieved from www.economist.com.

65 For more on the Thailand case, see *The Butterfly Defect*.

66 Chongvilaivan, Aekapol (2012). 'Thailand's 2011 Flooding: Its Impact on Direct Exports and Global Supply Chains'. *ARTNeT Working Paper Series, No. 113*. Retrieved from hdl.handle.net/10419/64271.

67 Thailand Board of Investment (2012). 'Expertise, New Investment Keep Thai E&E Industry at the Top'. *Thailand Investment Review*. Retrieved from www.boi.go.th.

68 Abe, Masato and Linghe Ye (2013). 'Building Resilient Supply Chains against Natural Disasters: The Cases of Japan and Thailand'. *Global Business Review* 14: 567.

69 Ibid.

70 Smalley, Eric (12 December 2011). 'Thai Floodwaters Sink Intel Chip Orders'. *Wired*. Retrieved from www.wired.com.

71 Thailand Board of Investment (2015). 'E&E Industry: Hard Disk Drive Export, 2005–2014'. *Thailand Investment Review*. Retrieved from www.boi.go.th.

72 Oxford Economics (2010). *The Economic Impacts of Air Travel Restrictions due to Volcanic Ash, Report Prepared for Airbus*. Oxford: Oxford Economics.

73 Kaplan, Eben (24 April 2007). 'America's Vulnerable Energy Grid'. *Council on Foreign Relations*.

74 US–Canada Power System Outage Task Force (2004). *Final Report on the August 14, 2003 Blackout in the United States and Canada: Causes and Recommendations*. Washington, DC and Ottawa: Department of Energy and Ministry of Natural Resources, p. 19.

75 Kharas, Homi (9 January 2015). 'The Transition from "the Developing World" to "a Developing World"'. *Kapuscinski Development Lectures*. Retrieved from www.brookings.edu.

76 Airports Council International (2015). 'Annual Traffic Data'. Retrieved from www.aci.aero/Data-Centre/Annual-Traffic-Data.

77 World Shipping Council (2015). 'Top 50 World Container Ports'. Retrieved from www.worldshipping.org/about-the-industry/global-trade.

78 EMC Corporation (2 December 2014). 'Over $1.7 Trillion Lost per Year from Data Loss and Downtime according to Global IT Study'. Retrieved from uk.emc.com/about/news/press/2014/20141202-01.htm.

79 Miller, Rich (July 2013). 'Who Has the Most Data Servers?' *Data Center Knowledge*. Retrieved from www.datacenterknowledge.com/archives/2009/05/14/whos-got -the-most-web-servers.

80 IBM (2015). *2015 Cyber Security Intelligence Index*. New York: IBM Security. Retrieved from public.dhe.ibm.com/common/ssi/ecm/se/en/sew03073usen/SEW03073US -EN.PDF.

81 Greenberg, Andy (2015). 'Hackers Remotely Kill a Jeep on the Highway – with Me in It'. *Wired*. Retrieved from www.youtube.com.

82 Symantec (2015). *2015 Internet Security Threat Report, Volume 20*. Mountain View, CA: Symantec. Retrieved from www.symantec.com/security_response/publications/threatreport.jsp.

83 Rogin, Josh (9 July 2012). 'NSA Chief: Cybercrime Constitutes the "Greatest Transfer of Wealth in History"'. *Foreign Policy*. Retrieved from www.foreignpolicy.com.

84 Ibid.; IBM, *2015 Cyber Security Intelligence Index*.

85 Rainie, Lee, Janna Anderson, et al. (29 October 2014). 'Cyber Attacks Likely to Increase'. Pew Research Center. Retrieved from www.pewinternet.org.

86 Ponemon Institute (2015). *2015 Cost of Data Breach Study: Global Analysis*. Traverse City, Michigan: Ponemon Institute.

87 Associated Press (23 September 2015). 'US Government Hack Stole Fingerprints of 5.6 Million Federal Employees'. *The Guardian*. Retrieved from www.theguardian.com.

88 Symantec, *2015 Internet Security Threat Report*.

89 Kushner, David (26 February 2013). 'The Real Story of Stuxnet'. *IEEE Spectrum*. Retrieved from spectrum.ieee.org/telecom/security.

90 Menn, Joseph (29 May 2015). 'US Tried Stuxnet-Style Campaign against North Korea but Failed – Sources'. *Reuters*. Retrieved from www.reuters. com.

91 Bundesamt fur Sicherheit in der Informationstechnik (2014). *Die Lage Der IT-Sicherheit in Deutschland 2014*. Berlin: German Federal Office for Information Security. Retrieved from www.bsi.bund.de.

92 Industrial Control Systems Cyber Emergency Response Team (2015). *ICS-CERT Year in Review*. Washington, DC: Department of Homeland Security. Retrieved from ics-cert.us-cert.gov.

93 Maddison, Angus (2003). *The World Economy: Historical Statistics, Vol. 2: Statistical Appendix*. Paris: OECD.

Chapter 8: Prophets and Bonfires

1 Savonarola, Girolamo (1452–1498) (1971). 'O Soul, by Sin Made Blind'. In *Italian Poets of the Renaissance*, edited by J. Tusiani. New York: Baroque Press, p. 81.

2 Viladesau, Richard (2008). *The Triumph of the Cross: The Passion of Christ in Theology and the Arts*. Oxford: Oxford University Press. p. 30.

3 Savonarola, Girolamo (1452–1498) (2005). 'Aggeus, Sermon XIII. Delivered on the 3rd Sunday of Advent, 12 December 1494'. In *Selected Writings of Girolamo Savonarola, Religion and Politics, 1490–1498*, edited by A. Borelli, D. Beebe and M. Passaro. New Haven, CT: Yale University Press.

4 Weinstein, *Savonarola*.

5 Ibid.

6 Ibid.

7 Cameron, Euan (2012). *The European Reformation*. Oxford: Oxford University Press.

8 Jones, Jonathan (19 October 2011). 'The Lusts of Leonardo Da Vinci'. *The Guardian*. Retrieved from www.theguardian.com.

9 Martines, Lauro (2006). *Scourge and Fire: Savonarola and Renaissance Florence*. London: Jonathan Cape.

10 Martines, Lauro (2006). *Fire in the City: Savonarola and the Struggle for the Soul of the Renaissance*. Oxford: Oxford University Press.

11 Black, Robert (2010). '(Review) Venice Besieged: Politics and Diplomacy in the Italian Wars, by Robert Finlay'. *English Historical Review* CXXV(512): 170–171.

12 Martines, *Fire in the City*.

13 Lean, Geoffrey (17 July 1999). 'The Hidden Tentacles of the World's Most Secret Body'. *Sunday Independent*. Retrieved from www.independent.co.uk.

14 World Trade Organization (1999). 'Document No. 99-55154: List of Representatives'. *Third Ministerial Conference*. Seattle: WTO. Retrieved from docs.wto.org

15 Piketty, Thomas (2014). *Capital in the 21st Century*. Cambridge: Harvard University Press.

16 Credit Suisse Research Institute (2010). *Global Wealth Report 2010*. Zurich: Credit Suisse.

17 Piketty, *Capital in the 21st Century*, Chapters 6 and 10.

18 OECD (2015). *In It Together: Why Less Inequality Benefits All*. Paris: OECD Publishing.

19 Saez, Emmanuel (2013). *Striking It Richer: The Evolution of Top Incomes in the United States (Updated with 2012 Preliminary Estimates)*. Stanford Center for the Study of Poverty and Inequality. Berkeley: Stanford University.

20 Rosenblum, Harvey, Tyler Atkinson, et al. (2013). 'Assessing the Costs and Consequences of the 2007–09 Financial Crisis and Its Aftermath'. *Federal Reserve Bank of Dallas Economic Letter* 8(7). Retrieved from www.dallasfed.org/research/eclett/2013/el1307.cfm.

21 CoreLogic (2013). *National Foreclosure Report*. Irvine, CA: CoreLogic. Retrieved from www.corelogic.com/research.

22 Simiti, Marilena (2014). 'Rage and Protest: The Case of the Greek Indignant Movement'. *Hellenic Observatory Papers on Greece and Southeast Europe, No. 82*. London: London School of Economics. Retrieved from www.lse.ac.uk/europeanInstitute/research/hellenicObservatory.

23 RTVE.es (6 August 2011). 'Más De Seis Millones De Españoles Han Participado En El Movimiento 15m'. *RTVE*. Retrieved from www.rtve. es.

24 RT.com (15 October 2011). 'Rome Descends into Chaos as Protests Turn Violent'. *RT*. from www.rt.com.

25 Rowley, Emma (16 January 2011). 'Bank Bail-out Adds £1.5 Trillion to Debt'. *The Telegraph*. Retrieved from www.telegraph.co.uk.

26 BBC News (7 January 2011). 'Bank Bonuses 'to Run to Billions in 2011'. *BBC*. Retrieved from www.bbc.co.uk.

27 BBC News (20 June 2015). 'Thousands Attend Anti-Austerity Rallies across UK'. *BBC*. Retrieved from www.bbc.co.uk.

28 Kassam, Ashifa (13 March 2015). 'Ciudadanos, the 'Podemos of the Right', Emerges as Political Force in Spain'. *The Guardian*. Retrieved from www.theguardian.com

29 Helm, Toby and Daniel Boffey (13 September 2015). 'Corbyn Hails Huge Mandate as He Sets out Leftwing Agenda'. *The Guardian*. Retrieved from www.theguardian.com.

30 OECD, *In It Together*, p. 240.

31 Centers for Disease Control and Prevention (2013). 'CDC Health Disparities and Inequalities Report – United States, 2013'. *Morbidity and Mortality Weekly Report*. Washington, DC: US Department of Health and Human Services.

32 Ineq-Cities Atlas (2015). 'Paris Socio-Economic Indicators and Mortality Maps'. *Socio-Economic Inequalities in Mortality: Evidence*

and Policies in Cities of Europe. Retrieved from www.ucl.ac.uk/silva/ineqcities/atlas/cities/paris.

33 Korda, Rosemary, Ellie Paige, et al. (2014). 'Income-Related Inequalities in Chronic Conditions, Physical Functioning and Psychological Distress among Older People in Australia: Cross-Sectional Findings from the 45 and up Study'. *BMC Public Health* 14: 741.

34 Martines, *Fire in the City*.

35 Whether Luther actually nailed his *Theses* to the church doors is disputed. What is known is that he wrote a letter to his superiors on that day to denounce the sale of indulgences, and included his *95 Theses* with it.

36 Strathern, Paul (2011). *Death in Florence: The Medici, Savonarola, and the Battle for the Soul of Man*. London: Jonathan Cape.

37 Luther, Martin (1483–1546) (1908). 'Letter to Christoph Scheurl, 5 March 1518'. In *The Letters of Martin Luther*, edited by M. Currie. London: Macmillan and Co., p. 23.

38 Edwards Jr., Mark U. (2005). *Printing, Propaganda, and Martin Luther*. Minneapolis: Fortress Press; Hsia, R. Po-chia (2006). *A Companion to the Reformation World*. Oxford: Blackwell.

39 MacCulloch, Diarmaid (2003). *Reformation: Europe's House Divided, 1490–1700*. London: Allen Lane.

40 Goldstone, Jack A. (1991). *Revolution and Rebellion in the Early Modern World*. Berkeley: University of California Press.

41 Te Brake, Wayne (1998). *Shaping History: Ordinary People in European Politics*. Berkeley: University of California Press.

42 Bethencourt, Francisco (2009). *The Inquisition: A Global History, 1478–1834*, translated by J. Birrell. Cambridge: Cambridge University Press, p. 444.

43 MacCulloch, *Reformation*, Chapter 17.

44 Ibid. pp. 671, 672.

45 Hall, Edward (1497–1547) (1904). *Henry VIII*. Edited by C. Whibley, *The Lives of the Kings, Volume 2*. London: T.C. & E.C. Jack, p. 43.

46 Frey, Carl Benedikt and Michael Oxborne (2015). *Technology at Work: The Future of Innovation and Employment*. New York and Oxford: Citigroup and Oxford Martin School.

47 OECD, *In It Together*.

48 Dabla-Norris, Era, Kalpana Kochhar, et al. (2015). 'Causes and Consequences of Income Inequality: A Global Perspective'. *IMF Staff Discussion Note*. Washington, DC: International Monetary Fund.

49 'Mine, All Mine'. *The Economist* (10 February 2011). Retrieved from www.economist.com.

50 Dabla-Norris, Kochhar, et al. Causes and Consequences of Income Inequality.

51 Federal Election Commission (13 January 2017). 'Statistical Summary of 21-Month Campaign Activity of the 2015–2016 Election Cycle'. *FEC*. Retrieved from www.fec.gov

52 Kutarna, Christopher (2016). 'Will Brexit Happen?' *YouTube*. Retrieved from https://youtu.be/9qHDtMJTL5k

53 Pew Research Center (16 September 2014). 'Faith and Skepticism About Trade, Foreign Investment'. *Pew Research Center Global Attitudes and Trends*. Retrieved from www.pewglobal.org.

54 Frontex (8 August 2015). 'Number of Migrants in One Month above 100,000 for First Time'. Warsaw: European Agency for the Management of Operational Cooperation at the External Borders of the Member States of the European Union. Retrieved from frontex.europa.eu/news

55 Much to the glee of autocratic regimes, like China's Communist Party, which are always happy to highlight democracy's chaotic potential in their state-run media.

Chapter 9: David

1 Twain, Mark (1975). *Mark Twain's Notebooks & Journals*, edited by F. Anderson, L. Salamo and B. Stein. Berkeley/Los Angeles: University of California Press, pp. 232–233.

2 Paoletti, John (2015). *Michelangelo's David: Florentine History and Civic Identity*. Cambridge: Cambridge University Press.

3 Ibid., p. 198.

4 Erasmus, Desiderius (c. 1466–1536) (1924). 'To Marcus Laurinus, February 1, 1523.' *Opus Epistolarum Des. Erasmi Roterodami. Volume V: 1522-1524*. Edited by P.S. Allen and H. M. Allen. Oxford: Oxford University Press, p. 277.

5 Strauss, Valerie (17 May 2014). 'The Greatest Commencement Speech Ever'. *The Washington Post*. Retrieved from www.washingtonpost. com.

6 Mokyr, Joel (1990). *Twenty-Five Centuries of Technological Change*. London: Harwood Academic.

7 NobelPrize.org (2015). 'List of Nobel Prizes and Laureates'. Retrieved from www.nobelprizc.org/nobel_prizes.

8 United Nations Department of Economic and Social Affairs (2015). *World Population Prospects: The 2015 Revision*. New York: United Nations.

9 Bhopal, Kalwant (2014). 'The Experience of BME Academics in Higher Education: Aspirations in the Face of Inequality'. *Leadership Foundation for Higher Education Stimulus Papers*. Retrieved from www.lfhe.ac.uk.

10 Rippon, Gina (5 September 2014). 'Prejudice, Not Brainpower, Is Behind the Gender Gap'. *The Times*. Retrieved from www.thetimes. co.uk.

11 XPrize (2015). 'Who We Are'. *XPrize.org*. Retrieved from www.xprize. org.

12 Barnett, Chance (9 June 2015). 'Trends Show Crowdfunding to Surpass VC in 2016'. *Forbes*. Retrieved from www.forbes.com.

13 Crowdsourcing.org (2015). 'Global Crowdfunding Market to Reach $34.4B in 2015, Predicts Massolution's 2015 CF Industry Report'. Retrieved from www.crowdsourcing.org/editorial.

14 World Bank (2013). 'Crowdfunding's Potential for the Developing World'. *Information for Development Program*. Washington, DC: The World Bank.

15 Ibid.

16 National Science Foundation (2014). 'Table 4-3: US R&D Expenditures, by Performing Sector, Source of Funds, and Character of Work: 2011'. *National Science Foundation*. Retrieved from www.nsf.gov; OECD (2015). 'Main Science and Technology Indicators'. *OECD.Stat*. Retrieved from www.oecd.org/sti/msti .htm.

17 Spickernell, Sarah and Clive Cookson (22 January 2014). 'R&D Suffers Biggest Cuts in Government Spending'. *The Financial Times*. Retrieved from www.ft.com.

18 OECD, 'Main Science and Technology Indicators'.

19 Alberts, Bruce, Marc W. Kirschner, et al. (2014). 'Rescuing US Biomedical Research from Its Systemic Flaws'. *Proceedings of the National Academy of Sciences of the United States of America* 111(16): 5773–5777; National Institutes of Health (2015). 'Research Project Grants: Average Size'. *NIH Data Book*. Retrieved from report.nih.gov/ nihdatabook/index.aspx.

20 National Institutes of Health (2012). *Biomedical Research Workforce; Working Group Report*. Bethesda, MD: National Institutes of Health.

21 Harris, Richard (9 September 2014). 'When Scientists Give Up'. *National Public Radio*. Retrieved from www.npr.org/sections/health-shots/2014/09/09/345289127/when-scientists-give-up?refresh=true.

22 Partridge, Loren (1996). *The Art of Renaissance Rome, 1400–1600*. New York: Harry N. Abrams.

23 Phelps, Edmund (2013). *Mass Flourishing: How Grassroots Innovation Created Jobs, Challenge and Change*. Princeton: Princeton University Press, pp. 316, 324.

24 Kharas, Homi (2010). 'The Emerging Middle Class in Developing Countries'. *OECD Development Centre Working Paper No. 285*. Paris: OECD; Cisco (2015). *The Zettabyte Era: Trends and Analysis*. San Jose: Cisco Systems Inc. Retrieved from www.cisco.com.

25 Terdiman, Daniel (11 February 2014). 'No, Flappy Bird Developer Didn't Give up on $50,000 a Day'. *CNET*. Retrieved from www.cnet.com.

26 ALS Association (29 August 2014). 'The ALS Association Expresses Sincere Gratitude to over Three Million Donors'. Retrieved from www.alsa.org/news/media/press-releases.

27 Ling, Jonathan (8 August 2015). 'Science AMA Series: Hi, I'm Jonathan Ling, a Researcher That's Here to Share Our New Breakthrough Discovery for ALS (Amyotrophic Lateral Sclerosis)'. *The New Reddit Journal of Science*. Retrieved from www .reddit.com/r/science/comments/3g4c7v/science_ama_series_hi_im_jonathan _ling_a.

28 Apple Events (2 June 2014). 'Apple Special Event: June 2, 2014'. Cupertino: Apple. Retrieved from www.apple.com/apple-events/june-2014; Phone Arena (10 June 2013). '6m Developers in Apple Ecosystem, $10B Paid in Revenue'. *Phone Arena*. Retrieved from www.phonearena.com/news.

29 Pettersson, Therese and Peter Wallensteen (2015). 'Armed Conflicts, 1946–2014'. *Journal of Peace Research* 52(4): 536–550.

30 Ungerleider, Neal (11 July 2014). 'IBM's $3 Billion Investment in Synthetic Brains and Quantum Computing'. *Fast Company*. Retrieved from www.fastcom -pany.com.

31 Carroll, John (11 September 2014). 'Google's Stealthy Calico Inks an R&D Deal for New Compounds Aimed at Neurodegeneration'. *Fierce Biotech*. Retrieved from www.fiercebiotech.com.

32 International Monetary Fund (17 July 2015). 'Counting the Cost of Energy Subsidies'. *IMF Survey*. Retrieved from www.imf.org/external/

pubs/ft/survey/so/2015/new070215a.htm; OECD (2015). *Agricultural Policy Monitoring and Evaluation 2015*. Paris: OECD.

33 OECD (2015). *In It Together: Why Less Inequality Benefits All*. Paris: OECD Publishing, Chapter 4.

34 Klapper, Leora, Luc Laeven, et al. (2006). 'Entry Regulation as a Barrier to Entrepreneurship'. *Journal of Financial Economics* 82(3): 591–629; Golec, J. and J. A. Vernon (2010). 'Financial Effects of Pharmaceutical Price Regulation on R&D Spending by EU versus US Firms'. *Pharmacoeconomics* 28(8): 615–628.

35 Winkler, Andy, Ben Gitis, et al. (2014). 'Dodd-Frank at 4: More Regulation, More Regulators, and a Sluggish Housing Market'. Retrieved from americanactionforum.org.

36 Spowers, Rory (2002). *Rising Tides: A History of Environmentalism*. Edinburgh: Canongate.

37 Haldane, Andrew G. (2012). 'Federal Reserve Bank of Kansas City's 36th Economic Policy Symposium, "The Changing Policy Landscape"'. *The Dog and the Frisbee*. Jackson Hole, Wyoming: The Bank of England.

38 Connell, William (2002). *Society and Individual in Renaissance Florence*. Berkeley: University of California Press, p. 111.

39 Arthur, Brian (2010). *The Nature of Technology*. London: Penguin.

40 Chandler, Tertius (1987). *Four Thousand Years of Urban Growth: An Historical Census*. Lewiston, ME: Edwin Mellen Press.

41 McKinsey Global Institute (2013). 'Urban World: A New App for Exploring an Unprecedented Wave of Urbanization'. Retrieved from www.mckinsey.com/insights.

42 Ferguson, Niall (20 January 2016). 'Florence.' Interviewed by I. Goldin, Davos.

43 Statistics Canada (2011). 'NHS Focus on Geography Series – Toronto'. *National Household Survey 2011*. Ottawa: Statistics Canada.

44 Downie, Michella (2010). *Immigrants as Innovators Boosting Canada's Global Competitiveness*. Ottawa: The Conference Board of Canada; Dungan, Peter, Tony Fang, et al. (2013). 'Macroeconomic Impacts of Canadian Immigration: Results from a Macro Model'. *British Journal of Industrial Relations* 51(1): 174–195.

45 Murray, Sarah (2015). 'The Safe Cities Index 2015: Assessing Urban Security in the Digital Age'. *The Economist Intelligence Unit*. London: The Economist.

46 Wile, Rob (14 June 2014). 'It's Clear That the Future of Bitcoin Is Not in the US'. *Business Insider*. Retrieved from www.businessinsider.com; SourceForge (2015). 'Bitcoin'. Retrieved from sourceforge.net/projects/bitcoin/files/stats/timeline.

47 International Monetary Fund (2015). 'House Price-to-Income Ratio around the World'. *Global Housing Watch*. Retrieved from www.imf.org/external/research/ housing.

48 Allen, Kate and Anna Nicolaou (16 April 2015). 'Global Property Bubble Fears Mount as Prices and Yields Spike'. *The Financial Times*. Retrieved from www .ft.com.

49 Passel, Jeffrey S. and D'Vera Cohn (2010). 'Unauthorized Immigrant Population: National and State Trends, 2010'. *Pew Research Center Hispanic Trends*. Retrieved from www.pewhispanic.org.

50 Platform for International Cooperation on Undocumented Migrants (22 April 2013). *PICUM Submission to the UN Committee on the Protection of the Rights of All Migrant Workers and Members of Their Families*. Geneva: PICUM.

51 US Department of Homeland Security (2006). *Report on H-1B Petitions: Fiscal Year 2004, Annual Report October 1, 2003 – September 30, 2004*. United States Citizenship and Immigration Services. Washington, DC: US Department of Homeland Security.

52 Brynjolfsson, Erik and Andrew McAfee (2014). *The Second Machine Age: Work, Progress, and Prosperity in a Time of Brilliant Technologies*. New York: W.W. Norton & Company.

53 Charette, Robert N. (30 August 2013). 'The Stem Crisis Is a Myth'. *IEEE Spectrum*. Retrieved from spectrum.ieee.org; *The Wall Street Journal* (19 March 2007). 'Does Silicon Valley Need More Visas for Foreigners'. *The Wall Street Journal*. Retrieved from www.online.wsj.com.

54 Congressional Budget Office (2013). *The Economic Impact of S. 744, the Border Security, Economic Opportunity, and Immigration Modernization Act*. Washington, DC: CBO. Retrieved from www.cbo.gov.

55 Lisenkova, Katerina and Marcel Merette (2013). 'The Long-Term Economic Impacts of Reducing Migration: The Case of the UK Migration Policy'. *National Institute of Economic and Social Research, Discussion Paper No. 420*. London: NIESR.

56 Pew Hispanic Center (2013). 'A Nation of Immigrants: A Portrait of the 40 Million, including 11 Million Unauthorized'. *Pew Research Center*. Retrieved from www .pewhispanic.org.

57 Meissner, Doris, Donald M. Kerwin, et al. (2013). *Immigration Enforcement in the United States: The Rise of a Formidable Machinery*. Washington, DC.: Migration Policy Institute.

58 Kynge, James and Jonathan Wheatley (3 August 2015). 'Emerging Markets: Redrawing the World Map'. *The Financial Times*. Retrieved from www.ft.com.

59 Riffkin, Rebecca (12 March 2014). 'Climate Change Not a Top Worry in US'. *Gallup*. Retrieved from www.gallup.com/poll/167843/climate-change-not-top-worry.aspx; Lomborg, Bjorn (9 March 2014). 'EU Likes to Say "Climate Change Is One of the Greatest Challenges of the Modern Age"'. *Facebook*. Retrieved from www .facebook.com/photo.php?fbid=10152349665523968.

60 Pew Research Center (14 July 2015). 'Climate Change Seen as Top Global Threat'. *Pew Global Attitudes & Trends*. Retrieved from www.pewglobal.org.

61 World Health Organization (2015). *Programme Budget 2016–2017*. Geneva: WHO. Retrieved from www.who.int/about/finances-accountability.

62 Rainforest Conservation Fund (2015). 'How Much Biodiversity Is Found in Tropical Rainforests'. Retrieved from www.rainforestconservation.org/rainforest -primer/2-biodiversity/b-how-much-biodiversity-is-found-in-tropical-rainforests; Hood, Laura (8 October 2010). 'Biodiversity: Facts and Figures'. *SciDev.Net*. Retrieved from www.scidev.net/global/biodiversity/feature/biodiversity-facts-and-figures-1.html.

63 della Mirandola, Pico (1463–1494) (2012). *Oration on the Dignity of Man: A New Translation and Commentary*, translated by F. Borghesi, M. Papio and M. Riva. Cambridge: Cambridge University Press.

64 Hector, Helen (4 December 2014). 'Trillion Dollar Scandal: The Biggest Heist You've Never Heard of'. *ONE.org*. Retrieved from www.one.org/scandal/en/report.

65 First proposed by the Oxford Martin Commission for Future Generations (2014). *Now for the Long Term*. Oxford: Oxford Martin School.

66 Machiavelli, Niccolò (1469–1527) (2005). 'Chapter XXV: Of Fortune's Power in Human Affairs and How She Can Be Resisted'. In *The Prince*, edited by P. Bondanella. Oxford: Oxford University Press.

67 Virgil (70 BC–19 BC). *The Aeneid*. Book 10, verse 284.

68 Machiavelli, 'Chapter XXV', in *The Prince*.

69 Ibid.

70 Oxford Martin Commission for Future Generations, *Now for the Long Term*.

71 Thompson, Bard (1996). *Humanists and Reformers: A History of the Renaissance and Reformation*. Cambridge: William B. Eerdmans.

72 Cicero, Marcus Tullius (106 BC–43 BC) (1961). *De Officiis*, translated by W. Miller. New York: Macmillan, Book I, Section 7.

73 Cohen, Jere (1980). 'Rational Capitalism in Renaissance Italy'. *American Journal of Sociology* 85(6): 1340–1355.

74 Rosen, Sherwin (1981). 'The Economics of Superstars'. *The American Economic Review* 71(5): 845–858.

75 Beardsley, Brent, Jorge Becerra, et al. (2015). *Global Wealth 2015: Winning the Growth Game*. Boston: Boston Consulting Group; Oxfam (2015). *Wealth: Having It All and Wanting More*. Oxford: Oxfam International.

76 Hudson Institute Center for Global Prosperity (2013). *Index of Global Philanthropy and Remittances 2013*. Hudson Institute.

77 Baker, Vicki, Roger Baldwin, et al. (2012). 'Where Are They Now? Revisiting Breneman's Study of Liberal Arts Colleges'. *Association of American Colleges & Universities*. Retrieved from www.aacu.org/publications-research/periodicals/where-are-they -now-revisiting-brenemans-study-liberal-arts.

78 UN Refugee Agency (2016). 'Evolution – Mediterranean Sea – Dead/Missing Persons'. *Refugee/Migrants Emergency Response – Mediterranean*. Retrieved from data.unhcr.org/mediterranean/regional.php.

79 Mohammed, Omar (27 August 2015). 'A Kenyan Won the Gold Medal in Javelin after Learning How to Throw on YouTube'. *Quartz Africa*. Retrieved from qz.com.

80 Nauert, Charles (2012). 'Desiderius Erasmus'. In *The Stanford Encyclopedia of Philosophy (Winter 2012 Edition)*, edited by E. N. Zalta. Retrieved from plato.stanford.edu /archives/win2012/entries/erasmus.

81 della Mirandola, *Oration on the Dignity of Man*.

82 Machiavelli, Niccolò (1469–1527) (2005). 'Chapter XXVI: An Exhortation to Seize Italy and to Free Her from the Barbarians'. In *The Prince*, edited by P. Bondanella. Oxford: Oxford University Press.

INDEX

Note: The letter 'f' following locators refers to figures.